COMMON SENSE AND LEGAL JUDGMENT

Common Sense and Legal Judgment

Community Knowledge, Political Power, and Rhetorical Practice

PATRICIA COCHRAN

McGill-Queen's University Press
Montreal & Kingston • London • Chicago

ISBN 978-0-7735-5088-9 (cloth)
ISBN 978-0-7735-5089-6 (paper)
ISBN 978-0-7735-5231-9 (ePDF)
ISBN 978-0-7735-5232-6 (ePUB)

Legal deposit fourth quarter 2017
Bibliothèque nationale du Québec

Printed in Canada on acid-free paper that is 100% ancient forest free (100% post-consumer recycled), processed chlorine free

This book has been published with the help of a grant from the Canadian Federation for the Humanities and Social Sciences, through the Awards to Scholarly Publications Program, using funds provided by the Social Sciences and Humanities Research Council of Canada. Funding was also received from the University of Victoria.

McGill-Queen's University Press acknowledges the support of the Canada Council for the Arts for our publishing program. We also acknowledge the financial support of the Government of Canada through the Canada Book Fund for our publishing activities.

Library and Archives Canada Cataloguing in Publication

Cochran, Patricia, 1977–, author
Common sense and legal judgment : community knowledge, political power, and rhetorical practice / Patricia Cochran.

Includes bibliographical references and index.
Issued in print and electronic formats.
ISBN 978-0-7735-5088-9 (cloth).–ISBN 978-0-7735-5089-6 (paper).–ISBN 978-0-7735-5231-9 (ePDF).–ISBN 978-0-7735-5232-6 (ePUB)

1. Common sense. 2. Judgment. 3. Justice. 4. Law–Political aspects. 5. Sociological jurisprudence. I. Title.

K370.C63 2017 340'.115 C2017-904731-0
C2017-904732-9

This book was typeset in Sabon.

Contents

Acknowledgments

I express my profound gratitude to everyone who assisted and supported me throughout the graduate studies and scholarly work that constitute this book. Many thanks to my doctoral committee at the University of British Columbia – Margot Young, Robin Elliot, and Bruce Baum – for their support and mentorship and especially for their patience and spirit of adventure as I learned to speak in multiple disciplinary languages. I also want to thank my colleagues at the University of Victoria for their support and collaboration in rising to the challenge of connecting legal theory with the concrete demands of justice. For their mentorship with respect to my research, particular thanks go to Rebecca Johnson and Jeremy Webber. For financial and institutional support, many thanks to the University of British Columbia, the University of Victoria, the Social Sciences and Humanities Research Council of Canada, and the Law Foundation of British Columbia. I thank my two anonymous reviewers for investing the time to constructively engage with my work in a way that has meaningfully advanced my thinking. I also thank Kate Plyley, Sylvie Vigneux, and Steven Davis for their outstanding research and editorial assistance, as well as the editors at McGill-Queen's University Press for sharing their knowledge and skill.

This book is about how words can work to build and sustain communities, and I am grateful to be part of so many respectful and inspiring communities. To my friends and family, especially Mark, Joseph, and Norah, I offer these words: *thank you.*

COMMON SENSE AND LEGAL JUDGMENT

Introduction

Common sense is a complex notion and a powerful rhetorical tool. In the late eighteenth century, when the phrase "common sense" began to appear in the works of some of his fellow philosophers, Immanuel Kant famously wrote the following scathing comments:

> It is indeed a great gift of God to possess right or (as they now call it) plain common sense. But this common sense must be shown in action by well-considered and reasonable thoughts and words, not by appealing to it as an oracle when no rational justification for one's position can be advanced. To appeal to common sense when insight and discovery fail, and no sooner – this is one of the subtile discoveries of modern times by which the most superficial ranter can safely enter the ranks of the most thorough thinkers and hold his own. But as long as one particle of insight remains, no one would think of having recourse to this subterfuge. Seen clearly, it is but an appeal to the opinion of the multitude, of whose applause the philosopher is ashamed, while the popular charlatan glories and boasts in it.[1]

Some two hundred years later, Scottish law lord James Reid addressed the Society of Public Teachers of Law on the topic of "The Judge as Lawmaker." During this speech, he said,

> We should, I think, have regard to common sense, legal principle and public policy in that order. We are here to serve the public,

> the common ordinary reasonable man ... Sometimes the law has got out of step with common sense. We do not want to have people saying: "If the law says that the law is an ass."[2]

These two quotations, although apparently opposed in terms of their direct argument about the value of common sense, come together in their illustration of some of the most important aspects of common sense as part of human judgment and discourse. In this conversation about common sense, the cast of characters includes "the most thorough thinker," "the philosopher," and the "common ordinary reasonable man." We also encounter the "superficial ranter," the "popular charlatan," and the "people saying ... 'the law is an ass.'" A whole host of personalities circulates around the idea of common sense. In a satire entitled *Pasquin*, written in 1736 by English playwright and magistrate Henry Fielding, common sense is itself embodied in the character of "Queen Common-Sense."[3] In that play, Queen Common-Sense readies herself for battle with the invading Queen Ignorance, only to meet an untimely death at the hands of traitorous advisors, who are none other than "Law," "Physick," and "Firebrand." Common sense, whether as pseudo-philosophical subterfuge, the fundamental basis for the common law, or a symbol of popular political will, carries with it an undeniable rhetorical power.

Given this power, when judges in courts of law use the language of "common sense" to explain their reasons for judgment, which character are they inhabiting? The "philosopher"? The "charlatan"? The "common ordinary reasonable man"? Further, who is the "public," or who are the "people," who constitute the "multitude" for a legal judgment? In the following pages, I interrogate many of these characters who speak of "common sense" by considering the way that they inhabit the work of scholars and judges. I reflect on how their words and actions relate to practices of good legal judgment.

When Kant wrote the passage quoted above, his worries were mostly about the capacity of common sense to interfere with the quality of philosophical discourse and thereby to impede the search for truth. My concerns are different. Although I am also interested in questions about communication and rhetoric, my central concerns are not with the practices of philosophy but with the practices of legal judgment and with questions about justice in a society characterized by diversity and inequality. The words "common sense" invoke claims about knowledge, about community, and about the value of different modes of reasoning; all of these claims relate directly to the value and legitimacy of our practices of legal judgment and to their capacity to effect justice.

"Common sense" is a powerful phrase, and when it is invoked in legal judgment without adequate reflection, it can harbour stereotypes, reproduce unjust power relations, and silence marginalized people. When legal judgment engages with the deep injustices of poverty, inequality, and social marginalization, unreflective reliance on common sense poses a significant threat to the quality and legitimacy of legal judgment. Yet, at the same time, common sense carries with it multiple intellectual and political histories, and when different aspects of common sense are explored with careful critical attention, its democratic, egalitarian, and community-sustaining components are also brought to light. In this book, I offer a critical account of common sense in legal judgment and seek to generate new ways of thinking about and using common sense as part of fully reflective and accountable legal judgment.

The social and historical reality of contemporary societies gives all of these issues further significance. In the contemporary Canadian society that forms the social and legal background for this book, claims about common sense are set in a context characterized not only by commonality but also by marginality and inequality. It is a context characterized not only by the obvious, or the self-evident, but also by deep disagreements about what is known and about what should be known by impartial legal judges. How can legal judges[4] use their common sense when this knowledge may not be held in common with the individuals and communities that are subject to the law? From the perspective of justice and good legal judgment, the use of common sense in legal judgment is problematic on its face.

To investigate this problem most fully, I explore common sense in a context that dramatically challenges the boundaries of common sense claims: the injustices of poverty. Here, not only is common sense problematic and easily misused, but it is also operating in spaces where people are already denied access to essential resources and political participation and where people cannot withstand further injustice. Here, there can be no tolerance for practices of legal judgment that further silence people already marginalized in public life. Indeed, this book is animated by the claim that the existence and persistence of poverty, and the discrimination, marginalization, and oppression that accompany it, are some of the most urgent challenges for justice in contemporary Canadian society.

This book is grounded in feminist and anti-poverty political commitments and theoretical frameworks. Such commitments have both substantive and methodological consequences. Substantively, I adopt an approach to "justice" that seeks equality throughout collective life, including in economic distribution, cultural status, and political participation.[5] Poverty is an injustice that implicates all of these dimensions of justice. I suggest that moving toward justice – however this contested notion is understood – is the central concern of law and of legal institutions. Therefore, the best practices of legal judgment are those that are most able to respond to the demands of this broad understanding of justice in a diverse and unequal world. Good legal judgment should effect just outcomes.

However, in this book I take a largely procedural approach to the question of legal judgment: I am interested in *practices* of judgment and in ideas that can be used to make those practices better. I argue that practices and procedures of judgment have implications for justice not only in their indirect contributions to specific legal outcomes but also in the way that they support or undermine certain understandings of power and community and in the way that they generate models for accountability. There are ways that judgment practices and rhetorical strategies can be evaluated directly with respect to equality and social justice. Thus I focus on the ways that feminist and anti-poverty approaches generate criteria for assessing practices of judgment *as such*. These approaches demand attention to power, attention to social context, and critical self-reflection. In response to these demands, when evaluating practices of legal judgment, I prioritize equality and social inclusion, and I refer to criteria such as transparency, accountability, and reflexivity. From a feminist and anti-poverty perspective, the issues raised by thinking about common sense – about knowledge, power, community, difference, reasoning, and persuasion – are absolutely central to practices of good legal judgment.

Thus the methodological approach that I have adopted paves the way for a complex understanding of the relationship between form and content, method and outcome. As noted above, it becomes central to my argument in this book that judging and rhetorical practices have meaningful connections to justice, quite apart from their instrumental connection to particular legal outcomes.[6] At the same time, the methodology I rely on insists that theoretical questions about practices never leave behind the political, moral, or philosophical perspectives that motivate the questions in the first place. Thus, when I assess the value of judging practices and propose criteria for *good* legal judgment, those value judgments connect back to concerns about social justice and must ultimately be defended on that basis.[7]

My focus on questions of procedure and practice also reveals a sustained focus on the potential for law and legal practices to respond to the demands of justice. This focus does not, in my view, reflect an uncritical optimism about the capacity of liberal legal institutions to achieve social justice – although this concern should never be too far from a reader's mind. I do take seriously the emancipatory potential of law as a set of human practices and institutions. I am interested in exploring *legal judgment* as a distinct, embodied human activity that is at once situated in diverse political communities and also situated within the particular constraints of the legal system in which I am most immersed: the Canadian state legal system. Studying practices of legal judgment provokes questions about the relationship between law and justice, between individuals and communities, and between political power and the historical instantiations of legal values.

All of these questions about the role of common sense, legal judgment, and the injustices of poverty materialized in the Supreme Court of Canada's 2002 decision in the case of *Gosselin v. Quebec (Procureur général)*.[8] This case is significant in this book for a number of reasons. It is an example of how the legal system continues to struggle with how best to address the injustices of poverty. It is an example of just how important questions of knowledge, community, and rhetoric can be when talking about the quality of legal judgment. And it is a provocative example of the use of the phrase "common sense" in legal judgment. In *Gosselin* the court was asked to determine the constitutionality of certain aspects of the social assistance regime that operated in Quebec during the 1980s. The claimant alleged that the legislation was unjust and discriminatory in the way that it left some young adults to subsist on a meagre $170 per month.[9] In upholding the legislation, the judgment of the majority of justices prominently invoked the words "common sense."[10] In the context of this case – which dealt with the politically charged question of welfare programs, involved complex and disputed social scientific evidence,[11] and included the deeply distressing testimony of Louise Gosselin herself[12] – the use of the language of "common sense" is remarkable and provocative. Indeed, this language has been the subject of comment from anti-poverty activists and scholars, and it served as the catalyst for much academic work, including this book.

The *Gosselin* case engendered a range of responses. Some responses, adopting a view along the lines of Kant's, accused the court of pandering to a kind of shallow majoritarianism and of endorsing stereotypes of people living in poverty – an "appeal to the opinion of the multitude."[13] Others, with Lord Reid, argued that the court was merely applying a kind of sensible reasonableness to legal claims that threatened to lose touch with reality or get "out of touch with common sense."[14] Yet, throughout this conversation, it seems that not all of the characters mentioned at the beginning of this chapter are represented. Where is the "philosopher"? Where is the "thorough thinker"? Where is the one who claims "to serve the public"? Do we see the rhetorical elements of ranting, shame, boasting, glory? The *Gosselin* case illustrates the need to subject common sense to expansive critical scrutiny and to broaden the range of perspectives we take when assessing the meaning and role of common sense for legal judgment. Without this scrutiny, we lose opportunities to understand the nature of legal judgment, especially when the injustices of poverty and inequality are at issue.

Some of the ways that common sense is problematic for legal judgment are made particularly acute in the contexts of poverty, inequality, and social marginalization. In these contexts, we are challenged to raise the critical question "common to *whom*?" Further, common sense has a particular salience in political and legal discourses about poverty, where it often operates in the service of conservatism, populism, or majoritarianism, all of which pose problems for a vision of law that seeks to transform unjust social relations.[15] For these reasons and others, it is crucial to identify the ways that the invocation of "common sense" constitutes significant challenges to good legal judgment.

At the same time, critical scholars and anti-poverty activists would be remiss to ignore or reject common sense as part of progressive political and legal discourse about poverty and justice.[16] To do so would be to relinquish common sense to a specific, dominant political ideology and to lose important resources for talking about what it means to exercise good judgment in the context of complex social life. Rather than abandoning common sense as merely an artifact of material power relations or the source of unsustainable universal claims, this book seeks to investigate the language of "common sense" in a robust and reflective manner. I aim to expand the possibilities for subjecting common sense to critical and feminist analysis. I explore whether, in addition to being worthy of critical analysis, common sense can also be a tool for making legal judgment more fully reflective and responsive to the needs of diverse communities. Motivated by an appreciation of the political and theoretical consequences of abandoning common sense to theoretical captivity or to the proponents of a conservative majoritarianism, the following chapters seek to generate new ways of thinking about common sense in legal judgment.

In this book, I seek insight about common sense from two primary sets of sources. First, I engage with three major thinkers from different disciplines whom I have chosen because common sense is central to their work: philosopher of common sense Thomas Reid, political thinker and activist Antonio Gramsci, and political theorist Hannah Arendt. Second, I draw insight from judgments of the Supreme Court of Canada in which judges have used the words "common sense" to explain their findings. I read these two sets of texts against criteria for good legal judgment, with particular attention to justice concerns arising from poverty, inequality, and social marginalization. By looking carefully at different aspects of common sense that become visible in scholarly texts and in written legal judgments, I open up this concept to critical view and create space for common sense to fulfil its potential as part of critical and reflective legal judgment.

CHAPTER OVERVIEW

Chapter 1 describes in more detail the nature of the problem I address in this book, which I describe as the "paradox of common sense." Chapter 1 also explains the research methodology that underlies my substantive arguments. I adopt a version of the methodology that Ludwig Wittgenstein calls "perspicuous representation," understood and modified by the feminist and anti-poverty political commitments that motivate this research.[17] I take the phrase "common sense" and explore its meaning and consequences in different contexts.[18] In each of the subsequent substantive three chapters, I present the work of a single theorist of common sense and argue that it allows us to see a particular aspect of common sense. In each of those chapters, I argue that when this aspect of common sense is considered in the context of legal judgment, we learn something specific about legal judgment, particularly about the relationship between legal judgment and poverty and social justice. This insight assists us in challenging our captivity to a picture of common sense that is of limited usefulness. Once debate is opened up in this way, we can generate alternative criteria for the use of common sense in legal judgment that are oriented toward the democratic and emancipatory potential of law.

Chapter 2 engages with the work of eighteenth-century Scottish philosopher Thomas Reid. Reid's perspective on common sense describes it as a form of knowledge that is rooted in daily life and equally accessible to everyone. He argues that the knowledge that people use to ground their judgments in daily life is the same knowledge that grounds other kinds of judgment, such as philosophical judgment. Reid also argues that common sense knowledge is what we use to determine the boundaries of rational debate. Placed in the context of legal judgment, the aspect of common sense that we see in Reid, including the valuation of universality and everyday life, is both helpful and problematic. To explore how this aspect of common sense operates in legal judgment, I read his theory against legal judgments in which judges use the language of "common sense" to describe how judges and juries should assess the credibility of witnesses. This is one area of Canadian law in which "common sense" is frequently invoked and in which the themes raised by Reid are also at work. As in Reid, this body of law tends to place common sense in opposition to expertise or technical knowledge, and it raises many of the same questions about universality, the legitimacy of everyday judgment, and the proper relationship between common knowledge and specialized expertise. When issues of poverty and social marginalization arise, these questions about common sense take on a special importance because of the ways that "common" knowledge can be inadequate to the task of judging in this context. Reid's writings bring our attention to how common knowledge and expert knowledge should be approached in legal judgment, as well as how important it is to understand what criteria are used to stake out the boundaries of legitimate debate in law.

Chapter 3 is about the work of Antonio Gramsci, the Marxist theorist and political actor who wrote about common sense while imprisoned in Italy in the 1930s. For Gramsci, "common sense" refers to a shared "conception of the world"[19] that is constructed through historical experience and relations of social and economic power. Gramsci argues that common sense knowledge has specific, class-contingent content and is an important component of the political hegemony of dominant classes. At the same time, common sense knowledge helps to constitute communities and can be transformed, through critical reflection, into "good sense,"[20] which can serve to ground progressive social change. The aspect of common sense we see by reading Gramsci concerns its historically contingent nature, the role of political power, as well as the potential and limitations of critical reflection. I explore these themes in legal judgments in which the court describes whether and how "common sense" can be invoked to justify the infringement of a constitutionally protected right. These judgments are also concerned with power, marginalization, what counts as "evidence," and the strengths and weaknesses of critical reflection as a judging practice.

Chapter 4 engages with the complex writings of political theorist Hannah Arendt, whose theory of human judgment relies importantly on her idea of common sense. Arendt's approach to common sense describes it as part of the practice of judgment, in which a judging person imaginatively references the collective views of one's community when coming to a judgment. The common sense of a community is what enables judgment to become valid beyond an individual and thus to have legitimate meaning for a community. Arendt also argues that engagement with common sense not only reflects the boundaries of existing communities but also works to create those communities in the first place. This aspect of common sense shifts attention away from epistemology and bodies of community knowledge and toward communicability and persuasion. In this context, I engage with legal judgments about how the common sense of individual judges can or should relate to the legal requirements for judicial impartiality. I look specifically at the way that judicial subjectivity and the human practice of judgment relate to common sense and to the criteria for legitimate legal judgment.

Chapter 5 concludes the book by reflecting on how these different aspects of common sense allow us to see it in a new light. I draw my arguments together to create a "perspicuous representation" of the concept that takes some steps toward freeing us from the intellectual captivity created by common sense and its self-referential and self-justifying characteristics. Legal judgment, particularly in the context of economic and social inequality, benefits from these new ways of thinking about common sense because this engagement helps to generate useful criteria for legitimate and critical invocation of "common sense" in legal judgment. Using the context of poverty and law in the Canadian legal system as the grounds for my exploration, I draw connections between common sense claims and aspirations to social justice. "Common sense," properly invoked, has the potential to open our practices of legal judgment to the complexities of our diverse, unequal society and thereby to make legal judgment more responsive to the demands of justice.

1

Common Sense: Self-evident and Inscrutable

We enter the Haymarket Theatre in London on 5 March 1736 to see the opening performance of Henry Fielding's satire Pasquin.[1] *As we make our way through the boisterous crowd, we are joined by the philosopher Ludwig Wittgenstein, arrived from twentieth-century Europe. Wittgenstein takes a seat but emits a kind of energetic intensity that makes him seem constantly in motion. The play begins, and the conspiracy to murder Queen Common-Sense, enacted by Law, Physick, and Firebrand, unfolds. The traitorous advisors complain about the erosion of their power in the face of common sense. Wittgenstein's eyebrows prick up when Lord Law addresses the power of language to shape the relationship between law, reason, and society.*[2]

Law.
Thou know'st, my Lord of *Physick*, I had long
Been privileg'd by Custom immemorial,
In Tongues unknown, or rather none at all,
My Edicts to deliver thro' the Land;
When this proud Queen, this *Common-Sense*, abridg'd
My Power, and made me understood by all.

Phys.
My Lord, there goes a Rumour thro' the Court,
That you descended from a Family
Related to the Queen; Reason is said
T' have been the mighty Founder of your House.

Law.
Perhaps so; but we have rais'd our selves so high,
And shook this Founder from us off so far,
We hardly deign to own from whence we came.[3]

At the conclusion of the play, Wittgenstein pulls out a notebook and records a few thoughts before venturing into the crowd to find Fielding himself.

THE PARADOX OF COMMON SENSE

Common sense is both self-evident and inscrutable. On the one hand, common sense describes that which is simple, straightforward, and obvious. We use the phrase "common sense" to describe what "everybody knows" or judgments that require no special expertise to be known and understood because they are readily apparent from the practice of daily life. Common sense judgments therefore require no further explanation or justification; common sense is self-evident.

On the other hand, the *meaning* of the phrase "common sense" is actually complex and dynamic; it means different things in different historical, social, and discursive contexts. For example, sometimes we invoke "common sense" to refer to a basic kind of reasoning or good judgment that almost everyone possesses because it is grounded in our daily life experiences ("just use your common sense"). At other times, we use the phrase "common sense" to mean the content of judgments, or knowledge, or facts that one arrives at by using the faculty of common sense ("it's a matter of common sense"). Further, the phrase "common sense" naturally provokes questions about community ("common to whom?"). However, any complexity in the phrase, or questions that might be asked, tend to be obscured by the way that common sense claims present themselves as self-evident. Even as it bears a host of different meanings, common sense carries with it the rhetorical force of the self-evident. In this way, investigation of common sense is often thwarted from the start or caught in a circle of reasoning; it is inscrutable. Anthropologist Clifford Geertz aptly captures this phenomenon in his influential essay "Common Sense as a Cultural System": "[I]t is an inherent characteristic of common-sense thought ... to affirm that its tenets are immediate deliverances of experience, not deliberated reflections upon it ... Religion rests its case on revelation, science on method, ideology on moral passion; but common sense rests its case on the assertion that it is not a case at all, just life in a nutshell. The world is its authority."[4] Thus common sense, like the two-faced god Janus, looks in two directions at once: toward the simple and self-evident and toward the complex and unseen.

This tension, nested in the phrase "common sense," has a particular salience when considering how it is deployed in the context of law and legal judgment. When judges invoke "common sense" to articulate their judgment, what does this mean? Is common sense a type of evidence that can support a legal argument? Is it a type of reasoning? Is it justified by its reference to community consensus? Consensus of what community? These questions are important for both the legitimacy of legal judgment and the justice of legal conclusions. But because of the apparent simplicity and self-evidence of common sense, these questions are rarely answered or even acknowledged in written reasons for judgment. In legal judgment, as elsewhere, "common sense" is much more often invoked than explained.[5] Thus the two-faced nature of common sense – self-evident and inscrutable – makes its way into legal judgment.

The nature of the practices we engage in when undertaking legal judgment are worthy of scrutiny: we need concepts and criteria for determining what will count as *good* legal judgment.[6] Many concepts help to serve this function in common law jurisdictions. Some are oriented to the content of legal decisions, including the idea that a judge must have knowledge of the law and an understanding of the role of the judiciary in a democratic society. Other criteria for good legal judgment are oriented directly to the *practices* of legal judgment, such as the requirement for judicial impartiality, the obligation to provide reasons for decisions, and the rules of evidence.[7] Judges must decide impartially, transparently, and with reliance on the right knowledge. Core concepts like judicial impartiality are articulated in jurisprudence and also elaborated through professional conduct guidelines like those published by the Canadian Judicial Council. For example, in the document *Ethical Principles for Judges*, the council identifies as essential the principles of judicial independence, integrity, diligence, equality, and impartiality. These principles describe how judges should approach the task before them and how we can evaluate judging practices in relation to the overarching purposes of legal judgment. The council notes the connections between procedure and substance in part of its discussion of the principle of "equality": "Equality according to law is not only fundamental to justice, but is strongly linked to judicial impartiality. A judge who, for example, reaches a correct result but engages in stereotyping does so at the expense of the judge's impartiality, actual or perceived."[8]

The Canadian Judicial Council's guidelines and commentary on "equality" demonstrate the inherent connections between substantive legal values such as equality and practices or procedures of judgment. In this book, I take this interconnection to be both inevitable and fruitful, as well as generative of both methodological and substantive insights. I proceed on the understanding that even though I focus on practice and procedure, all of the normative assessments offered in this book are ultimately grounded in a specific understanding of justice, and my methodology asserts that it is ultimately a matter of political choice, not objective truth, that prioritizes some practices over others. In this book, I advocate for the usefulness of this perspective for opening up the range of questions that can be asked about the relationship between judgment and justice.

Although a proper defence of my understanding of "justice" falls outside the scope of the present work, it is important that the approach to justice that animates this book calls for a contextualized assessment of legal judgment. Contemporary society is characterized by fundamental political and moral disagreement, as well as by relations of unequal power. Assessment of judging practices has to take place against this context; we need to understand "impartiality," for example, so that it makes judgment better *in our diverse and unequal society*. What matters is how our understanding affects things in the real social context in which we find ourselves. In this book, I focus on the specific context of contemporary Canadian society and make reference to the Canadian state legal order and to the Canadian social and economic realities of poverty and inequality. This is the context in which I find myself and against which I test the usefulness of my theoretical interventions. The insights and questions arising about common sense and legal judgment, however, are not necessarily bound in their application to this specific context, and I invite readers to consider my criteria for the use of common sense in good legal judgment against the social context and political commitments that are of concern to them.

Moreover, my approach to justice recognizes – indeed, insists – that no universal or conceptually unified approach to evaluating judgment can be meaningfully proposed under conditions of radical social diversity and inequality. However, it is still possible to talk about better and worse practices of judgment – practices that bring us closer to or push us away from ways of thinking and acting that reflect the demands of justice. This approach places particular importance on practices of judgment that have the potential to recognize power imbalances, generate critical reflection, and open the judging process to voices that might otherwise remain unheard.

Common sense has an ambiguous relationship with criteria for *good* legal judgment. On the one hand, common sense, understood as the practice of sensible judgment, surely seems like a good candidate for inclusion as part of good judgment in general and of legal judgment in particular. As noted by Lord James Reid at the beginning of the Introduction, common sense also seems to relate to the common law tradition in particular, in which connections to the local community are valued as part of legal reasoning.[9] On the other hand, the particular requirements of legal judgment sit uneasily with some characteristics of common sense. For example, whereas common law legal judgment is supposed to be grounded in facts proven at trial according to the rules of evidence,[10] common sense knowledge is unlikely to fall into this category and may be impossible to "prove" in this manner. Common sense appears to be about both form and content, pulling legal judgment in multiple directions.

Further, the unexamined appeal to common sense in a legal judgment allows the tension between the self-evident and the inscrutable to operate freely, leaving unanswered or unacknowledged questions about evidence, reasoning, and consensus. This practice creates the potential for partial, illegitimate, or nontransparent judgment. Indeed, these risks are particularly likely to manifest in those areas of law where the commonality of common sense is most in question. It is precisely what can happen when legal judgment encounters poverty and social marginalization. In this context, unreflective reliance on common sense is most likely to degrade our practices of legal judgment, and acts of poor judgment have the potential to cause the most damage. When legal judgment is put under stress by the social and legal challenges of poverty and social marginalization, it is especially urgent that we attend to the adequacy of our judging practices.

COMMON SENSE IN CANADIAN LAW AND THE CASE OF *GOSSELIN V. QUEBEC (PROCUREUR GÉNÉRAL)*

Judges use the language of "common sense" to explain their reasons in a variety of contexts, with a variety of rhetorical effects. Indeed, one empirical study in the United States found that "common sense" was the single most commonly cited "authority" for legal argument.[11] In Canadian judgments, this phrase tends to appear frequently in the law of evidence, in which "common sense" is understood as a foil for expert evidence.[12] The phrase "common sense" is also used to describe the concept of "reasonable doubt" in criminal law,[13] as well as the concept of negligence.[14] Further, the phrase "common sense" appears notably in constitutional law,[15] including as a way to describe the type of proof that must be offered to establish whether something is consistent with the "principles of fundamental justice" under section 7 of the Canadian Charter of Rights and Freedoms,[16] as well as to justify the breach of a right under section 1 of the Charter.[17] Certain specific propositions have been accepted as matters of "common sense" at various times, including the idea that "children of tender years" should live with their mothers[18] and the inference that one intends the consequences of one's physical actions.[19]

The language of "common sense" was notably and provocatively invoked in the constitutional case *Gosselin v. Quebec (Procureur général)*, described in the Introduction.[20] The explicit and repeated use of the phrase "common sense" makes *Gosselin* exceptional among poverty-related cases at the Supreme Court of Canada.[21] *Gosselin* is also exceptional in that it is one of only a handful of cases in which the Supreme Court of Canada has reviewed the content of a provincial welfare regime, and it is the only case in which the adequacy of welfare payments or programs has been assessed under the Charter of Rights and Freedoms.[22] The *Gosselin* case is useful for a study of common sense in legal judgment not because it is representative of a class of cases but because its treatment of poverty themes and its invocation of "common sense" provide insight on the role of common sense in legal judgment. Further, the *Gosselin* case is worthy of detailed scrutiny because of the way it fits with a larger jurisprudence on poverty issues.[23] In some respects, the use of "common sense" in *Gosselin* brings to the surface issues that pervade legal judgments on poverty and equality issues, such as questions of community, access to justice, and the legitimacy of the varied forms of knowledge relied upon by courts. Finally, *Gosselin* is useful for a study of common sense in legal judgment because it compels us to ask questions about the exceptionality of this case. If the Supreme Court rarely invokes "common sense" when talking about social justice, why is this the case? What would happen if the Supreme Court explicitly invoked "common sense" in other cases where social justice is at stake?

In *Gosselin* the Supreme Court of Canada reviewed Louise Gosselin's claims that her rights to equality and security of the person were compromised by her treatment under provincial welfare laws. The impugned law was a regulation that paid individuals receiving social assistance who were under the age of thirty a much lower amount than those who were thirty and over, unless the younger individuals were able to participate in certain training programs. Without such participation, the amount available to people under thirty was approximately $170 per month. Gosselin was a young woman who had attempted to survive on this amount, and she argued that the regulation in question violated sections 7 and 15 of the Canadian Charter of Rights and Freedoms.[24] The Supreme Court of Canada's judgments in this case were divided in complex ways.[25] However, the majority of justices found that the regulation was constitutional.

One of the main issues before the court involved the interpretation and application of section 15 equality rights. On this issue, the majority judgment, authored by Chief Justice Beverley McLachlin, found that that the legislation was not discriminatory because it did not offend Gosselin's dignity.[26] McLachlin accepted the government's assertion that the purpose of the law was to provide an incentive for young people to leave welfare in favour of paid employment.[27] She found that this supported, rather than harmed, the dignity of young adults because it communicated a favourable expectation of their potential.[28] McLachlin found that a reasonable person in Gosselin's position would take this factor into account and thereby experience no injury to her dignity.[29]

The *Gosselin* case discloses a series of different pictures of the world. It is very hard to reconcile the picture presented by Gosselin's evidence, which describes significant infringements on her physical and psychological integrity, such as hunger, extreme stress, and degrading survival strategies,[30] and Chief Justice McLachlin's picture of Gosselin as someone who should have understood her experiences in light of the government's well-meaning objectives. Gosselin's experience was one of fundamental disempowerment, yet the majority justices essentially claim that she should have experienced this disempowerment as empowerment. The writers of the majority and dissenting judgments describe their disagreement in strong terms, sometimes adopting a tone of incredulity. For example, in her dissent, Justice Claire L'Heureux-Dubé writes, "I cannot imagine how it can be maintained that Ms. Gosselin's physical integrity was not breached."[31]

In this context of deeply contested understandings of the impugned law and its effects, it is striking that at several crucial points, Chief Justice McLachlin uses the words "common sense" to articulate her findings. The phrase appears in three significant passages in the judgment, to which I will be returning throughout this book.[32]

First, while addressing the role of the purpose of the law in assessing its impact, McLachlin finds,

> *As a matter of common sense*, if a law is designed to promote the claimant's long-term autonomy and self-sufficiency, a reasonable person in the claimant's position would be less likely to view it as an assault on her inherent human dignity.[33]

Second, on the question of whether the law properly responded to the claimant's actual circumstances, she writes,

> Even if one does not agree with the reasoning of the legislature or with its priorities, one cannot argue based on this record that the legislature's purpose lacked sufficient foundation in reality and *common sense* to fall within the bounds of permissible discretion in establishing and fine-tuning a complex social assistance scheme. Logic and *common sense* support the legislature's decision to structure its social assistance programs to give young people, who have a greater potential for long-term insertion into the work force than older people, the incentive to participate in programs specifically designed to provide them with training and experience.[34]

Finally, in addressing the critique raised by the dissenting justices that the regulation failed to respond to the claimant's circumstances, she writes,

> [W]e cannot infer disparity between the purpose and effect of the scheme and the situation of those affected, from the mere failure of the government to prove that the assumptions upon which it proceeded were correct. Bastarache J. argues that the distinction between people under 30 and older people lacks a "rational basis" because it is "[b]ased on the unverifiable presumption that people under 30 had better chances of employment and lower needs" (para. 248). This seems to place on the legislator the duty to verify all its assumptions empirically, even where these assumptions are reasonably grounded in everyday experience and *common sense*. With respect, this standard is too high ... The legislator is entitled to proceed on informed

> general assumptions without running afoul of s. 15 ... provided these assumptions are not based on arbitrary and demeaning stereotypes.[35]

These passages show that common sense plays a significant role in the judgment, particularly in grounding the majority's resistance to the idea that an inappropriate government response to poverty might violate constitutionally protected rights. It also provides a lens for the assessment of evidence. At the same time, there is no definition or explanation of "common sense," nor any reflection on its role.

The *Gosselin* decision was met with considerable criticism,[36] including some that specifically focuses on the majority's use of the phrase "common sense" in critiquing the decision. Constitutional scholar David Schneiderman argues that the Supreme Court's reliance on "common sense" signals its willingness to adopt dominant views about poverty and welfare in its understanding of evidence in constitutional cases.[37] He argues that, when faced with contentious social issues, such as the relationship between poverty and constitutional rights, the Supreme Court is more likely to follow established common sense than to act as a leader in forming or reforming Canada's constitutional culture.[38] Schneiderman points to mainstream media reports on the case as sources of common sense and argues that these reports indicate a fairly wide social consensus about poverty and social welfare programs that disposes society against the claims of anti-poverty litigants.[39]

In her critique of *Gosselin*, legal scholar Sheila McIntyre also argues that the majority justices demonstrate a willingness to uncritically accept dominant notions of the world. Further, McIntyre specifically ties this practice to the requirements of legitimate legal judgment and argues that, through their reliance on common sense, the majority justices have essentially abdicated their responsibility to judge and have instead relied on stereotypes. She writes that "judicial complacency in invoking or accepting 'common sense' notions about historically marginalized, stigmatized or stereotyped groups amounts to bad judging."[40] McIntyre argues that legitimate practices of legal judgment, particularly in the context of constitutional review, cannot tolerate reliance on stereotypes, or "privileged innocence," about the experiences of marginalized people and that resort to common sense precipitates precisely this problem.[41]

In a similar vein, legal scholars Natasha Kim and Tina Piper argue that "one of the hallmarks of systemic discrimination is the ability to cloak itself in 'common sense' and to erase the realities of those suffering from discrimination."[42] And in response to *Gosselin*, the Victoria Anti-Poverty Coalition stated, "This truly bizarre 'common sense' economic insight on the part of Canada's Supreme Court will no doubt come as a tremendous shock to ... many thousands of Canadians."[43] These comments are all directed at slightly different theoretical and doctrinal targets, and they reveal different approaches to common sense and law. However, there is a general sense in which all of these critiques of the *Gosselin* case direct their analyses of judicial invocation of "common sense" to the question of whether the purported "common sense" is in fact "common," and, if so, to whom.

The question "common to whom?" is an essential one and plays a central role in this book. However, it also leaves many issues unaddressed. For example, in relation to *Gosselin*, I agree with Schneiderman that the case and the media reports about it reveal a partial (and problematic) social consensus around poverty and rights in Canada. However, I also think that the court's invocation of "common sense" is about more than this consensus. Further, I question whether the use of common sense necessarily restricts judges to dominant knowledges. In this context and others, important questions remain unanswered. What is the relationship between common sense and good judgment? How is common sense connected to specific communities? What is the measure of the "commonality" of common sense? What *effects* do claims about common sense have in social discourses, including legal discourse? Further, the framework for debate appears to make it difficult to even ask these questions. In this way, the claim that common sense makes about itself – that it is self-justifying – effectively serves to insulate it from critical scrutiny.

POVERTY AND THE CONSEQUENCES OF THE PARADOX OF COMMON SENSE

When our understanding and use of common sense are constrained by a framework that limits the scope of our questions, the quality of our judgment suffers. This problem takes on a particular significance in the context of poverty and social marginalization for two main reasons. First, the issues surrounding poverty in Canada raise major justice concerns. The persistence of poverty and the discriminatory patterns associated with deep or ongoing poverty in specific communities raise questions that strike at the heart of a constitutional democracy that values political participation and equality before the law. The questions raised in this book about the role of common sense in legal judgment gain much of their significance when they are placed against the backdrop of the realities of poverty in Canada and the ways that the experiences of poverty and social marginalization constitute injustice.

In this book, I use the term "poverty" to indicate a broad range of injustices in which there is a material component, including material hardship, economic inequality, and class marginalization. It is useful to refer to the definition of "poverty" developed by the United Nations Committee on Economic, Social and Cultural Rights, which describes it as "a human condition characterized by sustained or chronic deprivation of the resources, capabilities, choices, security and power necessary for the enjoyment of an adequate standard of living and other civil, cultural, economic, political and social rights."[44] Thus poverty is not simply about lack of income or material deprivation; it is also about exclusion, anxiety, oppression, and marginalization. Although Canada does not have an official "poverty line," by most measures millions of people of all ages live in poverty.[45] The nonprofit advocacy organization Canada Without Poverty describes this experience in the following terms:

> To live in poverty in Canada is to live with insufficient and often poor quality food. It is to sleep in poor quality housing, in homeless shelters, or on city streets. It is on a daily basis to have to

> make difficult and painful decisions involving trade-offs, such as whether to "pay the rent or feed the kids," pay the electric bill or go to the dentist, buy a new monthly bus pass or forego inviting friends over for dinner. No Canadian should have to suffer such anxiety.
>
> To live in poverty in Canada is to be at much greater risk of poor health, violence and a shorter lifespan. It is to be unable to participate fully in one's community and greater society. And it is to suffer great depths of anxiety and emotional pain, borne by young and old alike.[46]

Further, the risk of poverty is not shared equally among Canadians. Indigenous people, people with disabilities, single mothers, and recent immigrants are among the groups that are at higher risk of becoming poor.[47] Thus poverty relates not only to deprivation but also to discrimination and colonialism.[48] Indigenous communities dispossessed of their lands and economies encounter a range of the social, cultural, and material harms of poverty. Poverty is a gendered phenomenon, in which girls and women are significantly more likely to experience poverty during their lifetimes.[49] Moreover, the experience of poverty in Canada is shaped by gendered aspects of social life, such as unequal benefit from paid employment,[50] disproportionate responsibility for caregiving labour,[51] and vulnerability to intimate violence.[52] Poverty interacts in complex ways with other forms of social inequality to generate and sustain injustice.[53]

Thus it becomes clear that when judges must assess the rights of individuals living in poverty, practices of legal judgment are tied to very high stakes because of the *content* of the legal issues. For individuals and communities living in poverty, interaction with the law may be part of what determines their access to basic necessities like food, medical care, or housing, their ability to provide for their families, and their opportunity to participate in community life. Legal judgments about those issues might address, for example, the equality rights of women receiving social assistance,[54] the appropriate sentences for impoverished and marginalized women who commit crimes,[55] or the constitutional status of panhandling.[56] Although all kinds of legal judgments can carry important consequences for litigants and for society as a whole, it is not an exaggeration to say that, in some cases, poverty and law interact in relation to life and death matters.[57] The quality of our practices of legal judgment in this context is of great significance.

The second way that the dilemma of common sense in legal judgment carries special significance in the context of poverty has to do with judging practices and the form of judgment; poverty tends to complicate our understanding of legal judgment itself. For example, judgments about poverty bring into sharp relief the question of judicial subjectivity.[58] Legal questions about poverty are particularly likely to highlight the demographic differences between low-income Canadians and those Canadians sitting on the bench. Judges in Canada are overwhelmingly white and middle- or upper-class.[59] About two-thirds of judges are men.[60] The likelihood that a judge has direct personal experience of living in poverty is especially low, and thus the commonality of "common" sense becomes particularly suspect.

Judgments about poverty also have the potential to raise broader questions about the relationship between "poverty" and "law" in a constitutional democracy. There are rich bodies of literature addressing this subject and a whole constellation of concerns and approaches.[61] These literatures include discussion of rights discourse,[62] the relationship between judicial and legislative lawmaking for social justice,[63] the capacity of the Canadian Charter of Rights and Freedoms to respond to the challenges of poverty and inequality,[64] the institutional capacity of the court,[65] and the ways that poverty impacts other axes of injustice, such as sexism, racism, and colonialism.[66]

This book does not address these questions directly. However, scholarship on law and poverty provides the context for my examination of common sense and helps to determine what is important in my assessment of the adequacy of practices of legal judgment. This literature does inform my overall approach, and on occasion I reference it to highlight the significance of common sense for legal judgment. I adopt the view that law, legal judgment, and legal institutions are implicated in all aspects of collective life, including economic relationships and the creation, maintenance, and dismantling of social hierarchies. Thus attention to poverty and inequality is important for the study of law and legal judgment. Further, although actions addressing the injustices of poverty and social marginalization also and importantly take place outside the courtroom, I suggest that these issues are properly part of judicial as well as legislative lawmaking. That is, material circumstances and economic inequality are not merely the context for the assertion of legal claims and for the resolution of disputes but are also a core problem faced by any social institution that has "justice" as one of its organizing principles. Poverty and social marginalization raise central questions about the quality of legal judgment.

COMMON SENSE AS A SUBJECT OF INQUIRY

As noted above, the phrase "common sense" is much more often invoked than explained,[67] and the claim that something is a matter of common sense has a way of being self-justifying. However, even cursory reflection reveals that "common sense" is a rich and dynamic phrase, with shifting meanings and functions, even in everyday life. For example, "common sense" is often used to describe a body of facts that are known by almost everyone in a community. One might say, "Everyone knows that if you go for a walk in the rain, you'll get wet. It's just common sense." There is no need to look up such information in a book, nor could most people recall a specific moment in which they learned it.

At the same time, "common sense" is also used to describe not a body of knowledge but a type of judgment or sensibility.[68] Thus one might say, "She went out in the rain without her umbrella. She may be smart, but she really has no common sense." In this context, the speaker is not saying that the person lacks any particular piece of *knowledge*, such as "if you go for a walk in the rain, you'll get wet," but rather that she lacks good *judgment* in relation to everyday affairs.[69]

This seemingly banal example about umbrellas demonstrates the inherent particularity of any piece of common sense; it impossible to give examples of common sense without drawing on particular background assumptions and cultural references. What about people who live in places where umbrellas are not a usual piece of personal technology? What about places where rain is understood as a rare blessing? What about people who prefer to travel light at the risk of getting wet? What about people who cannot afford an umbrella? Do the people in these further examples simply exhibit poor judgment? Surely not. Thus even an apparently noncontroversial example raises questions about the relationship between particular communities and knowledges, as well as about the normative, judgmental component of common sense.

Despite these questions that lie beneath the surface of common sense, there is no sustained historical scholarly conversation on common sense in the same way that there is about other related concepts, such as knowledge. Rather, common sense has appeared at different moments, in different contexts, to serve different intellectual and political purposes for scholarly writers.[70] For Aristotle, the phrase usually translated as "common sense" means a human faculty that can coordinate sensory information; the common sense is the "sense" that allows me to appreciate that the apple I can see is the same object as the apple I can smell.[71] The "common" aspect of common sense indicates a coordinating capacity and is essential for the ability to make judgments.

When the phrase "common sense" is used by writers in the rhetorical tradition, such as Giambattista Vico, it refers to knowledge that is shared in a community. "Common sense" is what is known or believed by everyone in the community and what helps to form the boundaries of that community.[72] For later Enlightenment thinkers such as John Locke, "common sense" had come to mean not a specific body of shared knowledge but any kind of knowledge that could be understood by nonexperts, or knowledge that was properly the domain of everyday people.[73]

In her writing on the political history of common sense, historian Sophia Rosenfeld describes how all three of these elements of common sense – Aristotelian, rhetorical, and Enlightenment – came together: "At the start of the eighteenth century, with the revival of all of these sources, common sense came also to mean, in English, those plain, self-evident truths or conventional wisdom that one needed no sophistication to grasp and no proof to accept precisely because they accorded so well with the basic (common sense) intellectual capacities and experiences of the whole social body."[74] Rosenfeld argues that the increasing centrality of common sense in Western political discourse is part of a shift in the meaning of politics itself. In contemporary democratic society, "[p]olitics has been recast ... as the domain of simple, quotidian determinations and basic moral precepts, of truths that should be self-evident to all."[75] Rosenfeld argues, persuasively, that common sense as part of political discourse has an ambiguous relationship with democracy, both upholding it and subverting it in different historical moments.[76]

In the context of law and jurisprudence, common sense also draws on this composite intellectual history.[77] Just as common sense in politics has an ambiguous relationship with democracy, common sense in law has an ambiguous relationship with justice. In legal scholarship, the phrase "common sense" has rarely served as the primary object of scholarly inquiry, compared with the extensive conversation among lawyers and legal academics about ideology,[78] discourse,[79] or knowledge.[80] Those writers who do turn their attention directly to the relationship between common sense and law can be placed in three general categories. Although these categories do not constitute "schools of thought" and individual thinkers may engage with issues falling into more than one category, these three broad strands still provide a useful way to think about the literature on common sense and law.

First, "common sense" is sometimes invoked by writers interested in the history or meaning of the common law tradition (as distinct from the civil law or other traditions). From some perspectives, the common law, properly understood, is actually the embodiment of the common sense of a given community. Speaking in 1918, William Renwick Riddell of the Supreme Court of Ontario claimed that Upper Canadians, in contrast to some other colonial settlers, were strongly attached to the common law because of its historical and ongoing connection to their "common sense":

> Is not the real reason [for this attachment to the common law] to be found in the belief that the common law is the perfection

> of human reason – in a word, that *the common law is common sense*? What we call "common sense" is not the old metaphysical common sense, nor is it the sentiment which might be conceived to flow from lofty and altruistic philosophy; but it consists in the application of the rules of justice and honesty to the things of this work-a-day world, so full of anomalies and of fallible, imperfect, human beings.[81]

This passage reveals an understanding of the common law as the embodiment of common sense rules applied to everyday lived realities. Riddell also wrote, "The common sense of the judge was not far away from the common sense of the mass of the people – and the *dicta* of the judge recommended themselves to the people because they were much the same as they would themselves have uttered had they been articulate."[82]

Law and psychology scholar Norman Finkel also connects common sense with common law legal judgment and focuses on the ways that legal judgment is hindered or precluded by legal rules that are excessively technical or rational.[83] Finkel argues that human judgment, including legal judgment, is always imbued with subjective factors that help to form the basis of real justice, which he calls "commonsense justice."[84] Finkel argues that commonsense justice is the home of these essential human elements of judgment and that these human elements find their way into the law through concepts like "intent." He argues that legal doctrines that try to exclude these subjective elements, such as strict liability or objective tests, can therefore be contrary to commonsense justice: "[M]ost [people] see the law as a distinctly human creation pertaining to human actions, thoughts, feelings, and motives. Expressed in the law's penumbra or subtext is a psychology of human nature. When that human nature stops being human, or ceases to have anything but a cardboard similarity to the real thing, it fails the community test."[85] In a similar vein, evidence scholar Ronald Allen argues that the common law emerges from common sense and indeed that the ongoing existence of the common law demonstrates its consistency with common sense: "The law provides a web of regulation that surrounds virtually all of life in these [contemporary common law] societies. If that web were not generated largely from and consistent with the conventional interactions of individuals, it would not survive."[86] Allen also argues that the law of evidence does a service to the law by protecting space for the free operation of common sense in legal judgment: "The body of law governing evidence may be the strongest bastion against sudden assaults on common sense. I would add that resisting sudden assaults on common sense may be one of the most important guarantors of the continuing progression of civilization."[87] These writers invoke "common sense" as the basis for law and even argue that if the law departed from such shared knowledge, it would not survive. From this perspective, the common law is evidence of the content of common sense. We can see in these claims many of the intellectual strands of common sense identified by Rosenfeld, including common sense as shared knowledge and common sense as the knowledge of ordinary people.

The second broad category of writing on common sense and law includes legal scholars who have taken up common sense as a basis not for defending the content of the law but for critiquing it and the ground upon which it stands. For example, in his polemical book *The Death of Common Sense: How Law Is Suffocating America*, lawyer Phillip Howard argues that the legal system of the United States is not based on common sense but is the product of its abandonment. He argues that contemporary law, particularly administrative law, is directed so much at achieving certainty that it forecloses the exercise of judgment, both by those the law governs and by those charged with enforcing it.[88] He writes that "[i]n the decades since World War II, we have constructed a system of regulatory law that basically outlaws common sense. Modern law, in an effort to be 'self-executing,' has shut out our humanity."[89] To support his argument, Howard offers a series of purportedly outrageous anecdotes of state officials, like building inspectors and environmental regulators, adhering to "the letter of the law" in cases where a broader and more pragmatic exercise of discretion would clearly, in his view, have resulted in better regulation or a more just outcome. Howard stresses that common sense is closely linked to the genuine exercise of judgment, in contrast to unreasonable deference to rules, and on this basis he uses the idea of common sense to critique the content of law. However, he does not turn his critical attention to common sense itself.

Indeed, Howard communicates very few hesitations about the scope or content of common sense knowledge and its ability to ground good legal judgment. Concerned as he is with defending common sense against *rules*, he devotes little attention to the question of whether common sense knowledge itself might be disputed or problematic in ways that are directly relevant to legal judgment. Howard's book does address some issues related to social diversity, but he is quite unrestrained in using sweeping generalizations, as well as in associating common sense with majoritarianism and marshalling it against minority groups: nonsense is what is opposed to "us." For example, he critiques the concept of "rights," particularly as employed by people with disabilities, because it results in the use of public money that "comes out of everybody else's hide."[90] Howard's argument that formal rules have displaced common sense judgment fails to attend to the exclusion and marginalization of people who do not fit within his idea of the community.

In contrast, other thinkers put the legitimacy of common sense itself at the centre of the analysis. For example, in an article that is in part a critique of Allen's approach, feminist evidence scholar Marilyn MacCrimmon argues that not all common sense knowledge is a legitimate part of legal judgment. Indeed, common sense knowledge can be racist, sexist, or otherwise imbued with discrimination and unjust partiality.[91] For example, she catalogues the range of racist sayings and proverbs about Indigenous people that find their home in North American common sense.[92] MacCrimmon argues that the laws of evidence exist not to protect and promote the exercise of common sense but to contest and regulate it.[93] MacCrimmon points to several legal concepts that work to regulate common sense in the interests of legitimate, impartial legal judgment, including by structuring the generalizations that can be used to link evidence and facts.[94] In MacCrimmon's approach, we hear echoes of those intellectual traditions that address common sense as part of the process of judgment, as well as common sense as the knowledge of the community. However, unlike Howard, MacCrimmon is concerned to ask to *which* community the knowledge attaches, as well as concerned to test common sense against *other* criteria for legitimate legal judgment.

A third category of writing on the relationship between common sense and law, which often overlaps with the others, creates a contrast between common sense, on the one hand, and legal theory or expertise, on the other. Legal scholar F.K.H. Maher, in an article reviewing the role of common sense in legal judgment, argues that judges should resort to both modes of thought when making decisions.[95] Other writers clearly privilege one way of thinking, or type of knowledge, over the other. For example, legal scholar Michael Salter critiques the tendency of legal practitioners to unduly reject the value of theory for legal judgment due to an uncritical acceptance of common sense.[96] He describes common sense as a latent and "self-concealing" mode of thought that resists the critical attention that law deserves. Like MacCrimmon, Salter argues that the adequate exercise of legal judgment requires not that we adopt or exercise common sense but that we scrutinize and constrain it. This third approach, which contrasts common sense with theory, reflects those intellectual strains in which common sense is understood as the knowledge or thinking of ordinary people rather than the knowledge of experts.

Although these three general categories reflect different priorities and focus on different aspects of law, there is a sense in which all of them present either a critical or a sympathetic view of common sense. Sometimes this view can be seen just as much in the language and tone of the writing as in the argument itself. For example, Maher quotes the 1972 speech by Lord Reid set out at the beginning of the Introduction, in which Reid says, "We should, I think, have regard to common sense, legal principle and public policy in that order. We are here to serve the public, the common ordinary reasonable man ... Sometimes the law has got out of step with common sense. We do not want to have people saying: 'If the law says that[,] the law is an ass.'"[97] This kind of language sets us up to think that surely common sense is properly part of legal judgment. In contrast, Salter talks about the use of common sense as obstinately unreflective: "My primary contention is that our possibilities for authentic legal understanding, interpretation and thus thought, can be shown to be retarded to the extent that lawyers – theorists as well as students and practitioners – remain under the unseen dominion of common sense."[98] This language is much less likely to make us embrace common sense reasoning when thinking about criteria for legal judgment. Some legal writers seem to defensively attack those who are unwilling to take the time to rigorously engage with legal theory. Others accuse lawyers and legal academics of slinging jargon and ignoring the meaning of the law for everyone in the real world. Note that both sides imply that their opponents are ignorant of something important and are unable or unwilling to see what is *really* going on. "Common sense" in both camps is a rhetorical tool tied to legitimacy and the way that legal judgment connects to the rest of the world. Once again, the paradox of common sense – self-evident and inscrutable – makes an appearance.

What is missing from the conversation on common sense is an approach that allows us to do more than simply accept or reject common sense as part of good legal judgment. Like MacCrimmon, I start from a critique of the inequality and marginalization that can come into play when "common sense" is invoked in legal judgment, and I too see the urgent need to scrutinize the discriminatory and oppressive content and consequences of common sense. However, noting the complex and even contradictory nature of common sense, I insist on the need to remain open to the multiple meanings and consequences of this phrase. Those writers who advocate or even privilege the role of common sense also reveal important aspects of common sense that should not be rejected out of hand but subjected to careful scrutiny against the criteria for legal judgment that can respond to the demands of justice.

THE PARADOX OF COMMON SENSE AS A CONSTRAINT ON OUR UNDERSTANDING OF LEGAL JUDGMENT

The constellation of works touching on common sense described above shows that there are a wide range of perspectives that can be brought to bear on the question of legal judgment. However, whether theorists want to critique, celebrate, or deny the role of common sense in legal judgment, there is a frequent return to the idea that the legitimacy of common sense relates to the potential universality of some form or other of common knowledge. I argue that this approach to common sense – in which common sense is a kind of knowledge – overshadows other approaches and that it limits the kinds of questions that are asked about common sense.

Confronted with this kind of problem, philosopher Ludwig Wittgenstein uses the language of "captivity" to describe our inability to break out of one way of thinking. Wittgenstein argues that our way of thinking and talking about something, such as common sense, can become "captive" to a particular "picture" and thereby lose its usefulness as a way for us to understand ourselves.[99] I think that debates about common sense are often constrained in this way. To break free of this captivity and to reclaim the creativity and productivity of our language, Wittgenstein argues that it is useful to look at something from new perspectives and to use theoretical approaches that can generate this opportunity. We are captive to a picture of common sense in which the legitimacy of common sense relates to the potential universality of some form or other of common knowledge. Our captivity to this picture prevents full debate on the way that common sense relates to legal judgment, thereby impeding our ability to evaluate common sense and its potential as a resource for good legal judgment.

The dominance of this picture of common sense as a type of common knowledge is evident in the context of legal judgments touching specifically on poverty and inequality. In many respects, this picture of common sense – as a form of knowledge – is extremely useful in this context because it allows us to ask the crucial question "common to whom?" For example, in the *Gosselin* case, the majority justices used the language of "common sense" to ground certain conclusions. By asking whose knowledge grounds those claims, it becomes possible to scrutinize the justice (or injustice) of invoking "common sense" in that context. Within the framework provided by the picture of common sense as a type of knowledge, it is possible to see, as Schneiderman notes, that in *Gosselin* common sense seems to be associated with a dominant cultural consensus about welfare and justice.[100]

However, the injustices of poverty also tend to provoke other questions and concerns that seem unanswered or unanswerable from within the framework provided by the picture of common sense as a type of knowledge. For example, writing in dissent in *Gosselin*, Justice L'Heureux-Dubé could also have claimed that her judgment was based on her common sense, ***but she did not***. Why not? Is it just a matter of social consensus, or is there a substantive match between the political ideology espoused by the Quebec government in that case and the idea of common sense? Is there a link between common sense and the economic class of political elites or of judges? What do we make of the rhetorical choice to invoke, or refrain from invoking, "common sense" in written reasons? Thinking about common sense as a type of knowledge gives, at best, an incomplete answer to these questions and does not provide a framework to fully address what seems to be at stake. To respond to this challenge, I have adopted methodological tools that allow for the exploration of multiple aspects of common sense as it relates to legal judgment.

METHODOLOGY FOR OPENING COMMON SENSE TO CRITICAL SCRUTINY

The following chapters of this book work to crack open the paradox of "common sense" by examining the use of this phrase in different historical, political, legal, and discursive contexts. Through this engagement, our captivity to a picture of common sense as knowledge begins to fall away, and new questions can be asked about the role of common sense in practices of legal judgment.

In each of the following three chapters, I engage with a theorist of common sense in order to reveal the "aspect" of common sense that becomes visible through his or her work.[101] Placed in conversation with legal judgments, each aspect of common sense allows us to learn something specific about legal judgment, particularly about the relationship between legal judgment and social justice. Noticing these specific insights arising from each aspect assists us in challenging our captivity to a particular understanding of common sense that is of limited usefulness. With debate opened up, we are liberated to develop alternative criteria for the use of common sense in legal judgment, oriented to the emancipatory aspirations of law.[102]

There are two key methodological points about this exploration of common sense in legal judgment. First, by investigating different aspects of common sense and juxtaposing them, I aim to question things that may seem most immune to scrutiny – self-evident and inscrutable. I want this process of juxtaposition to serve as a way to interrogate and ultimately relativize common sense in legal judgment. This undertaking is particularly significant in the case of common sense, which itself claims to take up space not at the margins but right in the middle of community knowledge and practice. I study something from the "centre" not to reinforce its significance but to reveal its particularity, its contingency, and its relationship to other social practices.[103]

Second, the goal of my exploration is to reveal as many aspects of common sense as possible, subjecting it to robust critical scrutiny. This effort requires resisting abstract definitions from the outset and attending to the meaning of the phrase "common sense" and to the consequences of its use in any given context. In Wittgenstein's words, I aim to "look and see" how the phrase functions in context.[104] Most pointedly, in relation to legal judgments, this approach means that I focus on judgments in which the phrase "common sense" *actually appears*. In another kind of study, it could make sense to explore the ways that judges rely on their common sense without actually invoking that language explicitly. For example, if I were to define "common sense" as "shared background knowledge," I could look for cases in which judges seem to rely in some way on shared background knowledge. But this approach would require a pre-existing conceptualization that could foreclose certain aspects of common sense that might otherwise appear. For instance, what aspects of common sense are not captured if we think if it as "shared background knowledge"? To do so would be to risk remaining captive to a picture of common sense that so often foils attempts at thorough scrutiny. Instead, I try to look at how language actually functions in context and try not to prematurely attribute meaning. An attendant consequence of this approach is that I treat different instances of the use of the phrase "common sense" as different examples of the same thing. I argue that Wittgenstein's approach to language and investigation of language gives support to the general notion that it is relevant that the language of "common sense" appears in these various, distinct contexts. It *matters* that this particular language is used, and this use of language is my methodological starting point.

In a related way, unlike in a doctrinal legal study, I do not purport to conduct a full survey into the meaning of the phrase "common sense" in legal judgment, nor are my cases selected because they *represent* "the law on common sense" in Canada. Rather, the cases are *examples* for comparison, and the criterion used to select them is their usefulness in illuminating some aspect of common sense.

The cases I discuss are all judgments of the Supreme Court of Canada, not judgments of trial courts or other appellate courts. This approach is taken in part simply to limit the scope of my study but also because the language of the Supreme Court is adopted and repeated by other courts, thus making its invocation of "common sense" significant for the legal system as a whole. But beyond this choice to privilege the Supreme Court, I engage with the legal judgments without, at least at the outset, particular regard for the doctrinal context that might render some examples more significant than others. For example, in chapter 2 I discuss the court's judgment in *Vetrovec v. The Queen*,[105] which, although a landmark case, has been modified by subsequent jurisprudence and would no longer be cited on its own to support submissions on the law of corroboration.[106] Similarly, although I attribute various judgments to the individual judges who authored them, I do not seek to make claims about the views of any one judge. For example, Chief Justice Beverley McLachlin is the author of several of the judgments I address, including *Gosselin*. However, I do not attempt to reconcile the judgments or claim to discover her "real" views on common sense. Instead, I approach each judgment as a textual instance of the phrase "common sense" and try to attend carefully to what each text says on its face.[107]

Careful attention to the exact words of a text is important for my methodological approach. Exploration of the multiple meanings and uses of words forms the content of this project as a whole. The key words "common sense" and "judgment" are used in different ways in various contexts and by different writers. Thus, even before embarking on this journey, a few introductory comments about these words are in order.

"Common Sense"

The primary source material for this book consists of scholarly writings and legal judgments that explicitly invoke the phrase "common sense." In English, the words "commonsense" and "commonsensical" also appear, and I have treated these words as intimately related forms of the phrase "common sense." For example, when Norman Finkel discusses "commonsense justice," I have allowed this to count toward the discussion of "common sense."[108] Thomas Reid (discussed in chapter 2), writing in English, uses the exact phrase "common sense."

The work of Antonio Gramsci (discussed in chapter 3) was translated into English from the original Italian by Quentin Hoare and Geoffrey Nowell Smith.[109] In translation, Gramsci uses the phrase "common sense" as well as the phrase "good sense."[110] In chapter 3, I explore Gramsci's treatment of both common sense and good sense as aspects of the phrase "common sense."

In chapter 4, I engage with the work of Hannah Arendt. Arendt writes in English and uses the exact phrase "common sense." However, Arendt traces a different intellectual trajectory of the concept, invoking the Latin phrase *sensus communis*, which she either calls "common sense"[111] or calls "community sense"[112] when she wants to focus attention on the special meaning she attributes to it.

"Judgment," "Judging," and "Judges"

This book takes a broad approach to the task of understanding legal judgment. In my view, it is useful to understand legal judgment as one form of a larger human practice, which would also include political judgment, moral judgment, and aesthetic judgment. I discuss the substantive consequences of adopting this view in other parts of the book, especially chapter 4's discussion of Hannah Arendt. But for now, I want to draw the reader's attention to the way that this approach affects my choice of language to describe legal decision making.

First, the decision to understand legal judgment as a form of a larger human practice of judgment means that I use the words "judgment" and "judgments," rather than other related terms such as "adjudication," "decisions," or "findings," when describing what judges in a court of law do and how it may relate to common sense. This approach invites a certain slippage between the noun "judgment" as used in legal parlance to refer to the written reasons of a court in a given case and the noun "judgment" as used to mean the practice of judging in general. A similar slippage can occur between the verb "to judge," meaning to engage in the act of judgment, and the noun "judge," meaning a person who judges. I think these potential slippages and overlapping meanings are productive because they provoke reflection on what legal judgment is all about.

Second, talking about judgment as a general human practice means that when I want to talk specifically about what happens in a court of law, I talk about "legal judgment" or sometimes about a "legal judge." This approach makes my claims narrower and more specific. At the same time, I continue to use very general language about judgment no matter what kind of decision making is going on in a legal case. For example, I describe it as an act of "judgment" when judges make findings of fact, when they offer interpretations of laws, and when they make rulings on the outcomes of disputes. All of these forms of reasoning could be mapped differently in relation to other kinds of judgment, such as moral judgment. However, I argue that they all engage this larger practice of judgment, which is about the evaluation of a particular fact, law, or situation. And depending on the circumstances, they may all engage with common sense. Therefore, in this investigation of common sense in legal judgment, it is useful to adopt this very broad view in order to see the various points at which common sense comes into play and the way that it affects how legal judgment works.

Finally, taking a broad view of judgment has methodological implications given the way that legal judgment is set alongside other forms of judgment. Understanding judgment as a human practice that transcends the boundaries of subject matter provides opportunities for interdisciplinarity – when literature from other areas may help to illuminate the meaning of judgment in law. Throughout this work, I rely on theorists from a wide range of disciplines, both methodologically and substantively.

WHAT DIFFERENCE DOES IT MAKE?

Wittgenstein argues that when we consider alternative pictures of the world, the important question is how these alternative pictures relate to alternative ways of life. The real question about challenging our captivity to a certain understanding of the world is "what difference does it make?"[113] That is, if we break free of our captivity and change the content of the system of beliefs that frames our judgment, how does doing so affect the specific social practices that form the context for the picture? What difference does it make to our lives, to our communities, and to our ability to change our practices of legal judgment? For feminist and critical social theorists, these different ways of living are subject to evaluation against political criteria, including the question of which communities are the relevant point of reference. Here, the real question is: what difference does it make, *to us, in ways that matter to us*?[114]

For me, political and social inequality motivate the attempt to better understand common sense in legal judgment. The problem with the way many questions are posed and addressed is not just that they result in philosophically unsatisfying answers but also that they fail to provide knowledge or analysis that is useful for understanding and thus challenging oppression and inequality.[115] What is at stake is our capacity to envision and realize alternative, more just, understandings of the world.[116]

2

Thomas Reid's Common Sense: Accountability for Judgment and the Boundaries of Debate

We jostle for seats at London's Haymarket Theatre in 1736. We find ourselves sitting beside Thomas Reid, a philosopher and Presbyterian minister, arrived from 1750s Aberdeen. Our neighbour observes most of the proceedings with a serious expression but breaks into raucous laughter at the biting satire. One character tries to awaken the sleeping Queen Common-Sense by describing how common sense protects against all kinds of nonsense and deceit. Reid nods his head wryly.

> Awake, great *Common Sense*, and sleep no more,
> ... for while thou art on Earth,
> The Convocation will not meet again.
> The Lawyers cannot rob Men of their Rights;
> Physicians cannot dose away their Souls:
> A Courtier's Promise will not be believ'd;
> Nor broken Citizens again be trusted.
> A thousand News-papers cannot subsist,
> In which there is not any News at all.
> Play-houses cannot flourish, while they dare
> To Nonsense give an Entertainment's Name.[1]

And as the play concludes, Queen Common-Sense now dead, Reid applauds the final speech of her ghost.

And all the Friends of Ignorance shall find,
My Ghost, at least, they cannot banish hence.
And all henceforth, who murder Common-Sense,
Learn from these Scenes that tho' Success you boast,
You shall at last be haunted with her Ghost.[2]

INTRODUCTION

In this chapter, I explore the aspect of common sense that becomes visible when looking at common sense from the perspective of the eighteenth-century Scottish philosopher Thomas Reid, whose writings are central in the political and intellectual history of common sense. Reid uses the phrase "common sense" to mean a body of shared knowledge grounded in daily life and possessed by most everyone. Reid argues that this practical common sense knowledge is a form of knowledge no less true or meaningful than the structured knowledges of experts, including philosophers. In some respects, his perspective on common sense shares a great deal with the general view on common sense that tends to capture discourse on law. For example, there is the notion of common sense as a body of shared knowledge, as well as an egalitarian impulse that sometimes manifests itself in the form of exasperation at elite or technical knowledges. But Reid is also interested in how common sense relates to the exercise of independent and accountable judgment and how it rhetorically shapes the boundaries of legitimate debate. Thus, when we take seriously Ludwig Wittgenstein's methodological exhortation to "look and see,"[3] Reid's approach turns out to be nuanced in interesting ways that begin to complicate the "picture" of common sense that tends to dominate debates on common sense and legal judgment.[4]

Reid's aspect of common sense – that is, common sense as a body of common knowledge – brings attention to accountability, expertise, and the boundaries of debate. Reid's approach places a high value on nonexpert knowledge and the experiences of daily life, which can help to generate criteria for good legal judgment in the context of diversity and inequality. Said another way, adopting Reid's approach would call on judges who invoke "common sense" to take seriously the common knowledge of ordinary people. In addition, Reid calls for close attention to the roles of language and rhetoric in legal judgment, allowing us to see how common sense can set the boundaries of legal debate.

Yet the encounter between Reid's approach and the use of common sense in legal judgment also provides a framework for critical consideration of Reid's writings. Thinking about common sense in *legal* judgment, in particular, shows that his arguments rely on broad generalizations across social groups and that they view human knowledge and conduct as transparently linked. These elements of Reid's approach allow common sense to fall too easily into uncritical majoritarianism, and they provide little assistance in the quest to make legal judgment more reflective. Reid's approach is as problematic as it is helpful.

This chapter has two parts. In the first part, I describe in more detail the aspect of common sense that becomes visible when reading Reid. I focus on three themes. First, I describe how Reid relates common sense to the practice of judgment. Reid argues that common sense, rather than rules or expertise, necessarily grounds the exercise of judgment and that common sense facilitates accountability for judgment. Second, I explore Reid's claim that common sense knowledge is, in some senses, universal and the ways that this claim to universality has the effect of setting the boundaries of legitimate debate. Third, I discuss some of the rhetorical effects of the language of "common sense" and Reid's qualified advocacy of ridicule as a rhetorical strategy in the search for knowledge.

In the second part of this chapter, I investigate how Reid's aspect of common sense – that is, the understanding of common sense as a body of shared knowledge that frames our judgment – speaks to legal judgment specifically. What happens to our understanding of legal judgment if we think of common sense *in this* way or *from this perspective*? In this part, I discuss the Supreme Court of Canada's decisions in *Vetrovec v. The Queen* and in *R. v. D.D.*,[5] in which the court appeals to "common sense" to explain the basis on which judges and juries should assess the credibility of witnesses. In these cases, "common sense" is invoked in contradistinction to expert evidence and to legal rules. I also return to the case of *Gosselin v. Quebec (Procureur général)* in order to explore the invocation of "common sense" in that case against the backdrop of this discussion of common knowledge and the assessment of credibility. Reid's approach focuses attention on the nature of judgment and on how it is structured or constrained by systems of rules and specific bodies of knowledge. His approach also focuses attention on the criteria we use to assess accountability for judgment and on the boundaries of legitimate legal debate. All of these issues are important when thinking about how to make common sense part of fully reflective legal judgment that can address the injustices of poverty and social marginalization.

This chapter argues that Reid's approach contains an inherent tension that is important for legal judgment. On the one hand, Reid is committed to a kind of democratic epistemology, in which everyone shares equally in common sense. On the other hand, his works reveal a nascent discomfort with what to do about purported common sense claims that may be misled by error or limited by unduly insular social discourse. Reid recognizes that even his own understanding can be so limited.[6] Yet the power of his notion of common sense comes from its claims to be universal and communal. This tension is what allows this first aspect of common sense to begin to shake us free of our captivity to an unsatisfying understanding of common sense, freeing us to develop one that is more complex and ultimately more useful for legal judgment.

THOMAS REID ON COMMON SENSE

Judgment and Accountability

Thomas Reid (1710–96) was a philosopher and Presbyterian minister whose work is central in the intellectual history of common sense and who was one of the founders of the Scottish School of "Common Sense Philosophy."[7] Reid spent the earlier part of his life in the small northern city of Aberdeen, which provided a very particular context for his intellectual work. Aberdeen in the eighteenth century, like the larger urban centres of Edinburgh and Glasgow, was part of the intellectual and social phenomenon known as the Scottish Enlightenment.[8] However, Aberdeen was more isolated both politically and economically, with strong connections to traditional, agricultural ways of life and to the institutions of the Presbyterian Church. In some ways, Aberdeen was a parochial and conservative place. At the same time, Aberdeen was also relatively free of some of the social and political conflicts of larger cities, which helped to generate a kind of intellectual tolerance and a commitment to freedom of inquiry.[9] It was in this context of strong social traditions and relatively unfettered intellectual inquiry that Reid helped to found the Philosophical Society of Aberdeen in 1758 (known as the Wise Club).[10] The members of this society met to discuss a wide range of topics with the goals of self-improvement and the advancement of society generally.[11] Particularly important to the group were questions about evidence and proof and the way that people came to know things.[12] Reid and his colleagues were critical of epistemological skepticism, including that of their Scottish contemporary David Hume, and they thought that skepticism undermined both intellectual inquiry and moral and community life.[13] The members of the Wise Club, including Reid, thought that truly free, evidence-based thought led not to skepticism but to common sense. In the doctrine of common sense, Reid and his colleagues found a way to ground both their traditional religious and moral beliefs and practices and their commitment to unconstrained, autonomous thinking.[14]

Reid's most important writings on common sense are contained in two books: *An Inquiry into the Human Mind on the Principles of Common Sense* (1764) and *Essays on the Intellectual Powers of Man* (1785). Reid employs the words "common sense" throughout his work.[15] However, his explicit discussion and definition of the phrase "common sense" appear in chapter 6 of the *Essays*, titled "Of Judgment."[16] Reflecting an interest in common language that is both substantive and methodological, Reid defines "common sense" according to how he understands it being used in the oridinary language he hears around him. Reid notes that for philosophers, the word "sense" often means "the power by which we receive certain ideas or impressions from objects."[17] But Reid thinks that the phrase "common sense" means more than this, and he points out that in common language, "sense" implies not only the receipt of sensory information but also some *evaluation* of that information.[18] From this perspective, common sense is necessarily bound up with assessments of what we perceive – that is, with *judgment*. Reid writes, "[I]n common language, sense always implies judgment. A man of sense is a man of judgment. Good sense is good judgment. Nonsense is what is evidently contrary to right judgment. Common sense is that degree of judgment which is common to men with whom we can converse and transact business."[19] Reid argues that there is no good reason for departing from common language when it comes to defining "common sense," and he thus pursues his discussion on the basis that common sense is intertwined with judgment and evaluation.[20]

Reid's idea of common sense emerges in the context of his ideas about the task of a philosopher and what it means to engage in philosophical thinking.[21] Specifically, Reid turns to common sense as a way to respond to the claims of philosophical skepticism.[22] Reid argues that common sense forms the background against which we assess other claims, including philosophical claims.[23] Against both idealist and empiricist versions of epistemological skepticism, which value only reason or raw sense data as determinative of truth, Reid defends common sense as a legitimate basis for testing philosophical claims.[24] For example, Reid argues that common sense knowledge leads us to have faith in the reliability of our senses. As a legitimate framework for assessing truth, this common sense knowledge provides us with good reason to be wary of the claims of skeptical philosophers who insist that our senses are fallacious or that we must assume that our sensory perceptions are meaningless for the purposes of real knowledge.[25]

Reid also argues that common sense necessarily plays a role in the actual practice of philosophy.[26] Turning again to the example of the common sense belief that we can rely on our senses, he argues that even those philosophers who claim to doubt their senses in their philosophical work never actually doubt them in their daily lives. In characteristically witty form, Reid writes that he "never heard that any sceptic run his head against a post, or stepped into a kennel, because he did not believe his eyes."[27] It is significant for Reid that philosophers who profess to doubt their senses are actual embodied human beings who do, in fact, rely on those senses. And he insists that philosophizing, just like walking, is an inherently human activity that should not be understood as divorced from other parts of life.

Reid argues that *both* the daily-life judgment that prevents one from walking into a post and the philosophical judgment that one practices in reflective thinking are grounded in common sense. Philosopher and religious scholar Nicholas Wolterstorff writes that according to Reid, "[p]hilosophers are related to the principles of common sense in the same way everybody else is – and in the same way that he, the philosopher, is related when not engaged in philosophy."[28] Further, for Reid, this common sense background is not only inevitable but also valuable. Disconnected from common sense, philosophy loses its ability to meaningfully speak to human life. Reid says, "Philosophy ... has no other root but the principles of Common Sense; it grows out of them, and draws its nourishment from them. Severed from this root, its honours wither, its sap is dried up, it dies and rots."[29]

At the same time, Reid does not describe common sense knowledge as infallible, and he is interested in exploring the boundaries of the usefulness of common sense. In his writings, he notes our tendency to overvalue authority[30] and to interpret new things in light of things with which we are already familiar.[31] The best way to approach these realities of human judgment is not to use them as the basis for rejecting everything about our common ways of thinking but to address them as part of a larger whole with strengths and weaknesses.

The function of Reid's common sense knowledge in judgment is to provide a kind of background against which we assess things. For Reid, we use common sense to decide whether to affirm or deny the plausibility of some other claim. When something seems to defy common sense, we are less likely to judge it true or meaningful. In this way, common sense knowledge creates a kind of burden of proof that other claims must meet.[32] This means that rather than forming a body of positive knowledge, common sense tends to remain invisible until challenged.[33] When challenged (e.g., by epistemological skeptics who argue that we cannot trust our senses), common sense knowledge comes into view and forms the basis of a judgment – here, a judgment that tends to reject those skeptical claims.

Reid argues that common sense knowledge is made visible not by our ability to state it in general or abstract terms but by our practical reliance on it in daily life. For Reid, the "inner conviction" evidenced by a person's actions reveals a judgment.[34] Reid argues that people who demonstrate faith in their senses have made a *judgment* that their senses are worthy of this credit: "When a man in the common course of his life gives credit to the testimony of his senses, his memory, or his reason, he does not put the question to himself, whether these faculties may deceive him; yet the trust he reposes in them supposes an inward conviction, that, in that instance at least, they do not deceive him."[35] Thus Reid's common sense is related to the practices of daily life because it is in daily life that common sense develops and because it is through daily life that common sense becomes visible.

The practical and quotidian nature of common sense knowledge also means that, unlike science or abstract philosophy, which rely more on certainty and clarity for their usefulness, common sense works well even though it is uncertain. If asked, few people could precisely identify the contents of their common sense in advance. Reid argues that the ways that common sense knowledge is ill defined do not work against common sense as true or meaningful but actually support its usefulness in context. In a passage foreshadowing Wittgenstein, Reid argues that the unclear boundaries of common sense do not pose a problem when understood in the right context: "What the precise limits are which divide common judgment from what is beyond it on the one hand, and from what falls short of it on the other, may be difficult to determine; and men may agree in the meaning of the word who have different opinions about those limits, or who even never thought of fixing them. This is as intelligible as, that all Englishmen should mean the same thing by the county of York, though perhaps not a hundredth part of them can point out its precise limits."[36] In this way, the vagueness and ill-defined boundaries of common sense knowledge do not detract from its value; rather, these moments of vagueness and imprecision contribute to the practical usefulness of common sense.[37]

Although undefined in advance, once challenged, common sense knowledge is revealed as self-evident.[38] This means that we generally accept common sense knowledge as obviously true. Common sense beliefs are self-evident in the sense that we do not generally have reasons for believing them, nor do we usually think that such reasons are required. For example, if challenged, I would say that I believe that my senses provide me with accurate information about the world. This belief comes from my daily-life experiences. I did not arrive at this belief by acquiring reasons to support it (e.g., learning information about how nerves function). I cannot fully explain or justify why I have such confidence in my senses, other than to point to my ongoing reliance on this belief in my life. Further, Reid argues, if we attempt to locate the reasons for our common sense beliefs or try to justify them on the basis of logic, we find that the reasons themselves are not as convincing as the original belief.[39] Thus all the reasons I can find in support of my belief in the reliability of my senses, ranging from neuroscience to metaphysics, are in themselves less certain to me than my original belief. Reid maintains that in this way common sense beliefs come to form the "first principles" of other kinds of knowledge.[40]

The fact that common sense beliefs are not held on the basis of reasons means that the content of common sense knowledge has to be approached differently and more carefully than other kinds of knowledge. Reid writes, "There are ways by which the evidence of first principles may be made more apparent when they are brought into dispute; but they require to be handled in a way peculiar to themselves. Their evidence is not demonstrative, but intuitive. They require not proof, but to be placed in a proper point of view."[41] Reid argues that the mistake of some philosophers, such as his skeptical contemporaries, is to confuse the boundary between self-evident, common sense propositions and the propositions of reason and philosophy that can be built upon them. Thus these philosophers have tried to seek *reasons* in support of common sense knowledge and, finding no adequate ones, have declared common sense knowledge invalid.[42] This is to misunderstand the notion of common sense.

Reid argues that if we refuse to acknowledge the role of common sense in all kinds of judgments and instead attempt to set it aside, we are not led to pure rationality, as some philosophers might have it. Rather, Reid says, we are led to absurdity. Skeptical philosophers mistakenly attempt to replace common sense with a philosophical "system" divorced from the reality of human practice. The attempt to build philosophical knowledge on such an ungrounded structure renders the resulting philosophy of little use.[43]

But, for Reid, the more serious problem arising from this approach is that, in effect, it precludes the practice of good judgment. Judgment requires the assessment of something as it appears in life. When philosophers attempt to build knowledge solely on the basis of logic, they claim to withhold judgment on questions that logic cannot satisfactorily resolve. Logic cannot, for example, establish with certainty the reliability of our senses. By claiming that we have no reliable basis on which to judge these questions, philosophers are, in fact, not judging at all.[44] That is, they are not assessing the value of a particular claim. Instead, they are deferring this responsibility to an artificial system of rules.

This abdication of judgment permits the mistaken rejections of an important part of human life. Reid argues, "In all matters belonging to our cognisance, every man must be determined by his own final judgment, otherwise he does not act the part of a rational being. Authority may add weight to one scale; but the man holds the balance, and judges what weight he ought to allow to authority. If a man should even claim infallibility, we must judge of his title to that prerogative. If a man pretend to be an Ambassador from heaven, we must judge of his credentials. No claim can deprive us of this right or excuse us for neglecting to exercise it."[45] Failure to exercise judgment leads to errors and, moreover, a failure to fulfil important parts of being human. Further, it is our genuine judgments for which we can be held to account; by failing to judge, we avoid taking responsibility for their consequences.

Normative and Empirical Commonality

Reid's common sense knowledge is a type of knowledge that is shared by almost everyone; for most purposes, it is universal. All people – or at least all sane adults – share in common sense knowledge. Those excluded are those who lack the "degree of reason ... that makes a man capable of managing his own affairs, and answerable for his conduct towards others."[46] Reid's claims about the universality of common sense knowledge have two important consequences. First, if common sense is universal, it can be used to ground claims about what everyone knows and what everyone should know. Second, the content of common sense knowledge must be severely limited; otherwise, it could not possibly be held universally.

Common sense knowledge is not only possessed by virtually everyone but is also possessed equally by everyone. When it comes to matters of common sense, "every man is a competent judge."[47] Moreover, the content of common sense knowledge is *the same* for everyone. Reid relies solely on masculine referents throughout his writings, without reflection on the gendered nature of his "universal" common sense knowledge. However, he does address directly some questions about class and education that raise related problems for the "sameness" of common sense. Reid does not hesitate to claim that "the learned and the unlearned, the Philosopher and the day-labourer, are upon a level, and will pass the same judgment."[48] Nonetheless, this last point comes with an important caveat: Reid always maintains the possibility that people can be mistaken about their common sense.[49] The full passage says, "To judge of first principles, requires no more than a sound mind free from prejudice, and a distinct conception of the question. The learned and the unlearned, the Philosopher and the day-labourer, are upon a level, and will pass the same judgment, when they are not misled by some bias, or taught to renounce their understanding from some mistaken religious principle."[50]

There is a strong, even radical, egalitarianism inherent in this argument; Reid insists that common sense is indeed *common*. In her account of the political history of common sense, Sophia Rosenfeld argues that the democratic political consequences of Reid's views on common sense were largely unintended but that, in the hands of Reid and his colleagues, common sense epistemology helped to propel a "democratic ethos into the realm of public judgment."[51]

This picture of common sense knowledge as self-evident to virtually all human beings has the consequence of setting the boundaries of what can constitute rational debate. Reid argues that opinions contrary to common sense knowledge "are not only false, but absurd."[52] Common sense knowledge consists of things that all rational people cannot help but believe; anything contrary to common sense knowledge is nonsense and unworthy of rational consideration. Common sense knowledge thus helps to set the boundaries of reasoned debate because of its normative claim to universality; Reid's common sense knowledge consists of those things that every rational person *should* believe.

Reid also argues that common sense knowledge is "common" in the sense that it is empirically *shared*, and this is a large part of why common sense is valuable. Reid argues that "before men can reason together, they must agree in first principles; and it is impossible to reason with a man who has no principles in common with you."[53] Reid also talks about common sense forming the shared ground upon which people might "converse" or "transact business."[54] Reid sees this type of common knowledge as essential in order for people to understand one another and therefore essential for community and for developing other forms of knowledge.[55]

From this perspective, Reid's notion of common sense becomes more sensitive to the distinction between common sense knowledge and beliefs that are merely commonly held. If knowledge is not, in fact, actually shared among individuals, it fails to fulfil its role as a creator of common ground or facilitator of conversation and business. Like the "common sense" invoked by Hannah Arendt to demonstrate the communal character of human judgment (discussed later in chapter 4), Reid's common sense must be linked to a real community. Reid understands common sense knowledge to be useful in large part precisely because it facilitates our communal lives, which he values highly.[56] When speaking in defence of the common sense principle that gives credit to our senses, he points to our belief in each other's existence as central to human life and to all kinds of meaningful communication: "It is evident that we can have no communication, no correspondence or society with any created being, but by means of our senses."[57] Further, he writes, "When I consider myself as speaking to men who hear me, and can judge of what I say, I feel that respect which is due to such an audience. I feel an enjoyment in a reciprocal communication of sentiments with candid and ingenious friends, and my soul blesses the Author of my being, who has made me capable of this manly and rational entertainment."[58] For Reid, common sense is the precondition for the respectful, reciprocal communication that is necessary for "transacting business" and relationships of friendship.

Reid's concern that common sense knowledge be *actually*, as well as normatively, shared requires him to grapple with the question of how contradictory versions of common sense knowledge coexist. For Reid, this is a question of *error*; when common sense contradicts itself, this indicates that a mistake has been made about whether something can properly count as common sense knowledge. Reid argues that although common sense knowledge is real and meaningful knowledge that we can and should rely on, common sense knowledge is not infallible: "But is it not possible, that men who really love truth, and are open to conviction, may differ about first principles? I think it is possible, and that it cannot, without great want to charity, be denied to be possible."[59] It will always be necessary to take certain things for granted. But, when dealing with taken-for-granted principles, we should treat our judgments, even our common sense ones, as open to scrutiny. Drawing, interestingly enough, on a legal metaphor, Reid writes,

> We do not pretend, that those things that are laid down as first principles may not be examined, and that we ought not to have our ears open to what may be pleaded against their being admitted as such. Let us deal with them, as an upright judge does with a witness who has a fair character. He pays a regard to the testimony of such a witness, while his character is unimpeached. But if it can be shown that he is suborned, or that he is influenced by malice or partial favour, his testimony loses all its credit, and is justly rejected.[60]

In this way, Reid treats common sense as properly benefiting from a *presumption* of reliability, and he regards any proposition that goes against common sense as properly bearing the burden of proof. Common sense knowledge remains primarily invisible until challenged. And when challenged, real common sense knowledge will seem self-evident. But on other occasions, the challenge can provoke reflection on our opinions, leading to the rejection of something that had previously been harboured with our common sense.

Reid argues that we can be led astray by "prejudices," which are the cause of errors in relation to the principles of common sense. Although it is not our natural way to be led into error, there are times when this happens, just as good health can be corrupted by disease.[61] Reid enumerates a number of different kinds of prejudice, which he thinks might affect our proper judgment and our common sense. Two of these are particularly relevant for present purposes because they relate to the problems of knowledge and marginality that are posed when legal judgment speaks to poverty.

First, Reid argues that people have a natural tendency to overvalue authorities of various kinds, including legal, scientific, and religious authorities. He writes that "[m]en are prone to be led too much by authority in their opinions."[62] Reid notes that although deference to authority and expertise can be useful and indeed essential in some contexts, overvaluing authorities abdicates responsibility to determine one's own judgments. Reid clearly disdains the notion that one might follow the "authority" of one's social group or that one's judgments might be determined by one's circumstances.[63] Reid argues that it is essential for people to determine their own judgments and not to defer to authorities without careful consideration. Thus, he argues, "authority ... ought to have more or less weight, in proportion to the evidence on which our own judgment rests, and the opinion we have of the judgment and candour of those who differ from us, or agree with us."[64] Here, the egalitarian and potentially democratic consequences of Reid's approach become clear. Reid's doctrine of common sense as a form of common knowledge provides a justification for valuing the knowledge of ordinary people and their capacity to exercise good judgment within the realm of common sense.

Reid's approach, like that of Antonio Gramsci (explored in chapter 3), explains why ordinary individuals have the capacity, the right, and even the obligation to scrutinize and challenge what is accepted as "knowledge." If some knowledge claim – either purported common sense or part of something more formalized – contradicts my own common sense, I have the right and capacity to examine that part of my common sense and come to a judgment about whether it has stood up to the test. If my common sense belief seems to stand up, I can use it to assess the validity of the other claims I encounter. Regardless of what I hear from "authorities" like experts and regardless of the commonly held beliefs in my community, I can and should consider the situation myself and come to an independent judgment. Moreover, everyone else has this same right and obligation to exercise their judgment.

Second, Reid identifies the tendency to reason by analogy as a possible prejudice that might skew our appreciation of common sense principles. Reid accepts that, like reliance on authority, analogical reasoning is an essential tool. However, it carries with it certain kinds of risks: "It would be absurd to lay aside this kind of reasoning altogether, and it is difficult to judge how far we may venture upon it. The bias of human nature is to judge from too slight analogies."[65] It is natural and somewhat inevitable that we judge new things in terms of things we already know, but this way of thinking can also cause us to misjudge. To address this problem, Reid argues that opinions contrary to *true* common sense are made vulnerable by our exposure to a more diverse social context. In particular, the prejudices that result from our tendency to understand new things in terms of things we already know can be moderated if we test our beliefs against a wider group of others: "Men judge other men by themselves, or by the small circle of their acquaintance ... It is commonly taken for granted, that this narrow way of judging of men is to be cured only by an extensive intercourse with men of different ranks, professions, and nations; and that the man whose acquaintance has been confined within a narrow circle, must have many prejudices and narrow notions, which a more extensive intercourse would have cured."[66]

Reid's approach to the problem of overreliance on analogy and the risks of insular communities has notable connections to the views of Hannah Arendt (explored in chapter 4). The aspect of common sense that comes to light by reading Arendt is essentially focused on this process of "acquaintance" and "intercourse" that shapes one's judgment; Arendt calls this process "enlargement of mind," and for her it is at the heart of discovering and developing a community's common sense.[67] For Reid, the practice of human conversation and exchange is not so much the essence of common sense as a corrective practice that can help to identify those anomalous moments when errors or prejudices are masquerading as common sense.

It is also important to note that Reid's claims about the virtual universality of common sense lead him to describe the province of common sense as quite circumscribed. Since something can count as a common sense belief only if it is self-evident, shared, and not generated by prejudices, the range of common sense knowledge is fairly narrow. Examples of things Reid thinks have a "just claim" to the character of "common sense" are "that I *think*, that I *remember*, that I *reason*, and, in general, that I really perform all those operations of mind of which I am conscious," and "by consciousness we know certainly the existence of our present thoughts and passions; so we know the past by remembrance."[68] Reid also counts among his "first principles" the idea of self-identity:

> I take it for granted that all the thoughts I am conscious of, or remember, are the thoughts of one and the same thinking principle, which I call *myself*, or my *mind*. Every man has an immediate and irresistible conviction, not only of his present existence, but of his continued existence and identity, as far back as he can remember. If any man should think fit to demand a proof that the thoughts he is successively conscious of belong to one and the same thinking principle. If he should demand a proof that he is the same person today as he was yesterday, or a year ago, I know no proof that can be given him: He must be left to himself, either as a man that is lunatic, or as one who denies first principles, and is not to be reasoned with.[69]

This observation highlights once again the connection between common sense, everyday experience, philosophy, and appropriate modes of reasoning.

On the question of the value of shared knowledge, Reid also argues that the fact that some belief is widely shared is, by itself, reason to think it is a reliable belief. He argues that when a piece of knowledge is held in common across places and times, this commonality speaks in favour of its value as legitimate knowledge: "The consent of ages and nations, of the learned and unlearned, ought to have great authority with regard to first principles."[70] Theorists who engage more directly with history and political power, such as Antonio Gramsci, may see the fact that a belief is very widely shared as a sign of its embeddedness in a dominant cultural view or its relation to specific historical conditions. For Gramsci, the dominance of a belief is a red flag, calling for particular scrutiny. In contrast, Reid sees the fact of a belief's widespread presence as evidence of its usefulness and reliability for large groups of people, and this utility speaks to its value as common sense knowledge.[71] Gramsci agrees that a widespread belief is "useful" for a large group of people, but his socialist and egalitarian politics lead him to ask "useful for what?" and "useful to whom?" Reid's form of egalitarianism takes him in a different direction: he argues that for an "expert" or a philosopher to doubt a widespread belief without good reason (e.g., by insisting that it be proven rather than demonstrating it to be false) reveals a kind of arrogance or hubris that devalues the lived experiences of all of the people who rely on that belief in their daily lives. Reid writes, "But if, in spite of Nature, we resolve to go deeper, and not to trust our faculties, without a reason to shew that they cannot be fallacious, I am afraid, that seeking to become wise, and to be as gods, we shall become foolish, and being unsatisfied with the lot of humanity, we shall throw off common sense."[72] To disdain the value of common sense knowledge in this way is to lose valuable opportunities to develop our knowledge.

Ridicule and Debate

When we are presented with apparent conflicts in the content of common sense knowledge, Reid says that we are at a "peculiar disadvantage" because we do not have recourse to our usual way of resolving such disputes. That is, we cannot point to reasons in order to decide which belief should count as common sense knowledge.[73] Since common sense knowledge forms the "first principles" of other kinds of knowledge, we cannot resolve controversies about common sense with resort to first principles. However, Reid argues, there are other, compensating characteristics about disagreements on common sense that make it possible to engage in meaningful debate. To begin, although disputes about common sense cannot generally be resolved with recourse to rational argument, there are some forms of logical reasoning that are still effective, such as tests of internal consistency.[74] Moreover, Reid argues, logical reasoning does not exhaust the resources available for assessing knowledge. In particular, Reid points to the "emotion of ridicule" as an aspect of the human disposition that equips us to deal with debates about common sense.[75]

Reid's defence of ridicule as a rhetorical strategy is provocative because of the way that ridicule so often functions to exclude not the grandiose claims of high-status people like philosophers but the claims of marginalized people who challenge more powerful groups in society. For example, in the eighteenth century, writer and activist Mary Wollstonecraft's argument that women should be understood as equal with men in a liberal polity was met with ridicule in many communities.[76] Women advancing essentially the same liberal arguments about women's participation in contemporary politics are also met with derision and dismissal. Even powerful women whose actual political views fit very neatly with dominant perspectives find it impossible to participate in politics without facing ridicule of their appearance, sexuality, and femininity.[77] There is good reason to be concerned about Reid's advocacy of ridicule as a way to support legitimate knowledge in society.

At the same time, the methodology I am working with points back to the text and careful attention to what Reid actually says about ridicule. This strategy yields some interesting results: although the caution about the capacity of ridicule as a tool for the powerful still stands, Reid's defence of ridicule as a rhetorical strategy also has links to the democratic and egalitarian character of his common sense.

Reid argues that opinions that contradict common sense are not only false but also absurd or nonsensical and thus vulnerable to ridicule. Although he acknowledges that ridicule, like rational argument, can be abused, Reid writes, "This weapon, when properly applied, cuts with as keen an edge as argument. Nature hath furnished us with the first to expose absurdity; as with the last to refute error. Both are well fitted for their several offices, and are equally friendly to truth when properly used."[78]

Reid's explicit defence of ridicule as a rhetorical device – and indeed his own employment of the *reductio ad risum* – corresponds to his argument that common sense knowledge is made up of self-evident things that we believe without reasons:

> All men that have common understanding agree in such principles, and consider a man as lunatic or destitute of common sense, who denies, or calls them in question. Thus, if any man were found of so strange a turn as not to believe his own eyes; to put no trust in his senses, nor have the least regard to their testimony; would any man think it worth while to reason gravely with such a person, and, by argument, to convince him of his error? Surely no wise man would. For before men can reason together, they must agree in first principles; and it is impossible to reason with a man who has no principles in common with you.[79]

Ridicule has the effect not necessarily of persuading the people whose words are ridiculed that they are wrong but of helping to draw the boundaries around legitimate argument. Ridicule communicates that the person's perspective is not worthy of consideration. Further, the evaluative character of common sense means that ridiculing a belief on the grounds that it is contrary to common sense can also communicate the unworthiness of the speaker since common sense knowledge is what every rational person cannot help but believe.

Reid acknowledges the potential weaknesses of ridicule as a rhetorical strategy. He notes that it can be stifled by the competing emotion he calls "sanctity," with which people unreasonably insulate some particular belief from scrutiny.[80] Reid also acknowledges that ridicule, just like reasoned argument, can be "abused to serve the cause of error."[81] However, Reid argues that when we are not blinded by prejudices, ridicule can be effective to uncover absurdities for what they are, leaving them to dissolve on their own and leaving true common sense knowledge to "gain rather than lose ground among mankind."[82] The ridiculousness of a belief is a clue that it is wrong, and ridicule can help to make this evident in a way that reasoned argument never can.[83]

Reid wants to endorse the capacity of ordinary people to hear a philosophical claim (e.g., the idea that we have no way to know whether our senses are reliable) and to judge it from within the framework of knowledge that they use in their daily lives – to say "that is ridiculous" and to rely on that judgment. Further, he argues that philosophers should pay heed to such judgments and should abandon views that turn out to be absurd or ridiculous when judged against real common sense. This is the egalitarian component of common sense judgment, and it can be served by ridicule.

Reid is attentive, to some extent, to the prejudices potentially associated with authority and insular society. However, he gives no real consideration to the risk that ridicule can serve to silence marginal, alternative, or nontraditional views not because they are necessarily *wrong* but for other, potentially illegitimate or unjust, reasons. Reid's commitment to egalitarianism and to the common sense of his community thus carries with it the risk of entrenching knowledge that is linked to injustice. With this complexity in mind, I turn in the next sections to the task of placing Reid's common sense in conversation with the requirements of legal judgment.

REID'S COMMON SENSE IN LEGAL JUDGMENT: EXPERTISE, ACCOUNTABILITY, AND CREDIBILITY

In Reid's writings, common sense and judgment are often contrasted with the practice of reaching a decision by unthinking reference to a set of technical rules, or by deference to the opinions of experts. For Reid, the failure to exercise judgment leads us into error. In law, the failure to exercise real judgment leads not only to errors but also to the failure to meet some of the basic demands of the legal system. The obligation of the judge and/or jury to decide, to *judge*, is more than a matter of good epistemology but also a matter of justice. In this section, I read Reid's theory of common sense in conjunction with legal judgments that invoke the phrase "common sense."[84] In particular, I explore Reid's approach to common sense in the context of Supreme Court of Canada judgments on the assessment of witness credibility, an area of law in which the phrase "common sense" is repeated and endorsed by the court. As the remainder of this chapter shows, these cases and Reid's writings on common sense reveal overlapping concerns about judgment, accountability, and the reliability of common knowledge.

The challenge of assessing the credibility of witnesses is a complex one, which judges and juries must undertake in almost every legal proceeding. Assessing credibility is challenging, a task described by the Supreme Court of Canada as a "notoriously difficult problem."[85] When a witness testifies in a court of law, the finder of fact must decide to what extent that person is trustworthy and reliable.[86] There is little doubt that this is one area where common sense knowledge plays a major role. According to socio-legal scholar Richard Thompson, "The concept of 'credibility' is the legal curtain behind which common sense lurks ... Determining what is plausible or worthy of belief requires a context of interpretation, a context that is itself not open to belief or tests of plausibility because it determines same. This context is the system of common sense, and when a judge rules that a witness's testimony lacks credibility, she is saying, without of course actually saying, that such testimony goes against or doesn't square with common sense."[87] Thus legal judgments about credibility assessment are a fruitful place to explore the meaning of "common sense" in law.

Vetrovec v. The Queen

The case of *Vetrovec v. The Queen* is a landmark decision about the assessment of witness credibility. In *Vetrovec* the Supreme Court of Canada made some fundamental changes to the law on "corroboration," or the rules of evidence concerning how the testimony of suspects or "unsavoury" witnesses (e.g., accomplices) should be treated. Prior to *Vetrovec*, a rule of law had developed that required judges to issue a specific kind of instruction to juries, warning them not to convict an accused person by relying solely on the testimony of an accomplice, unless that testimony was "corroborated" in the required manner. A complex body of law had developed to answer questions about who counted as an "accomplice," what counted as "corroborating evidence," and what, exactly, that evidence had to corroborate.[88] This set of rules was born out of the concern that juries might not fully appreciate just how compromised the testimony of an accomplice might be and that unjust convictions could result. These rules on corroboration were intended to provide some structure for juries, as well as to allow juries to benefit from the expertise of trial judges, whose experience in the courtroom purportedly gave them special knowledge about credibility and about accomplices.[89] Many critics, including a report by the Law Reform Commission of Canada, alleged that the jury instructions emerging from these rules were excessively technical and, rather than assisting juries in the task of assessing credibility, distracted them with legal terms of art.[90] In *Vetrovec*, Justice Brian Dickson addressed this problem head on when he wrote, "The result [of the current rules] is that what was originally a simple, *common sense proposition* – an accomplice's testimony should be viewed with caution – becomes transformed into a difficult and highly technical area of law. Whether this 'enormous superstructure' (to use the description of the Law Reform Commission) has any meaningful relationship with the task performed by the jury is unknown."[91]

Here, as in Reid's writings, "common sense" knowledge is invoked in opposition to a body of determinative rules. A body of rules may lead to a conclusion, but it does not assist in the practice of *judgment*. Indeed, a set of rules may actively hinder the genuine exercise of judgment. In *Vetrovec*, the Supreme Court rejected the idea that the trial judge had a duty to describe a complex set of rules to the jury. Instead, following on the "common sense proposition" noted above, Dickson articulated a discretion to warn the jury, in general terms, about the potential problems with relying on uncorroborated evidence from a suspect witness like an accomplice.[92] In Dickson's judgment, one can see something like Reid's distinction between genuine, human judgment, on one side, and unreflective adherence to rules, on the other, with common sense firmly located on the side of judgment.

A more complex picture emerges when considering the question of the content of common sense knowledge itself. Recall that Reid, in his own work, is careful to circumscribe what counts as common sense knowledge. Although the scope of common sense knowledge is unclear in advance, there is a definite boundary delineating those things that are the proper subject of common sense and those that are not. Further, by identifying possible prejudices that might lead us to harbour *wrong* beliefs under the auspices of common sense, Reid calls on us to exercise our considered judgment when identifying common sense knowledge.

Similarly, Dickson does not advocate for reliance on totally unstructured resort to common sense knowledge for the assessment of credibility in a legal case. Rather, he argues that this exercise must be bound by the particular requirements of judgment *in the context of legal judgment.* This reflects a concern about boundaries, context, and difference that is always relevant to common sense knowledge but is made particularly acute in the case of law because of the way that fact finding is related to the requirements of legitimate legal judgment. In legal judgment, we care not only that the judgment be epistemologically correct but also that it be just. If a jury assessing the credibility of a witness relies on something that purports to be a matter of common sense but is actually a result of mistake or prejudice, injustice results. Further, in a way not fully accounted for by Reid, this problem becomes especially acute when we try to apply the justice values of the legal system, such as equality and the rule of law, in a context involving the marginalization of certain social groups. In this context, common sense is especially likely to overstep its jurisdiction because the knowledge in question may not be shared between majority and minority groups. And so it is here that injustice is especially likely to be unnoticed, reified, or reinforced. Thus, although Reid's approach supports the idea that the genuine exercise of judgment is related to common sense, not to rules, it also supports the idea that, in legal judgment especially, attention must be paid to the boundaries of common sense knowledge.

Dickson appears to be seeking a middle ground between unstructured reliance on common sense and imposition of technical rules. He notes the tension inherent in trying to establish guidelines for exercising legal judgment: "All this takes one back to the beginning and that is the search for the impossible: a rule which embodies and codifies common sense."[93] In some respects, Dickson's words in *Vetrovec* reflect the idea that the common sense of a judge or jury can play a positive role in *legal* judgment only if common sense has been structured, to some degree, by an understanding of the relevant legal principles and standards. The court's findings in *Vetrovec*, like Reid's arguments on common sense, are motivated not by opposition to rules per se but by the search for good judgment. In the context of law, some kinds of formal rules are necessarily part of judging practice.

Reid's approach is useful in negotiating the relationship between formal rules and common sense because of the way that common sense and judgment are linked to *accountability*. Deference to rules also allows abdication of responsibility; when we exercise judgment, we can be held to account for our decisions. Part of Reid's argument about the strength of common sense knowledge as a basis for judgment is that it facilitates our exercise of independent judgment and, in so doing, facilitates accountability for the choices we make.[94] Advocates of common sense such as Norman Finkel and Phillip Howard (described in the Introduction) follow this line of argument into the legal realm,[95] showing how excessively detailed rules allow us to forgo making difficult choices and thereby to avoid our responsibilities as citizens or as adjudicators.[96] However, these writers stop before asking the critical questions of accountability *for what* and *to whom*. If we adopt Reid's perspective that common sense is valuable in part because of its close ties to the genuine exercise of human judgment, including accountability for that judgment, then these questions are of major significance. Common sense advocates like Finkel and Howard take up the first part of this argument but stop before reaching the pressing question of what is really meant by "accountability."

In the context of legal judgment that aims to address problems of inequality, a more nuanced account of the relationship between formal rules and accountable judgment is needed. One such account can be found in the work of feminist and critical race legal scholar Patricia Williams.[97] Williams's approach is useful here because it provides a way to think through the relationships between rules, judgment, and accountability that directly addresses questions of oppression and inequality. It also speaks to the question of what "accountability" for judgment might look like in the context of the complex diversity and inequality that characterize our public life.

Williams's work is a much larger project about the relationship between race and rights in the United States. Here, I am interested in how her approach speaks to a narrower question about the best role in legal judgment for formal structures of rules, on the one hand, and for common sense, on the other. As part of her discussion of the role of "rights" – which I count here as falling on the side of legal "rules" – Williams provides a compelling alternative model of how formal rules and accountability might work together in legal judgment.

Williams argues that one's orientation to the formality of legal rules, laws, and rights is grounded in part in one's personal experiences and social location. In particular, "one's sense of empowerment defines one's relation to the law."[98] People whose social experiences confirm the legitimacy of their needs may have fewer concerns about dispensing with formal rules in favour of organizing social relations less formally, such as through acts of trust and friendship.[99] In contrast, those with a history of engagement with law that threatens or actively denies their entitlement, even to the extent of denying their personhood, may have an entirely different perspective on rights discourse.[100] This approach complicates our assessment of how formal rules should relate to good legal judgment, broadly understood. Thus Williams argues that "[a]lthough rights may not be ends in themselves, rights rhetoric has been and continues to be an effective form of discourse for blacks."[101] Williams argues that the value of rights language comes in part from its rhetorical role in public debate. Rights can be understood as publicly identified political and moral commitments: "rights are to law what conscious commitments are to the psyche."[102]

Williams's defence of formal rights – both as the basis of legal action and as a form of political discourse – suggests that, when the social reality of inequality and oppression is taken into account, good legal judgment cannot afford to dispense with rules in favour of common sense. To do so would be to set aside an important tool for identifying and challenging inequality. Does this endorsement of rules mean that legal judgment is doomed to operate with unreflective formality, foresaking the independent exercise of human judgment and becoming unconnected to common sense of any kind, as Howard seems to imply (i.e., the "death of common sense")? Williams's approach, I suggest, tells us this is not the case.

Williams describes an approach to legal judgment in which our subjectivity as particular, contextualized human beings is actively engaged. Williams challenges us to develop an approach to law and legal judgment in which we learn to engage with our own subjectivity, and with legal constructs such as "rights," in a more complex manner. She writes, "What is needed, therefore, is not the abandonment of rights language for all purposes, but an attempt to become multilingual in the semantics of evaluating rights."[103] We need to be able to see and express more than one way of engaging with rights.

Moreover, this approach to social and legal analysis, which allows us to adequately take into account questions of subjectivity and social context, will have the consequence of generating "a more nuanced sense of legal and social responsibility."[104] I suggest that this approach can be used to generate a more nuanced understanding of the accountability that Reid hopes will follow from basing judgment on common sense. Although Reid himself did not go down this path, his interest in having criteria for independent and genuine judgment, linked to accountability, provides an opening for taking his thought in this direction.

R. v. D.D.

In *Vetrovec*, Dickson begins to address the balance between judgment and rules by insisting that common sense knowledge must be understood in relation to certain kinds of legal principles.[105] In the following section, I further explore the relationship between common sense and judgment by engaging with the case of *R. v. D.D.* In this case, "common sense" is understood as being not just in opposition to technical rules but also in possible opposition to other forms of knowledge, such as scientific expertise, or in opposition to itself, with multiple bodies of common sense knowledge existing together.

Central to Reid's account is the idea that common sense is normatively universal and thus works to shape the boundaries of legitimate debate. If common sense consists of everything that everyone should already know, nothing is gained by exchanging and discussing reasons on those points. The challenge of delineating the proper scope for debate, or the proper range of things for which we should demand reasons, also emerges in legal judgments concerning witness credibility.

The case of *D.D.* provides an instructive example for discussion of this issue. In that case, the Supreme Court of Canada was asked to decide on the admissibility of expert evidence on the issue of the credibility of child witnesses in criminal trials. The accused was charged with the sexual assault of a child, who testified during the trial. During the case, the accused argued that the child's delay in disclosing the abuse took away from the credibility of her testimony and that this conclusion was simply a matter of "common sense."[106] In response, the Crown offered the evidence of a psychologist, who testified that in his expert opinion, the timing of a child's disclosure of abuse had no relationship to the question of whether the abuse in fact occurred.[107] The Supreme Court was asked to determine whether the trial judge had properly admitted this expert opinion evidence.[108]

Speaking for the majority, Justice John C. Major found that the expert evidence was inadmissible because the issue could be fully dealt with by a direct instruction to the jury; no expertise was needed to support the "undeniable" concept that a delay in reporting has no effect on credibility.[109] The dissenting judgment, authored by Chief Justice Beverley McLachlin, did find that the expert evidence was necessary and therefore admissible.[110]

The phrase "common sense" appears in several paragraphs of this dissenting judgment. McLachlin begins by describing "common sense" as one way of determining the "facts" of a situation, which can be counterposed to the evidence of experts. Specifically, in addressing the defence argument that the expert evidence was unnecessary, McLachlin rejects the idea that "common sense" involves "inferences" that need only be offered rather than "facts" that must be proven. She finds that factual claims, whether made through inferences supported by common sense or through expert evidence, must all meet the necessary legal criteria:

> It is argued that the relevance requirement is not met because the "fact in issue" – that a child's delay in reporting suggests the events did not occur – is not a fact but a common sense inference. This argument is not persuasive. How the inference is made does not affect whether there is an issue of fact at stake. Issues of fact include both facts and the logical inferences which may (or may not) be drawn therefrom. At trial, defence counsel made an issue of the reason for the delayed allegation, cross-examining the child and asking the jury to infer from the delay that the events did not occur. For the purposes of determining relevance, it does not matter whether the inference is made by counsel, drawing on "*common sense*," or with the assistance of expert evidence. Either way, what is at issue is a factual proposition put by the defence – namely, that a child's delay in reporting abuse makes it more likely that the abuse did not occur.[111]

Following on this finding, McLachlin argues that the expert evidence was necessary, partly because it could provide jurors with the information they might need to critically examine the content of their own common sense knowledge. The expert evidence was necessary, not because the claim in question was contestable but because the jurors needed to understand the *reasons* underlying the claim:[112]

> Dr. Marshall testified, in essence, that contrary to what the ordinary juror might assume, there is no "normal" child response. Some abused children complain immediately, others wait for a period of time, and some never disclose the abuse. Thus the timing of the complaint, he testified, does not help to diagnose

> whether it is true or fabricated. He also outlined the factors that may lead to delay in disclosure, such as fear of reprisal, lack of understanding, fear of disrupting the family, the nature of the child's relationship with the abuser, and the nature of the abuse. *Some of these explanations might have occurred to ordinary jurors as a matter of experience and common sense, but some might not have been apparent to them without expert assistance.* Having heard on the *voir dire* what Dr. Marshall proposed to say, it was open to the trial judge to conclude that his evidence would assist the jurors by giving them an understanding of the issue of delay in reporting that their ordinary knowledge and experience might not provide.[113]

Thinking about these passages from the dissent in *D.D.* in light of Reid's understanding of common sense shows both the explanatory power and the limitations of Reid's approach. McLachlin's invocation of "common sense" here overlaps with Reid's understanding in that Reid places common sense in opposition to expertise as a possible framework for judgment. On first glance, it seems that McLachlin departs from Reid's approach insofar as she endorses expertise, rather than common sense, as the basis for good judgment in this case. However, Reid might simply agree with McLachlin that the proposition at hand – that the timing of a child's disclosure of abuse has no relationship to whether the abuse occurred – is *not* within the province of common sense and rightly the subject of expertise.[114]

This approach is fully available to Reid, who is quite careful to circumscribe his own claims about the content of common sense knowledge.[115] Reid's justification of the universality of common sense knowledge lies with the fact that he includes *only* those beliefs that appear as self-evident to all rational people. If we stick faithfully to this restriction, the content of common sense knowledge is actually quite sparse, including things such as the "judgment" that we can rely on our senses and other things without which we start to lose our ability to think about how we live our daily lives. However, unlike Reid, many of those who invoke the normative universality of common sense are not so circumspect. Indeed, as we see in the *D.D.*

case, claims about common sense extend far beyond this universality to include things that are, in fact, deeply contested.

Reid could also argue that in this context purported common sense suffers from certain prejudices, such as reasoning from improper analogy, and should be challenged. As noted in the previous section, Reid is committed to the idea that we are obligated to exercise our judgment in a reflective manner. However, Reid's theory suggests that it will usually be quite easy to determine whether something can count as common sense; once challenged, common sense propositions will appear self-evident. For Reid, the issue of potentially "incorrect" common sense is one about *error*. When common sense knowledge turns out to be wrong, we have simply made a mistake about something, and this error can be corrected with reference to the transparent, actual state of affairs.

For Reid, true common sense knowledge is self-evident, so we need only refer to it in order to say, "Aha, now I see how I was misled before." So Reid does allow for the possibility of purported common sense knowledge that is, in fact, wrong. But Reid's insistence that we can resolve the question of whether something should count as common sense knowledge in a very straightforward way lays bare his underlying (problematic) assumptions about the relationship between thought and behaviour and the relative independence of judgment from social relations.

Not addressed directly by McLachlin (or by Reid) are the ways that these disputes about the meaning of a child's conduct in disclosing or not disclosing abuse are set in a context of inequality and the exercise of political power. Children who disclose abuse by an adult face a variety of stereotypes and misconceptions that are best understood not just as *errors* but also as consequences of a social structure that systematically devalues the testimony of victims of sexual abuse.[116] Those aspects of Reid's approach that focus on self-evidence and nonexpertise appear to be of little assistance here.

The juxtaposition of Reid's theory of common sense with the invocation of the phrase "common sense" in *D.D.* also highlights the relationship between common sense knowledge, daily life, and reasoning. Reid argues that the rootedness of a belief in the everyday life of groups of people gives that belief the benefit of a presumption of reliability. He argues that to think otherwise, or to structure a system of argument from a different starting point, is not just mistaken but also fundamentally disrespectful of those people. People and communities, as well as "experts," are the sources of true knowledge, and this reality should be taken seriously by thinkers of all kinds. I suggest that Reid's opposition of common sense knowledge to expertise generates a normative expectation that everyday knowledge should benefit from a presumption of reliability, with countervailing expertise carrying a burden of proof. In the context of legal judgment, this expectation actually corresponds quite well with the doctrinal requirement that expert opinions must be "necessary" before they should be admitted as evidence.[117]

Recall that, for Reid, anything that is properly the subject of common sense judgment will appear as self-evident and not amenable to proof or disproof via rational reasons. Following from this understanding, Reid argues that access to common sense does not improve with expertise.[118] However, McLachlin's approach in the *D.D.* case contemplates precisely this possibility: that the nonexpert framework that judges and jurors use to assess credibility may, in this context, be inaccurate, misleading, or incomplete and that these deficiencies can be remedied with reference to scientific expertise. Further, the dissenting judges appear to acknowledge that many people will need *reasons* to displace the presumption of reliability with which they habitually invest their common sense knowledge. This finding sits uneasily with Reid, who insists that we hold our common sense views because of our daily-life experiences, *not* because we hold convincing reasons to support them. Reid does perceive that our daily lives (e.g., the diversity of our social experiences) can affect the quality of our common sense knowledge. But he does not perceive that *those things we believe without reasons* might be structured not just by their reliance on daily living but also by their reliance on particular social structures. He does not consider how social inequalities might produce particular patterns of inadequate common sense knowledge. These questions are of primary concern to Antonio Gramsci, whose aspect of common sense is considered in the following chapter and whose perspective becomes increasingly essential when legal judgment is placed in a real life context characterized by social and political inequalities.

These reflections show some of the shortcomings of Reid's approach as a way to understand common sense in legal judgment. However, Reid's interest in the rhetorical value of common sense does offer a constructive way to think about common sense and legal judgment in a context of inequality. Reid argues that part of the value of common sense knowledge is its ability to set the terms of reasonable debate. Reid argues that since common sense knowledge consists of those things we believe not on the basis of reasons but on the basis of our everyday experience, we can reasonably debate only those things lying *outside* the jurisdiction of common sense. But for things that are properly contained within common sense knowledge, debate is inappropriate. Most times, we cannot offer reasons for our common sense beliefs, but for Reid, this lack of reasons just demonstrates the nature of the belief as rooted in practice, which speaks to its *value*, not to any problem with its epistemological credentials. Thus, when claims arise that are counter to common sense knowledge, the appropriate response is not reasonable debate – which may indeed be impossible – but something else entirely, including questions about the speaker's membership in the community of rational people or questions about whether the belief is rooted in a "prejudice" such as undue deference to authority. In such cases, perhaps the appropriate response is simply ridicule.

The rhetorical effects of common sense claims are worthy of particular scrutiny in the context of legal judgment. Written legal judgments in a common law jurisdiction have particular rhetorical purposes of their own, such as persuading readers that a just result has been reached in a particular case, providing an example of the proper functioning of the legal system, and contributing in a general way to the legitimacy of the judicial process.[119] For the Supreme Court of Canada, these rhetorical tasks are also directed at multiple audiences: lawyers and judges, who must interpret and apply the law in the future; the parties to the litigation, who should feel that the process has been fair; and the general Canadian public, for whom the judgment is also a symbolic statement about justice.

The language of "common sense" plays a complex role in such a context. Reid describes the rhetorical strategy of ridicule as a way to dissolve nonsensical claims. But even without the more extreme form of ridicule, it is true that almost any claim about common sense has rhetorical effects that are related to ridicule. In particular, it is significant that claims invoking "common sense" are more strongly polemical than persuasive.[120] Addressing the role of common sense rhetoric in the constitutional law of the United States, Terry Maroney writes, "[A]sserting that one's own view is commonsensical never will persuade someone to whom it appears otherwise, but it will instead come across as maddening, wrongheaded, even insulting."[121] When presented with a claim that something is a matter of common sense knowledge, those who have a contrary view may not be persuaded to change their minds, or even to reconsider their view, if the claim is presented as an obvious truth that any rational person cannot help but believe.

Further, the power of the normative universality of common sense claims can still work even when the "knowledge" in question is wrongly counted as part of common sense knowledge. By invoking "common sense" as the basis for his argument, the accused in *D.D.* relies on this language to make the underlying claim that any other assertions are so wrongheaded as not to merit consideration. In the context of a debate about the admissibility of expert evidence, the defence argument appeals to the idea that this question can and should be decided on the basis of existing everyday knowledge and that scientific expertise will only distract or mislead. This rhetorical move poses enormous risks to the legitimacy of legal judgment. Put starkly, the defence argument appeals to a powerful prejudice against children in order to foreclose debate on the credibility of the child's testimony.

For the dissenting justices in *D.D.*, the rhetorical impact of the claim that "common sense" impelled an inference against the credibility of the child witness had to be directly confronted by drawing the issue back into the realm of reasoned debate. By contrasting purported common sense knowledge with the knowledge offered by the expert witnesses, McLachlin frames the question as one that does indeed merit rational scrutiny, opening opportunities to expose the limits of dominant views on sexual abuse and child witnesses.[122]

The majority judgment in *D.D.* does not use the language of "common sense," so it does not speak directly to the rhetorical value of this phrase. However, because the majority and minority judgments are framed against each other, and explicitly address the defence arguments about common sense, Major's judgment does provide the opportunity for some reflection on this point. I argue that by rejecting the need for expert evidence, the majority justices are, in essence, claiming that common sense, *for the purpose of legal judgment*, does contain the "knowledge" that the timing of a child's complaint about abuse has no relation to its credibility.

Major does draw a line around the reasoned debate that might happen in this case, and he places this issue firmly outside its bounds. This is done, essentially, to make the legal and normative claim that a juror, exercising proper legal judgment, *should* accept this fact and that no argumentation on this question is necessary. That children should be disbelieved when they delay reporting sexual abuse is not a *logical* absurdity. But perhaps it is something that the law should label as a *normative* absurdity, something outside the realm of good legal judgment, not just on the basis of empirical information but also, more importantly, on the basis of the normative claim that justice, and thus good legal judgment, requires the judge to reject any association between the timing and credibility of abuse complaints.

According to Reid, one rhetorical consequence of common sense claims, and indeed the whole purpose of engaging in ridicule, is to foreclose debate on certain points. Doing so serves the purpose of clarifying the boundaries of what can be justified with reference to reasons and what must be justified on other grounds. But in legal judgment, particularly on a matter that has been pursued all the way to the Supreme Court of Canada, we are dealing with questions on which people clearly disagree. To invoke "common sense" in this context can undercut the rhetorical purpose of a judgment related to fair process because it may appear that debate has been unfairly constrained or precluded from the outset. At the same time, the foreclosure of debate on certain points can be used to transparently establish the normative values that will ground fact determination for legal judgment; certain things are simply not up for discussion in a court of law, and this circumstance might serve either progressive or oppressive ends, depending on the context.

When we consider legal cases involving complex social issues and the problems of inequality, the risks and benefits of common sense claims as rhetorical devices are shown in particularly sharp relief. This is the case partly because, in Reid's terms, the risk of our common sense knowledge being corrupted by "prejudices" is particularly high. When dealing with issues arising from social marginalization, there is a greater risk that common sense knowledge will reflect undue deference to authority – especially to dominant or majority views – or the tendency to decide on the basis of "too slight analogies."[123] If these prejudices operate without constraint in legal judgment, we risk undermining substantive legal principles such as equality. Thus, given its rhetorical power, the phrase "common sense" should be invoked with caution and diligent attention to equality.

Gosselin v. Quebec (Procureur général)

In the introduction to this book, I quote those passages from *Gosselin v. Quebec (Procureur général)* that invoke "common sense." In this section, I return to these passages and read them specifically in light of Reid's approach to common sense. As with *Vetrovec* and *D.D.*, I read *Gosselin* here in order to ask what is learned about legal judgment by looking at "common sense" from Reid's perspective.

In one passage, in which she addresses how the purported purpose of the law can affect its impact, Chief Justice McLachlin writes, "As a matter of common sense, if a law is designed to promote the claimant's long-term autonomy and self-sufficiency, a reasonable person in the claimant's position would be less likely to view it as an assault on her inherent human dignity."[124] This passage overlaps with many of the themes raised by Reid in his discussion of common sense. McLachlin frames a modified subjective test (i.e., "what would a reasonable person in the claimant's position believe?") in terms of "common sense." With Reid's picture of common sense in mind, framing this analysis in terms of "common sense" transforms it into a question about what any reasonable person *should* believe. Rhetorically, it places anyone who sees things differently outside the realm of rational debate. Anyone exercising judgment on the basis of common sense knowledge would find that the law in question did not infringe their human dignity. Louise Gosselin, who specifically claims that she did, in fact, view the law as an assault on her human dignity, is excluded from the rational community to whom the legal judgment is addressed.

In another passage from *Gosselin*, McLachlin invokes "common sense" as a source of legitimate and reliable knowledge:

> Even if one does not agree with the reasoning of the legislature or with its priorities, one cannot argue based on this record that the legislature's purpose lacked sufficient foundation in reality and *common sense* to fall within the bounds of permissible discretion in establishing and fine-tuning a complex social assistance scheme. Logic and *common sense* support the legislature's decision to structure its social assistance programs to give young people, who have a greater potential for long-term insertion into the work force than older people, the incentive to participate in programs specifically designed to provide them with training and experience.[125]

In a later passage, McLachlin writes,

> [W]e cannot infer disparity between the purpose and effect of the scheme and the situation of those affected, from the mere failure of the government to prove that the assumptions upon which it proceeded were correct. Bastarache J. argues that the distinction between people under 30 and older people lacks a "rational basis" because it is "[b]ased on the unverifiable presumption that people under 30 had better chances of employment and lower needs" (para. 248). This seems to place on the legislator the duty to verify all its assumptions empirically, even where these assumptions are reasonably grounded in everyday experience

> and *common sense*. With respect, this standard is too high ... The legislator is entitled to proceed on informed general assumptions without running afoul of s. 15 ... provided these assumptions are not based on arbitrary and demeaning stereotypes.[126]

In these passages, McLachlin asserts in part that we *can* draw conclusions in law based on knowledge we hold as nonexperts; we do not always need "empirical" information on which to base our judgments. Reid would endorse this general view of common sense knowledge as a legitimate resource for judgment. This is a crucial step in defending the capacity and indeed obligation of individuals to render their own judgments without undue deference to authority – which might appear here in the form of some kind of social scientific data. At the same time, Reid's picture of common sense invites consideration of whether the beliefs in question are actually shared in some relevant way. In the context of the *Gosselin* case, the "common sense" knowledge invoked by McLachlin is clearly not universal. Indeed, it sits on a dividing line that has a great deal of social and legal significance, bearing markers of class, gender, and age. Common sense knowledge, mistakenly claimed across these communities, does not provide common ground but functions to imply a consensus where there is none.[127] "Common sense," as invoked in *Gosselin*, takes common sense beyond Reid's narrower claims about things we cannot help but believe and heeds none of his cautions about the boundaries of common sense knowledge.

The consequences of attributing a false consensus in this context are not just to paper over *difference* but also to reiterate inequality and hierarchy. Although Reid's aim is to have common sense form the basis for a practice of judging that is empowered, pragmatic, and accountable, this accountability evaporates when the opinions of a dominant group come to be equated with common sense. In this context, claims about common sense knowledge can subvert, rather than support, practices of good legal judgment.

Invoking the language of "common sense" in a legal judgment can also pose challenges for one of the main rhetorical functions of written judgment: persuading the people who are bound by the law, including the litigants who have lost their case, that justice has been done. In *Gosselin* the rhetorical consequences of invoking "common sense" include the exclusion of Louise Gosselin, and many other Canadians living in poverty, from the community of rational people to whom the courts owe a duty of justification. It also has the effect of erasing many kinds of experiences from the constitutional imagination: common sense does *not* tell us that poverty affects dignity, security, or equality. Insofar as they have any legal value at all, the experiences of Louise Gosselin and others in her position are not "common" or matters of common sense.[128]

One way to respond to this problem from a perspective inspired by Reid – aside from simply saying that this knowledge lies outside the province of common sense – is to say that such a practice of judgment has not fully taken into account the requirements of common sense knowledge. In particular, the invocation of "common sense" knowledge in *Gosselin* does not adequately reflect a judging practice that takes responsibility for the *rhetorical* consequences of invoking "common sense," including drawing the scope of legitimate debate. In the context of legal judgment, reliance on common sense knowledge should be justified not only in terms of its standing as a basis for judgment in opposition to technical rules or scientific evidence but also in terms of the rhetorical consequences flowing from its use. Said another way, judges should justify their resort to common sense on the basis of the boundaries that it draws, namely the boundaries of legally and constitutionally appropriate debate and the boundaries of the communities that they speak to in their judgments. Taking insight from Williams's nuanced account of judgment and accountability, our approach to common sense requires attention to context and politics in order to make it a valuable resource for legal judgment.

These reflections on *Gosselin* show that the aspect of common sense that we see by reading Reid helps to confront some of the challenges of common sense in legal judgment but leaves others unaddressed. Reid's perspective provides a way to talk about judgment and accountability and about the way that common sense sets out the boundaries of debate. When McLachlin says "everyday experience and common sense," she is counterposing common sense with empirical or social scientific data, and we can use Reid's approach to make sense of this aspect of common sense. But this phrase is set in the context of a legal finding about the kind of evidence the state must produce to explain and justify a law that might breach the rights of citizens. What does it mean for the *legislature* to rely on its common sense? Whose common sense can or should prevail here, where the law in question – the interpretation of section 15 of the Canadian Charter of Rights and Freedoms – is precisely addressed to the protection of marginalized people from majority rule? Looking at common sense from Reid's perspective provides few resources for addressing these kinds of questions because it lacks a sufficiently nuanced understanding of how common sense is affected by history and power. To address this issue, I turn in chapter 3 to the work of Antonio Gramsci.

In relation to the rhetorical effects of invoking "common sense," Reid's approach provides rich fodder for debate about rhetoric, ridicule, and the boundaries of rational debate. There are ways that Reid's theory is very useful when assessing the consequences of invoking "common sense" in legal judgment. However, in addition to delineating the boundaries of rational debate, it is also the rhetorical function of a legal judgment to make a statement about the content of the law and to make a discursive contribution to the building of the legal system. From this perspective, claims about common sense are not just potentially persuasive but are also normative statements about law and the communities for whom the law exists. Reid's approach helps us to see why the use of the phrase "common sense" in the majority's judgment in *Gosselin* might be construed as discriminatory or offensive to many people living in poverty because of the way it articulates the scope of debate. However, Reid's approach, focused as it is on the possibility of near-universal common knowledge, provides little assistance when we try to draw the boundaries of community on the basis of political or legal principles. In constitutional equality law, whose common sense is most legally appropriate as the reference point for knowledge? What *should* the law treat as beyond dispute? To answer such questions, I turn in chapter 4 to the work of Hannah Arendt.

CONCLUSION

For Reid, the function of common sense knowledge is to provide a stable ground upon which we can collectively conduct the work of human life, from everyday conversation to philosophical analysis. When the language of "common sense" is improperly extended, we end up not with a stable ground but with an unstable edifice of some sort, which at once constrains our exercise of judgment and precludes us from seeing what is really at stake in our debates, and so we lose our ability to meaningfully communicate. The ongoing challenge is to find some middle ground between transforming too much into undoubtable first principles (as Reid thought Ancient philosophers did) and making everything subject to doubt (as he thought his skeptical contemporaries did).[129] For Reid, this challenge has to do with discovering truth. For this book, this challenge is about identifying the proper boundaries of debate *for the purpose of legal judgment.*

Reid understands common sense knowledge as the framework for good judgment, the reference point for meaningful debate, and the condition of social life. In legal judgment, all of these aspects of common sense knowledge are important, and common sense knowledge is a necessary and inevitable part of legal judgment. I conclude that, if examined in the context of legal judgments, the aspect of common sense that describes it as a form of shared knowledge has many pitfalls when it is assessed from the perspective of justice. Reid's common sense knowledge carries a strong risk of partiality and error, and when invoked, it can imply false consensus and impose not a "common" understanding but a dominant or majoritarian one. Reid's common sense lacks a sufficiently complex approach to social relations to fully respond to challenges about inequality and the relationship between power and knowledge.

However, those with an interest in seeking out criteria for good legal judgment ignore common sense as shared knowledge at their peril. The power of common sense claims to generate normative boundaries around legal debate and various communities must be attended to not only because of the attendant risks of exclusion and marginalization but also because of the potential for "common sense" to be invoked in the service of actively chosen principles of equality and access to justice. For example, a judge who invokes "common sense" can choose, on the basis of equality, to circumscribe debate in a manner that removes from marginalized litigants the burden of proving facts that are fundamental to the legal system, thus disallowing challenges that are based on oppressive beliefs or stereotypes. Further, claims about common sense, as understood by Reid, are characterized by normative commitments to respect for nonexpert knowledge and for the experiences of daily life.

The aspect of common sense revealed by Reid is undoubtedly at work in legal judgment and is most constructively understood as an opportunity for critical reflection on legal knowledge, rhetoric, and the criteria for good judgment in law. Although Reid's approach shares much with the dominant view of common sense that tends to hold us captive, a close look at what Reid actually says about common sense starts to dislodge some of the assumptions that hold this picture in place. Even for Reid, there are cracks in the "universal" and "self-evident" common sense knowledge arising from reasoning prejudices, and Reid calls on everyone to exercise their independent judgment in a full and meaningful way. But the aspect of common sense explored here – its status as a form of shared knowledge – is unable to address all of the implications of these dilemmas. If common sense benefits from a presumption of reliability because it is shared, how can those who do not share it challenge its legitimacy? If common sense is rooted in the fundamental reality and equal legitimacy of daily-life knowledge, what happens when people's daily lives differ dramatically? These important issues arise from questions about power and community, made significant by my focus on poverty and social justice in legal judgment. Thus, in my search for what Ludwig Wittgenstein calls a "perspicuous representation" of common sense, it is necessary to shift perspective in order to see a new aspect.[130]

3

Antonio Gramsci's Common Sense: History, Power, and Our Conception of the World

This time, our companion at London's Haymarket Theatre in 1736 is the socialist thinker and political activist Antonio Gramsci, arrived from Italy circa 1923. Gramsci glances around at the patrons gathered in the seats and galleries and at those watching from the floor. In act 4 of Henry Fielding's Pasquin, Queen Common-Sense debates Queen Ignorance and declares herself the protector of wisdom:

> Could Common-Sense bear universal Sway,
> No Fool could ever possibly be great.[1]

Gramsci mutters in exasperation. But at other points, he nods in agreement, as when Queen Common-Sense chastises Law for injustices brought upon poor citizens and for the unfair conduct of lawyers who act in their own private interest:

> *Q.C.S.*
> My Lord of *Law*, I sent for you this Morning;
> I have a strange Petition given to me;
> Two Men, it seems, have lately been at Law
> For an Estate, which both of them have lost,
> And their Attorneys now divide between them.
>
> *Law.*
> Madam, these things will happen in the Law.

Q.C.S.
Will they, my Lord? then better we had none:
But I have also heard a sweet Bird sing,
That Men, unable to discharge their Debts
At a short Warning, being sued for them,
Have, with both Power and Will their Debts to pay,
Lain all their Lives in Prison for their Costs.

Law.
That may perhaps be some poor Person's Case,
Too mean to entertain your Royal Ear.

Q.C.S.
My Lord, while I am Queen I shall not think
One Man too mean, or poor, to be redress'd.[2]

His inherited spinal condition causing him pain, Gramsci shifts uncomfortably in his seat. At the conclusion of the play, he makes his way into the crowd to hear the audience members debate the production.

INTRODUCTION

In this chapter, I persevere with the task of challenging our captivity to a particular understanding of common sense by juxtaposing multiple aspects of common sense. This chapter explores the aspect of common sense that we come to see by reading the work of Antonio Gramsci. Gramsci's writings on cultural hegemony, with common sense playing an important role, are some of the most influential socialist writings of the twentieth century.

In the previous chapter, I addressed the aspect of common sense provided by Thomas Reid: common sense as a form of shared knowledge. Focusing on this aspect of common sense proved to be quite useful when thinking about legal judgment; Reid's approach helps to direct attention toward everyday knowledge, accountability for judgment, and the way that common sense works to set the boundaries of debate.

Attention to these things reveals both the strengths and weaknesses of Reid's approach as a way to generate criteria for using common sense in legal judgment. Although Reid's approach overlaps considerably with the way that common sense is most often used and understood in relation to legal judgment, when we "look and see"[3] what Reid has to say, doing so starts to loosen the constricted conversation that sometimes holds us captive. For example, Reid endorses common sense knowledge as real and legitimate. However, he is very careful to limit the content of common sense knowledge. Moreover, he is alive to the possibility of prejudice and to our tendency to judge using unreliable analogies. At the same time, there are nascent or emergent questions about common sense in legal judgment that seem difficult to address or even formulate clearly within Reid's paradigm. For example, if common sense is what best grounds acts of accountable judgment, what is the best way to approach judgments in which there is a significant stretch between the daily-life knowledge of the judge and that of some broader community? What about the worry that a very widely held view might not be "common" but just dominant in some way? Studying common sense from Reid's perspective has shaken free some new issues that require attention in order for us to take further steps toward a more productive understanding of common sense. In this chapter, I shift perspective to look at the aspect of common sense that comes to light in the work of Antonio Gramsci. For Gramsci, "common sense" refers to a shared "conception of the world";[4] it is historically constructed and related to power.

Antonio Gramsci's theory of common sense emerges in the context of his evaluations of, and exhortations for, Italian socialism. Gramsci was born in 1891 on the island of Sardinia in the southern part of Italy, an area of widespread poverty among the peasants and miners who lived and worked there.[5] Gramsci attended university in Turin, where he grew both as an intellectual and as a political leader. Gramsci was active as a writer and political educator, working for various socialist newspapers and helping to organize workers' councils. In the 1920s he helped to found the Communist Party of Italy and was elected to the national legislature in 1924. In 1926 the fascist government of Benito Mussolini arrested Gramsci as part of an attempt to repress opposition parties. The prosecutor at his trial famously said of Gramsci that "we must stop this brain from working for twenty years!"[6] Gramsci was imprisoned, and his health, compromised by pre-existing problems, including a spinal condition, deteriorated. He was released to a hospital in 1934 but never recovered from his time in prison, and he died in 1937 at the age of forty-six. The prosecutor's success in convicting Gramsci resulted in his lengthy imprisonment but manifestly failed to stop his brain from functioning; during his imprisonment, Gramsci wrote thousands of pages of notes and essays, which have been collected and translated as the *Prison Notebooks*.[7] These writings contain Gramsci's thoughts on a wide range of subjects related to the role of Marxism in contemporary Italy, the history of the region, the social and cultural context of Italian socialism, and theoretical perspectives on politics, education, history, and culture.

Common sense plays a central role in Gramsci's analysis of social change and in his exhortations for political action. Unlike Reid, for whom common sense knowledge is primarily an epistemological concept, Gramsci's notion of common sense is aimed directly at specific political goals and at the emancipation of oppressed peoples. Gramsci argues that common sense must be subjected to critique in order for people to develop an understanding of the ways that common sense beliefs can stifle change and buttress the social dominance of certain groups. This critique is possible because common sense is heterogeneous and unstable, making it susceptible to transformation through critical reflection.

For Gramsci, common sense is not merely a body of shared knowledge but also a shared conception of the world that frames what we think and do. This aspect of common sense is also centrally concerned with power and the ways that power operates at the level of beliefs and knowledge as well as action. To grapple with the complexity of power, a notion that extends beyond political or state power and reaches into culture and society more broadly, Gramsci develops the concept of "hegemony," which explains how dominant social groups maintain their power not only through direct force and economic domination but also through culture and civil society.[8] Common sense plays an important role in both the maintenance of, and the resistance to, hegemonic worldviews.

Looking at common sense from Gramsci's perspective reveals how claims of common sense are connected to political power in terms of both their origin and their consequences. In legal judgment, this connection to power means that the common sense of judges comes from their own social experiences – including, most often, a position of relative power. This connection to power also means that invocation of the phrase "common sense" in a legal judgment affects how the judgment will relate to collective knowledge and practices in the future. This aspect of common sense – as a conception of the world inherently connected to power – presents huge challenges to legal judgment. It shows the potential for power, through common sense, to undermine legal values such as impartiality and the rule of law.

At the same time, Gramsci's vision of common sense presents opportunities for developing valuable criteria for legal judgment because it reveals the benefits and limitations of practices of critical reflection. Critical reflection relates quite directly to the practices and principles that might guide judicial engagement with common sense, such as the way that judges negotiate the relationship between common sense and evidence. In the context of poverty, inequality, and marginalization, it is valuable to understand the potential of such practices for the assessment and transformation of the use of common sense in legal judgment.

This chapter has two parts, parallel to the structure of the previous chapter on Thomas Reid. In the first part, I describe the aspect of common sense that emerges from Gramsci's writings in the *Prison Notebooks*. I focus on three themes. First, I describe how Gramsci's common sense is constituted through a process of "sedimentation," as knowledge and experiences gradually create the way that people perceive and interpret the world. For Gramsci, this process is inherently tied to social relationships of power, which makes common sense highly problematic as a source of knowledge or as the basis of action. Second, I address the ways that Gramsci nonetheless finds value in common sense, including its capacity to form collective consciousness and the kernels of "good sense" that are contained in common sense. Third, I describe Gramsci's assessment of critical reflection as a way to evaluate and transform common sense. Gramsci argues that the transformative potential of critical reflection is highly dependant on a set of enabling political conditions and on the practice of what he calls the "philosophy of praxis."[9]

In the second part, I take this aspect of common sense – as a conception of the world that is related to political power – and examine it in the context of legal judgment. I allow the scholarly and legal texts to shed light on each other. Against the backdrop of feminist and anti-poverty political values, what is learned about legal judgment by thinking about common sense in this way? Further, what does the context of legal judgment reveal about Gramsci's approach? In this part, I discuss *Chaoulli v. Quebec (Attorney General)* and *Sauvé v. Canada (Chief Electoral Officer)*,[10] both of which are Supreme Court of Canada decisions dealing with the question of what governments must do to justify the infringement of a constitutionally protected right. In these cases, "common sense" is invoked as a possible way for this justification to take place. I also return to the case of *Gosselin v. Quebec (Procureur général)* to reread this case in light of the aspect of common sense we see in Gramsci.[11] All of these cases provide opportunities to evaluate Gramsci's approach to common sense in the context of the institutions, values, and discourses of legal judgment. Further, all of these cases provide opportunities to interrogate how courts rely on common sense when negotiating the relationship between group and individual rights and interests. Sometimes the legal issue at hand deals with questions that concerned Gramsci quite directly, such as class inequality and poverty. Others are about marginalization more broadly understood and involve a wide range of issues, including gender and age discrimination, access to welfare, criminalization, democratic participation, and access to healthcare.

For legal judgment, the value of looking at common sense through the lens provided by Gramsci is that this approach requires sustained attention to power and social context. Adopting the perspective and priorities highlighted by this aspect of common sense makes mandatory the consideration of how relations of power affect all forms of judgment and knowledge, from practices of daily living to the structured decision making of legal adjudication. Reading legal judgments from this perspective illustrates the explanatory potential of Gramsci's approach as well as the enormous challenges posed by understanding common sense in this manner. Gramsci's perspective also points to the potential and limitations of critical reflection as a way to scrutinize and transform the common sense that underlies judgment, thereby transforming judgment itself.

GRAMSCI ON COMMON SENSE

Hegemony and Historical Residue

Gramsci begins his reflections on the "study of philosophy" by saying that it is not just professional philosophers or an elite group of intellectuals who have a "philosophy" that guides their interpretation of the world.[12] Instead, "everyone is a philosopher."[13] All carry with them a specific "conception of the world."[14] All kinds of people are intellectually and politically active in this sense.[15] Gramsci writes, "Each man, finally, outside his professional activity, carries on some form of intellectual activity, that is, he is a 'philosopher,' an artist, a man of taste, he participates in a particular conception of the world, has a conscious line of moral conduct, and therefore contributes to sustain a conception of the world or to modify it, that is, to bring into being new modes of thought."[16]

The conception of the world held by most people is contained not in a structured theory but in what Gramsci means by "common sense."[17] In Gramsci's view, we develop our common sense throughout our lives as we absorb knowledge and philosophies from various teachings and experiences. Gramsci argues that social events and philosophical movements all leave behind layers of historical "sedimentation" that build up in the collective consciousness of different groups of people; this is what comes to be known as "common sense."[18] Gramsci writes,

> Every social stratum has its own "common sense" and its own "good sense," which are basically the most widespread

> conception of life and of man. Every philosophical current leaves behind a sedimentation of "common sense": this is the document of its historical effectiveness. Common sense is not something rigid and immobile, but is continually transforming itself, enriching itself with scientific ideas and with philosophical opinions which have entered ordinary life. "Common sense" is the folklore of philosophy, and is always half-way between folklore properly speaking and the philosophy, science, and economics of the specialists. Common sense creates the folklore of the future, that is as a relatively rigid phase of popular knowledge at a given place and time.[19]

Thus Gramsci's common sense is connected to social context in a very immediate way. It emerges from our very specific life experiences and our responses to them: "One's conception of the world is a response to certain specific problems posed by reality, which are quite specific and 'original' in their immediate relevance."[20] But individual life experiences are not the only influences that shape the content of common sense. Rather, common sense – like almost all other kinds of knowledge and philosophy – is a *social* phenomenon and therefore related to one's membership in social groups.

Gramsci argues that all of our beliefs and approaches, including our common sense, are related to our membership in different groups: "In acquiring one's conception of the world one always belongs to a particular grouping which is that of all the social elements which share the same mode of thinking and acting. We are all conformists of some conformism or other, always man-in-the-mass or collective man."[21] Arising from its social character, common sense should be understood not as universal or transcendent but as highly contingent and adaptable. Gramsci writes that "common sense is a collective noun, like religion: there is not just one common sense, for that too is a product of history and a part of the historical process."[22] At any given time, with any given constellation of social relations, the content of what is called "common sense" will differ. Further, all of the "common senses" that are at work in a society are related to the different histories and political contexts of the people in that society.

But for all of these social groups, there is something called "common sense" that forms the "conception of the world" that most people have to guide their beliefs and actions.

In Gramsci's writings, the social and historical nature of common sense means that common sense is inherently related to power and power struggles between groups.[23] Gramsci was specifically concerned with the oppressive content of the common sense that dominated in his society and with the ability of this common sense to impede progressive political transformation of his society.[24] In this regard, Gramsci's understanding of common sense overlaps in significant ways with his notion of "hegemony."[25] Gramsci's concept of hegemony is complex and has been the subject of political and scholarly engagement in numerous disciplines.[26] At its heart is the idea that relations of domination cannot be explained only by reference to physical force or direct coercion. Rather, power relations affect all areas of human life, including culture, philosophy, and common sense.[27] A worldview is hegemonic when it extends into and dominates in all these areas. Similarly, a social group[28] can dominate in a society partly because it is able to make its views hegemonic.[29] This approach to social relations contrasts strongly with a mechanical or "economistic" Marxism, in which economic arrangements are fully determinative of social and cultural phenomena.[30] Offering this richer and more nuanced perspective on the relationship between economic relations and other forms of human thought and practice is one of Gramsci's most important theoretical contributions, one that has found a role in many socialist and postmodernist literatures.[31]

Gramsci's notion of common sense is related to power and domination but not in a straightforward or obvious way.[32] The idea of hegemony describes how less powerful groups come to embrace the worldviews of others, and common sense is a central part of this process. In unequal, capitalist societies, this means that less powerful groups come to participate in the cultural systems that contribute to their own oppression. Common sense is importantly related to hegemony because common sense is one of the main ways that the views of dominant groups come to be understood as natural and universal.[33] Sharing in common sense is part of how certain beliefs and perspectives come to feel like "ours," rather than alien or imposed, regardless of whether that common sense succeeds or fails to explain our own experiences and regardless of whether it buttresses the privileges of others. The beliefs and experiences of dominant social groups come to be universalized in the common sense that is held not only by those groups but by others as well.[34]

However, the hegemony of any one common sense is never complete. Dominant common sense reflects and naturalizes the interests and perspectives of dominant groups, but the content of common sense does not *merely* follow behind economic relations or patterns of political domination.[35] Common sense *also* contains aspects that arise "organically." This kind of common sense is not handed down from more powerful groups but emerges from actual life experiences. It is more meaningfully "ours" and reflects community consciousness. Gramsci argues that we tend to *act* on the basis of these ideas that make sense in context – what Gramsci sometimes calls "organic" philosophy[36] – but at the same time consciously affirm the ideas of another group because of the dominance of that group.[37] For example, because of the dominance of capitalist logic, I may believe that markets reward workers on the basis of merit and hard work, but I also find that my own hard work goes relatively unrewarded.

Gramsci argues that this dualism in our consciousness creates tensions between the different parts of our common sense: the "organic" parts that form the basis for action and the parts absorbed from dominant groups that are what we *think* we believe in. Gramsci writes that a contrast between thought and action "signifies that the social group in question may indeed have its own conception of the world, even if only embryonic; a conception which manifests itself in action, but occasionally and in flashes – when, that is, the group is acting as an organic totality. But this same group has, for reasons of submission and intellectual subordination, adopted a conception which is not its own but is borrowed from another group; and it affirms this conception verbally and believes itself to be following it."[38] Moreover, Gramsci observes that no single version of common sense is completely hegemonic in twentieth-century capitalist societies.[39] Therefore, some groups, more than others, find their experiences reflected in and meaningfully interpreted through the dominant common sense. People located in a position of social privilege will likely find many of their experiences reflected in and explained by common sense, but people in a marginalized position will probably not. Most people will come to experience at least some degree of conflict between what they think or believe and how they actually act in practice. Foreshadowing complex debates on concepts like "consciousness raising" or "false consciousness,"[40] Gramsci argues that the conflicts that arise between what we think, what we experience in practice, and what informs our actions are not merely a matter of self-deception, although in a few cases they may be. Rather, "in these cases the contrast between thought and action cannot but be the expression of profounder contrasts of a social historical order."[41] That is, conflicts between thought and action arise because the hegemonic norms that purport to explain the world actually serve the specific interests of dominant groups, including by falsely universalizing those very interests.

Discussion of the potentially contradictory nature of common sense provides a significant point of comparison between Gramsci and Thomas Reid. Reid agrees with Gramsci that the content of common sense emerges from one's practical experiences in daily life. Further, both thinkers argue that daily-life experiences provide a kind of evidence of one's genuine or "organic" beliefs, in contrast to beliefs that are held superficially or that one (merely) claims to hold.[42] For Reid, a conflict between one's explicitly held beliefs and the beliefs that must underlie one's actions has to do with *error*; when I claim to believe one thing, but by my conduct demonstrates that I believe its opposite, I have made a mistake. Further, Reid argues that this kind of error occurs when we become too deferential to authority, whether it be the authority of philosophers, religious dogmas, or our fellow members of social and cultural communities.[43] This kind of error demonstrates a failure to exercise good judgment, and it stands in the way of our fully understanding ourselves and the world around us.

Gramsci's focus on the role of power in shaping common sense points to consequences of this conflict – between our consciously held beliefs and the beliefs that underlie our actions – that reach far beyond questions of epistemological error. Indeed, he argues that the lack of a coherent and meaningful worldview is part of what makes less powerful groups vulnerable to domination and that it constitutes one of the more damaging consequences of this domination.[44] Gramsci argues that "the contradictory state of consciousness does not permit of any action, any decision or any choice, and produces a condition of moral and political passivity."[45] Conflicts between one's practice of living and one's consciously affirmed view of the world diminish one's ability to act as an intellectual and political agent.

Thus common sense is always partly, but never completely, captured by dominant perspectives. This circumstance leads to one of the key characteristics that Gramsci ascribes to common sense: fragmentariness. Common sense may affirm one thing and then also affirm its opposite. Gramsci writes, "Common sense is not a single unique conception, identical in time and space. It is the 'folklore' of philosophy, and, like folklore, it takes countless different forms. Its most fundamental characteristic is that it is a conception which, even in the brain of one individual, is fragmentary, incoherent and inconsequential, in conformity with the social and cultural position of those masses whose philosophy it is."[46]

Accordingly, to rely on common sense for one's philosophy or "conception" of the world results in a conception that is "disjointed" and "episodic" rather than "coherent" or "critical."[47] For example, Gramsci points out that dominant common sense in his political context was strongly religious in content but also materialist and "realistic."[48] In some respects, this notion of common sense bears some similarities to Reid's discussion of the limits of the county of York:[49] common sense cannot be assigned a unified or coherent definition in advance. However, whereas Reid suggests that the lack of unity or coherence is not a problem for the value of common sense, Gramsci argues that a disjointed or incoherent common sense or conception of the world does pose problems for people in understanding their lives and exercising political agency.

One of the consequences of the fragmentariness of common sense is that it is vulnerable to instrumental use in judgment.[50] That is, because "common sense" can be invoked to support all kinds of claims, even contradictory ones, it is a difficult standard upon which to base judgments. Gramsci argues that because of the compound and often contradictory content of common sense, it does not make sense to refer to common sense as evidence for the truth of any given proposition: "Common sense is a chaotic aggregate of disparate conceptions, and one can find there anything that one likes."[51] Further, "[w]hat was said above does not mean that there are no truths in common sense. It means rather that common sense is an ambiguous, contradictory and multiform concept and that to refer to common sense as confirmation of truth is a nonsense. It is possible to state correctly that a certain truth has become part of common sense in order to indicate that it has spread beyond the confines of intellectual groups, but all one is doing is making a historical observation."[52]

When placed in a social context of unequal power relations, the fragmentary and incoherent nature of common sense is made even more problematic. Gramsci argues that fragmentary common sense makes people vulnerable not just to instrumental reliance on common sense per se but also to manipulation by authoritarian exploitation of common sense for specific, oppressive ends.[53] Authority figures can appeal to "common sense" in order to create the illusion of unity between thought and action. In this way, common sense disguises the real social conflicts that are happening in society and blunts the ability of oppressed groups to understand their own situation. This can happen through the directly manipulative conduct of authority figures like employers or local religious figures. It can also happen when a hegemonic ideology extends its power through control of public institutions such as the media, schools, and religious institutions. Gramsci argues that a limited "unity" of theory and practice had been achieved through authoritarian means by the Catholic Church, which enforced its view through strict dogmas and "by imposing an iron discipline on the intellectuals."[54] Thus the fragmentary character of common sense means not only that it cannot serve as evidence for a truth claim but also that it can facilitate the subordination of some groups by others, limiting people's ability to make sense of their experiences and to act as political agents.[55] The fragmentary nature of common sense, linked to the political power of dominant groups, prevents some people from understanding and pursuing their own interests.

Collective Consciousness and "Good Sense"

Gramsci understood a *critique* of common sense as being a primary task for progressive political action. At the same time, the most compelling interpretations of Gramsci are ones that also recognize his notion of common sense as something with possible democratic value. This question of the possible positive value of common sense as Gramsci understands it is the subject of debate among interpreters of Gramsci's work.

For example, political theorist Andrew Robinson argues that Gramsci's comprehensive critique of common sense has been neglected or misunderstood in the literature, weakening the force of Gramsci's revolutionary message.[56] Robinson argues that those writers who understand common sense to be a neutral field of political debate or who give common sense positive political significance are misreading Gramsci, a mistake that "blunts the critical edge of Gramsci's remarks on common sense."[57] In Robinson's view, Gramsci's *critique* of common sense is connected to his interest in everyday life and to his insistence that systemic changes in political organization must be accompanied by, or even prefaced by, the transformation of everyday life and thought. Gramsci refers to this transformation as "intellectual and moral reformation,"[58] and by this phrase, Robinson argues that Gramsci "has in mind a thoroughgoing transformation and development of people's ways of thinking and acting in everyday life, a transformation fundamental enough to break the grip of bourgeois ideological formations and to transform the subaltern strata from a passive mass into an active historical force."[59] At the heart of this reformation is the critique of common sense. In essence, Robinson argues that Gramsci's commitment to taking everyday life seriously requires us to see the ways that common sense constrains political change and to subject it to scrutiny. We cannot transform politics without transforming common sense.

Theorist José Nun argues that Gramsci's interest in the significance of everyday life and everyday thinking supports not only a *critique* of common sense but also a recognition of the *value* that common sense has as a necessary part of everyone's thinking and practice.[60] Nun argues that Gramsci's writings on common sense reflect an underlying tension in his thought between a rationalist commitment to Marxism as a universally valid interpretive framework and a commitment to a more historicist view in which any philosophical claim must make sense of its particular social, economic, and cultural context.[61] Nun places Gramsci's writings on common sense in the context of this interest in the historicist approach to philosophizing and analyzes the resulting tension in Gramsci's work.[62] Common sense is oriented toward specific social contexts and toward the nonunitary, heterogeneous practices of daily life. This means that Gramsci's interest in valuing or preserving common sense (at least in some form) entails valuing some kinds of thinking that are not universal or purely rational.[63] Common sense must be subjected to critique, but, thus transformed, it also forms the basis of future social change because it is how people develop a meaningful conception of the world in which to ground their action. Nun writes, "Gramsci – like no other Marxist thinker of his time – is sensitive to the enormous resistances opposed by common sense to the progress of a rational logic; but he does not question, in the end, the very possibility of its access to philosophical reason, to 'a coherent and unitary conception of the world' ... Common sense is 'the folklore of philosophy,' but also the antecedent to the true philosophy which will be embodied in the masses."[64]

Common sense is heterogenous, even fragmentary, because it contains elements drawn from dominant perspectives and from organic experience; these contradictions arise from the political contradictions of capitalist society. However, common sense is also heterogenous for reasons that might survive socialist political transformations: it is tied to everyday life, to the sedimentary way that we build a conception of the world over a lifetime, and to forms of reasoning beyond the purely rational. People are by nature dynamic and diverse, and our common sense reflects these characteristics.[65] This insight suggests that we will *always* need to apply our critical attention to common sense, regardless of its specific content or our particular historical context. At the same time, we will always have access to common sense that can help to ground our communities and political movements. Gramsci writes that "implicit" in Marx's writings on common sense is "an assertion of the necessity for new popular beliefs, that is to say a new common sense and with it a new culture and a new philosophy which will be rooted in the popular consciousness with the same solidity and imperative quality as traditional beliefs."[66] Thus I suggest that the radical nature of Gramsci's critique is complicated, rather than blunted, by the recognition that common sense may have some progressive political value.[67] I take up this theme in the second part of this chapter, where I explore the potential to transform common sense through critical reflection in the context of legal judgment.

The value that Gramsci attributes to common sense can be understood in a number of ways. First, returning to the dominant general characteristic of common sense, we have seen that the fragmentary and heterogeneous nature of common sense is part of what makes it problematic and potentially oppressive. However, this same characteristic can also be seen as a potential value of common sense, or at least something that leaves it open to challenge and transformation. Political scientist Mark Rupert writes, "Popular common sense could become a ground of struggle because it is an amalgam of historically effective ideologies, scientific doctrines and social mythologies. Gramsci understood popular common sense not to be monolithic or univocal, nor was hegemony an unproblematically dominant ideology which simply shut out all alternative visions or political projects. Rather, common sense was understood to be a syncretic historical residue, fragmentary and contradictory, open to multiple interpretations and potentially supportive of very different kinds of social visions and political projects."[68] Thus common sense can support dominant social groups and their hegemonic social status. But it can also be used in the service of other political visions and purposes.

Gramsci also argues that common sense has value because it contains seeds of worthwhile knowledge and discourse, a "healthy nucleus," which Gramsci refers to as "good sense."[69] Good sense can serve as hints toward the truth, forming small pockets where common sense has gotten it right. An example of good sense is the general hostility that people sometimes feel toward "bosses" and authority figures in their lives.[70] Such general antipathy to authority figures reflects a kind of nascent appreciation of unjust power relations. By standing in contrast to the rest of common sense, such pieces of good sense provide a starting point for developing alternative views of the world. Good sense is too fragmentary to provide a full basis for an alternative philosophy, but it does provide openings for critique and ways to make philosophical critiques comprehensible to the masses.[71]

Gramsci also finds good sense in the way that common sense can identify basic principles of causation in the physical world.[72] Common sense is valuable in that it "does not let itself be distracted by fancy quibbles and pseudo-profound, pseudo-scientific mumbo-jumbo."[73] Like common sense resistance to "bosses," common sense resistance to "mumbo-jumbo" carries the seed of resistance to (unworthy or unjust) authority. On this theme, Gramsci expresses appreciation for the social context that motivated some common sense philosophers, including the seventeenth-century thinkers of whom Reid was an important example: "It was natural that 'common sense' should have been exalted in the seventeenth and eighteenth centuries, when there was a reaction against the principle of authority represented by Aristotle and the Bible. It was discovered indeed that in 'common sense' there was a certain measure of 'experimentalism' and direct observation of reality, though empirical and limited."[74]

Thus Gramsci finds in common sense some potential for grounding a new and transformative conception of the world. However, common sense, even the "good sense" that can be found at its "healthy nucleus," is never organized, critical, or coherent enough to do this on its own.[75] Rather, it is necessary for us to subject common sense to criticism in order to change it into something that *can* form the basis for a coherent and meaningful conception of the world. Good sense is precisely that part of common sense that is worthy of our critical attention and that "deserves to be made more unitary and coherent."[76] The task before us is not to reject common sense wholly but to scrutinize and transform it.

Critical Reflection and Its Political Conditions

Transformation of common sense takes place through a process of critical reflection, in which people can come to a more explicit awareness of how their common sense ideas are related to history and to politics. Gramsci writes, "The starting-point of critical elaboration is the consciousness of what one really is, and is 'knowing thyself' as a product of the historical process to date which has deposited in you an infinity of traces, without leaving an inventory."[77] Critical reflection makes it possible to understand the relationship between one's conception of the world and one's experiences of the world and therefore enables one to begin to make conscious choices about the content of one's conception. For Gramsci, this is "the reason why philosophy cannot be divorced from politics. And one can show furthermore that the choice and the criticism of a conception of the world is also a political matter."[78]

That criticism is a political matter means that the process that would make it possible to critique one's own common sense, or to distinguish valuable good sense from oppressive, misleading dominant common sense, can be conducted only under certain *political* circumstances. This process is a matter of grappling with hegemony – the mutually reinforcing patterns of political force and cultural domination. Gramsci places a great deal of significance on the freedom to seek and express knowledge, including how this freedom relates to education and the media and to the ways that institutions like schools and newspapers help to structure our understanding.[79] Gramsci himself was widely regarded as a journalist and worked on the editorial boards of socialist newspapers, which he thought were extremely important for the development of socialist thought.[80] Gramsci also wrote extensively about education and about the need for education to challenge traditional common sense not only by presenting alternative sources of knowledge but also by closing the gap between the curriculum and the life experiences of the students.[81]

Further, students – indeed, all people – need to develop the confidence to exercise their own judgment. Gramsci points out that common sense is "dogmatic and eager for peremptory certainties" and that this simplistic way of thinking undermines our ability to take up the intellectual challenge of the kind of dialectical thinking that is actually necessary.[82] Like Reid, Gramsci challenges people to step up to meet the demands of real judgment. However, unlike Reid, Gramsci sees that numerous political and social conditions, such as free expression and adequate education, are prerequisites for this possibility.

Gramsci's notion of common sense, partly because of its association with dominant social groups, benefits from a powerful presumption of reliability. This circumstance is related to the fact that most people experience common sense as a kind of faith in the goodness or sensibility of their fellow community members; so many people could not be wrong, or at least not as radically wrong as is being proposed.[83] This view means that conceptions counter to common sense must overcome a particular burden of proof. Philosophies propounding such conceptions thus need to repeat their arguments and must constantly work to improve the intellectual standing of their audiences.[84] Gramsci argues that any new conception of the world will be highly unstable and will need to rely on robust freedom of expression in order to gain traction in public life.[85]

This issue of the burden of proof points to another contrast between Gramsci and Reid. For Reid, it is entirely appropriate and indeed beneficial that propositions contrary to common sense carry the burden of proof. We should never be quick to reject what so many people already believe. In contrast, for Gramsci, that so many people believe something is actually a sign that there is a problem; in an unequal society, hegemonic perspectives are linked to dominant social groups and to the justification of their power, which makes those perspectives *suspect*, not worthy of deference.

The transformation of common sense into a coherent conception of the world that can support political change cannot be achieved simply by confronting one philosophy with another. It is not a matter of imposing "science" or "philosophy" (even Marxist science or philosophy) on the masses or offering a doctrinaire critique of what people already think. Rather, it is a matter of making "critical" what is already known through practice. This objective can be achieved through what Gramsci calls the "philosophy of praxis."[86]

The central characteristic of the philosophy of praxis is that it calls for scrutiny and critique of *both* the philosophy of the intellectuals and the philosophy of common sense.[87] Indeed, the philosophy of praxis requires an ongoing relationship between intellectuals and the masses, such that the intellectuals find within the experiences of the masses the problems that need to be addressed in philosophy and see it as their task to apply criticism and coherent structure to common sense.[88] At the same time, members of the masses must learn to subject their common sense knowledge to a heightened level of reflection and critique. Gramsci writes, "The philosophy of praxis does not tend to leave the 'simple' in their primitive philosophy of common sense, but rather to lead them to a higher conception of life. If it affirms the need for contact between intellectuals and [the] simple it is not in order to restrict scientific activity and preserve unity at the low level of the masses, but precisely in order to construct an intellectual-moral bloc which can make politically possible the intellectual progress of the mass and not only of small intellectual groups."[89]

The relationship between the "simple" and the "intellectuals" is likened to a student-teacher relationship in which each party is both a student and a teacher.[90] Notably, Gramsci specifically contrasts this relationship with a legal process. The progress of knowledge should *not* be conceived as a matter of prosecution and defence.[91] That is, philosophers should not think of their task only as one of defending a particular view but also as one of examining their own views in light of what they hear from others. Here, as in Reid, the theme of intellectual humility plays an important role.

Moreover, Gramsci argues that in a sense, everyone is an "intellectual." Everyone has a common sense "conception of the world,"[92] and everyone's work contains some intellectual component. Gramsci writes that "in any physical work, even the most degraded and mechanical, there exists a minimum of technical qualification, that is, a minimum of creative intellectual activity."[93] Gramsci's discussion of the philosophy of praxis works to break down the distinction between "intellectuals" and the "masses" itself.

At the same time, Gramsci recognizes that some work and some social roles are more strongly "intellectual" in character, or are at least labelled that way by the dominant culture. Gramsci sets out two categories of "intellectuals." On the one hand, there are "traditional intellectuals," who are defined by their professions and social roles and might include artists, scientists, professional philosophers, and ecclesiastics.[94] On the other hand, there are "organic intellectuals," who arise in every social group and are the people who develop, or elaborate, or organize certain aspects of the intellectual activity in which the social group engages. Organic intellectuals might include the capitalist entrepreneur, who understands certain aspects of economics and can instil confidence in investors, or the feudal lord, who has technical military knowledge.[95] Organic intellectuals emerge from social groups and help to provide the basis for that group's self-understanding.[96] In contrast, traditional intellectuals often conceive of themselves as autonomous from any social group because they experience a certain degree of historical continuity.[97] However, Gramsci argues, this independence or objectivity is largely illusory. In fact, traditional intellectuals are "conquered 'ideologically'" by the hegemonic perspectives of the dominant group.[98] For a hegemonic social group, traditional and organic intellectuals become "welded together."[99]

The philosopher of praxis is concerned with developing the organic intellectuals of subaltern social groups, both in terms of the number of people who have the opportunity to engage in critical reflection and in terms of the quality of this intellectual engagement.[100] With regard to common sense, the organic intellectuals arising from non-dominant social groups will embody the process of critical reflection that will allow those groups to challenge dominant common sense and to mobilize alternative conceptions of the world.[101] Organic intellectuals participate in the critique of hegemonic common sense and work to develop the good sense of their communities.

Organic intellectuals can play this role because they can link the everyday experience of subaltern groups – including manual labour – to the world of intellectual elites and to the practice of philosophical self-reflection.[102] Organic intellectuals also function to break down binary distinctions (e.g., between "theory" and "practice" or between "common sense" and "philosophy") so that all knowledges, practices, and modes of thinking can receive the necessary critical scrutiny. This process must be conducted with reference to the particular, situated knowledge of oppressed social groups, which has the potential not only to challenge hegemonic common sense but also to liberate those social groups and to transform the political landscape as a whole.[103]

Thus the role of an organic intellectual is to reflect upon and make coherent one's own experiences, as well as the experiences of one's social group, through critical thought. But it also involves leadership in organizing the social group toward self-understanding and therefore political transformation. In this regard, Gramsci sometimes calls the organic intellectuals of subaltern groups the "new" intellectuals, whose work will help to transform society: "The mode of being of the new [organic] intellectual can no longer consist in eloquence, which is an exterior and momentary mover of feelings and passions, but in active participation in practical life, as constructor, organiser, 'permanent persuader' and not just a simple orator."[104] The challenge for organic intellectuals is to think critically about their individual and group experiences, to communicate those experiences in a way that resonates with group members, and to contribute materially to the organization and activism of the group as a political body.

The critique of common sense and the development of good sense are essential parts of the philosophy of praxis. Looking at Gramsci's political analysis with particular attention to common sense focuses attention on the complexity of this undertaking: it is not a matter of simply rejecting "common sense" in favour of "philosophy" or simply reversing the positions of dominant and oppressed groups. Critique and transformation of thought and action are called for on all fronts. Rupert writes, "At the core of Gramsci's project was a critical pedagogy which took as its starting point the tensions and possibilities latent within popular common sense, and which sought to build out of the materials of popular common sense an emancipatory political culture and a social movement to enact it – not simply another hegemony rearranging occupants of superior/subordinate social positions, but a *transformative* counter-hegemony."[105]

In the following sections, I place Gramsci's theory of common sense in a different context: the practice of legal judgment. The aspect of common sense that we come to see by reading Gramsci provokes a number of questions. Are judges traditional intellectuals or are they ever "organic" ones? To what extent do judges uphold the hegemonic common sense that reinforces the privileges of dominant groups? And if the critique and transformation of common sense are essential to overcoming unjust power relations, what does it mean when "common sense" is invoked to articulate the judgment of a state court? What does doing so suggest about the process of generating evidence for courts? Whose testimonies and submissions are invited or welcomed?

GRAMSCI'S COMMON SENSE IN LEGAL JUDGMENT: JUSTIFICATION, EVIDENCE, AND STEREOTYPES

In this section, I explore Gramsci's aspect of common sense in the context of legal judgments concerning the justification of infringements of constitutional rights. This area of law is centrally concerned with questions about the relationship between individual and group rights as well as with the possibility of questioning, justifying, or transforming common sense on any given matter. Like the assessment of witness credibility (discussed in the previous chapter), the justification of infringements of constitutional rights, either under section 7 or section 1 of the Canadian Charter of Rights and Freedoms, is an area in which the justices of the Supreme Court of Canada have repeatedly employed the language of "common sense" to express their rulings and concerns.[106]

In this context, the court is often faced with a situation in which the government's justification of the law, including the purported "rational connection" between the government's objective and the legislation itself, is something that is not amenable to empirical proof.[107] In cases about the justification of the infringement of a right, "evidence" on the connection in question may be conflicting or otherwise not convincing, or the connection may be something that is simply "difficult, if not impossible, to measure scientifically."[108] However, the validity of those connections is contingent on whether they can be "justified," not on whether they can be measured scientifically.

So the court has had to articulate the standards for justification more broadly, including in terms of "common sense."[109]

I argued in the previous chapter that, in the area of the assessment of witness credibility, the Supreme Court of Canada has used the language of "common sense" to provide a counterpoint to systems of rules or scientific expertise to which jurors might unduly defer their judgment. Here, I argue that "common sense" in the context of the justifications under section 1 or section 7 of the Charter is counterposed not so much to systems of rules but to "evidence." This perspective suggests that in this context, common sense is not only a kind of information but also a framework for interpreting information – or in Gramsci's terms, a "conception of the world."

The prominence of the language of "common sense" in these cases is important. The justification of government action that infringes rights has to do with the way that courts negotiate the relationship between individual and collective interests, as well as between the judiciary and other branches of government. Questions about common sense and justificatory evidence take on particular significance in the context of constitutional debates that engage the rights and interests of marginalized individuals and communities. In the following passages, I discuss three constitutional cases that prominently feature the language of "common sense" and that bring up issues of class, poverty, and marginalization. In *Chaoulli v. Quebec*, which concerns the issue of private medical insurance, questions of class are quite central to the case. This is also true of *Gosselin v. Quebec*, which deals with the adequacy of income assistance programs and with poverty more directly. *Sauvé v. Canada* concerns the voting rights of federally incarcerated prisoners. Poverty and class arise only indirectly when considering *Sauvé*, but relevant questions about marginalization and stereotyping arise directly and in a way that clearly has implications for the meaning of "common sense."

Following Ludwig Wittgenstein's exhortation to "look and see,"[110] I read these cases not so much as sources for developing an accurate doctrinal picture – which is their most common role – but as *examples* of the use of the phrase "common sense." These tasks overlap, of course, but the goal is different. I read these cases not to discover "the law" on common sense or the evidentiary requirements of sections 1 and 7 of the Charter but to explore how common sense, understood from Gramsci's perspective, appears in legal judgment. I try to "look and see" what the text says on its face about the meaning and role of common sense, and I consider what it means for our broader understanding of legal judgment that common sense sometimes takes on that meaning and role.

Chaoulli v. Quebec (Attorney General)

In *Chaoulli v. Quebec (Attorney General)*, the Supreme Court of Canada addressed questions about the validity of legislation in Quebec that prevented individuals from purchasing private medical insurance to cover medical services that were part of the public system.[111] The claimants in this case were Jacques Chaoulli, a doctor who was frustrated by regulatory limits on his ability to practise medicine privately, and George Zeliotis, a man with heart and hip conditions who had experienced delays in accessing treatment in the public system. Both men challenged legislation that prohibited private medical insurance on the grounds that it violated the rights of Quebeckers as protected by the Canadian Charter of Rights and Freedoms and by Quebec's Charter of Human Rights and Freedoms.[112]

The claims of Chaoulli and Zeliotis were dismissed at trial and at the Quebec Court of Appeal. However, in a four-to-three decision, the majority of justices at the Supreme Court of Canada agreed with the appellants. All of the judges who addressed the Canadian Charter agreed that there were at least some circumstances in which some people would find their life, or "security of the person," put at risk because of the prohibition on private medical insurance.[113] However, they were divided on the question of whether the legislation accorded with the principles of fundamental justice and was therefore constitutional. The four majority justices found that the legislation was in violation of Quebec's Charter.[114] Three of those justices also found that the legislation was inconsistent with section 7 and not justified under section 1 of the Canadian Charter.[115] Three dissenting justices would have rejected the claims and upheld the constitutionality of the legislation.[116] Thus the doctrinal result of the case was that the prohibition on private medical insurance was struck down in Quebec as contrary to Quebec's Charter. The status of similar legislation in other provinces is uncertain.[117]

The phrase "common sense" appears in *Chaoulli* in the context of debates about the evidentiary requirements of section 7 of the Canadian Charter. Pursuant to section 7, legislation will be found unconstitutional when it deprives someone of "life, liberty and security of the person, ... except in accordance with the principles of fundamental justice."[118] If a section 7 right is interfered with in accordance with these principles (e.g., by restricting the liberty of someone convicted of a crime after a fair trial), it is constitutional. If, however, the deprivation of the right breaches the principles of fundamental justice (e.g., by being arbitrary), the law in question will be struck down.

In *Chaoulli* the claimants argued that the impugned provisions were *arbitrary* and that any infringement on their section 7 rights was therefore unconstitutional. In reply, the government argued that the prohibition on private medical insurance was not arbitrary but meaningfully connected to the goals of the public medical system. One of the central issues for the Supreme Court was whether this connection between the prohibition and the public system had been established in the appropriate way. In a number of instances, the phrase "common sense" appears when the justices address this connection, as well as when they debate whether legislation can be justified or challenged by resort to "common sense."[119]

There are a host of important doctrinal questions raised in this context about the evidentiary requirements of Canadian Charter claims, including the justification of a rights breach.[120] For example, when will the Supreme Court demand to see social science evidence to support a government claim about "rational connection"? Is common sense a type of evidence? Can it stand on its own, or must it work together with other sources of information or ways of reasoning? These questions highlight the necessity of a deeper understanding of how the phrase "common sense" is deployed by the justices in this case.

Turning now to the passages in *Chaoulli* in which the phrase "common sense" appears, I look first at the judgment of Chief Justice

Beverley McLachlin and Justice John C. Major (with Justice Michel Bastarache concurring), who found that the legislation in question was not constitutional. To begin, McLachlin and Major use the phrase "common sense" in their characterization of the competing claims of the litigants:

> In support of [its position] the government called experts in health administration and policy. Their conclusions were based on the "common sense" proposition that the improvement of health services depends on exclusivity ... They did not profess expertise in waiting times for treatment. Nor did they present economic studies or rely on the experience of other countries. They simply assumed, as a matter of apparent logic, that insurance would make private health services more accessible and that this in turn would undermine the quality of services provided by the public health care system.
>
> The appellants, relying on other health experts, disagreed and offered their own conflicting "common sense" argument for the proposition that prohibiting private health insurance is neither necessary nor related to maintaining high quality in the public health care system. Quality public care, they argue, depends not on a monopoly, but on money and management. They testified that permitting people to buy private insurance would make alternative medical care more accessible and reduce the burden on the public system. The result, they assert, would be better care for all. The appellants reinforce this argument by pointing out that disallowing private insurance precludes the vast majority of Canadians (middle-income and low-income earners) from accessing additional care, while permitting it for the wealthy who can afford to travel abroad or pay for private care in Canada.[121]

The justices then assess these claims against the evidentiary requirements of section 7:

> To this point, we are confronted with competing but unproven "common sense" arguments, amounting to little more than

> assertions of belief. We are in the realm of theory. But as discussed above, a theoretically defensible limitation may be arbitrary if in fact the limit lacks a connection to the goal.
>
> This brings us to the evidence called by the appellants at trial on the experience of other developed countries with public health care systems which permit access to private health care. The experience of these countries suggests that there is no real connection in fact between prohibition of health insurance and the goal of a quality public health system.[122]

McLachlin and Major go on to argue that the evidence from other countries, presented by the appellants, represents the only real evidence or "facts" available for grounding a decision, and they find that "[w]hen we look to the evidence rather than to assumptions, the connection between prohibiting private insurance and maintaining quality public health care vanishes."[123] Therefore, they find, the legislation is indeed arbitrary.

In the passages quoted above, McLachlin and Major characterize the disagreements between the litigants as a matter of competing and contradictory "common sense" beliefs. The case is decided not by evaluating the relative merits of these "common sense" beliefs but by determining which set of beliefs also has "facts" or "evidence" on its side. These passages characterize "common sense" in opposition to "facts" or "evidence," to what is "real," and to what is the case "in fact." In contrast, "common sense" is aligned with "unproven ... beliefs," with "assertions of belief," with what is "assumed as a matter of apparent logic," or with what lies "in the realm of theory." McLachlin and Major specifically relate this approach to the obligations of the court in undertaking judicial review: "The task of the courts, on s. 7 issues as on others, is to evaluate the issue in the light, *not just of common sense or theory, but of the evidence*."[124]

When we read these passages through the lens provided by Gramsci's approach to common sense, a number of things stand out. First, the invocation of "common sense" in opposition to "evidence" is suggestive of Gramsci's view that common sense cannot stand as an adequate justification of any particular factual assertion; here, it is claimed on behalf of contrasting views, and it is not fruitful to adjudicate between them on the basis of common sense alone. To say that something is confirmed by "common sense" leaves it still unproven. This approach recalls Gramsci's worries about the incoherent and heterogenous nature of common sense and about the inherent potential for the instrumental use of common sense in argument. Unlike most other references to "common sense" by judges, McLachlin and Major explicitly problematize this phrase by putting quotation marks around it, which further suggests a skeptical posture toward its value in legal judgment, at least as a way to defeat the charge of arbitrariness.

Second, McLachlin and Major's invocation of "common sense" also overlaps with Gramsci's in the sense that they characterize common sense not only as a potential source of information (contrasted with "evidence") but also as a way of looking at things, a type of logic or theory. The passages cited above suggest that common sense can be understood as a framework for seeing the world, or for a "conception of the world" in Gramsci's language. The use of "common sense" in these passages suggests that a common sense approach to the world will be *inadequate* to ground a government's justification without essential support from a more systematic and fact-based approach informed by "evidence."

The dissenting judgment in *Chaoulli*, authored by Justices Ian Binnie and Louis LeBel, with Justice Morris Fish concurring, objects to McLachlin and Major's characterization of the issue as a matter of competing claims of common sense, with nothing more than the appellant's evidence to distinguish them:

> Our colleagues the Chief Justice and Major J. write:
>
> The task of the courts, on s. 7 issues as on others, is to evaluate the issue in the light, not just of common sense or theory, but of the evidence. [para. 150]
>
> This, of course, is precisely what the learned trial judge did after weeks of listening to expert testimony and argument. In general,

> we agree with her conclusions. There is nothing in the evidence to justify our colleagues' disagreement with her conclusion that the general availability of health insurance will lead to a significant expansion of the private health sector to the detriment of the public health sector.[125]

In particular, Binnie and LeBel go on to defend the "evidentiary" quality of the government's submissions, primarily by reciting at length the expert credentials of the government witnesses, and they call for deference to the trial judge's findings: "Our colleagues the Chief Justice and Major J. dismiss the experts accepted by the trial judge as relying on little more than 'common sense.' Although we agree that the experts offered 'common sense,' they offered a good deal more ... The respondent's experts testified and were cross-examined. The trial judge found them to be credible and reliable. We owe deference to her findings in this respect."[126]

This argument, supporting the trial judge's conclusion that the legislation was not arbitrary, also has interesting implications for the meaning of "common sense." Binnie and LeBell accept, without quotation marks, that the government's assertions accord with common sense. Then they go on to say that the government's arguments *also* have evidence in their favour. Thus, in some respects, both the majority and dissenting judgments affirm that "common sense" is something *other* than "evidence" when it comes to legal judgment.[127] And for the most part, both judgments agree that it is evidence that should ground the justification exercise.[128] However, in the judgment by Binnie and LeBel, there is also some room for identifying common sense on a given matter and endorsing it ("we agree that the experts offered 'common sense'"), as well as for claiming common sense as one's own in addition to what the evidence might say.

Gramsci's concerns about the contradictory content of common sense and its unreliability as a source of evidence are thus partly played out in the various judgments of the *Chaoulli* case. The majority judgment does reflect Gramsci's idea that common sense is vulnerable to instrumental use and cannot be used as evidence of any given proposition. But in the judgment, common sense is described as problematic because it is *empty* as far as this legal argument is concerned; it cannot, on its own, push us one way or the other. For Gramsci, common sense is *not empty* but overflowing with ideas and perspectives that need careful scrutiny from a political perspective.

Thus this case also works well to facilitate discussion of Gramsci's approach to common sense precisely because of what is missing from the judgments: analysis of power. The *reason* that Gramsci is concerned about the heterogenous and contradictory content of common sense is that it undermines the capacity of certain social groups to have a worldview that meaningfully explains their experiences. Gramsci's concern is that the conception of the world that frames our vision reifies and perpetuates the oppression of some groups by others. It is on *this* basis that Gramsci rejects resort to common sense on its own as a way to prove an argument. McLachlin and Major also reject common sense in *Chaoulli*. However, *Chaoulli* is not a case in which common sense becomes a vector for transporting hegemonic perspectives into legal judgment in order to obtain a result favourable to dominant groups. In contrast, in this case, the majority judgment *rejects* "common sense" in favour of "evidence" but nonetheless reaches a result that tends to support the class interests of wealthier Canadians.[129] Moreover, the class and equality elements of the case, such as the accessibility of healthcare and the ability of the wealthy to advance their claims in court, are strangely invisible in the decision itself.[130] Common sense is apparently not the only concept requiring more transparent treatment.

Gramsci asks that we be critical of common sense, subjecting it to careful scrutiny. But his approach to common sense does not stop there. Gramsci's common sense is connected to history and power. A vague or generalized skepticism will not do; we have to engage with common sense in a contextualized, specific, and dialogical manner. The goal is to critique common sense in order to understand its powerful implications and undermine them by allowing other kinds of information or evidence to come into dialogue with common sense. Moreover – and this is what is missing in *Chaoulli* – *both* common sense and evidence, or science, or philosophy should leave the encounter transformed.

This process of relational transformation is captured by Gramsci's "philosophy of praxis" – a dialogical process that he likens to a student-teacher exchange. In contrast, the judgments in *Chaoulli* lack this kind of transformational approach. McLachlin and Major reject "common sense" because of its unclear content and its vulnerability to instrumental use in reasoning, but they do not apply this same critique to the "evidence" on which they do rely. Gramsci would ask us to consider whose common sense is being offered to support the prohibition on private medical insurance? Whose common sense is being offered to oppose it? Whose interests are at stake? And further, whose interests are advanced by the demand for scientific "evidence"? What evidence is understood as persuasive or legitimate? What kinds of assumptions underlie the scientific claims offered in contrast to common sense? For example, in their comment on the case, legal scholars Colleen Flood and Sujith Xavier argue that the majority justices assume, falsely, that a government monopoly on health services causes wait lists.[131] This is a crucial part of the case but receives little in the way of clear scrutiny.

Gramsci's idea of hegemony describes how the interests of dominant groups come to be inscribed not only in common sense but also in all kinds of social and cultural institutions and practices, including science, philosophy, religion, and education. The critique he levels at common sense is crucial because of the way that common sense can appear as the natural and default "conception of the world" that most ordinary people possess. But the content and function of other "conceptions of the world" are by no means exempt from the historical-political critique that is necessary to uncover domination and generate the conditions for political transformation. Moreover, Gramsci's idea of common sense provides criteria for determining what parts of common sense are valuable toward this goal and can count as "good sense," which is the theme that I explore next.

Sauvé v. Canada (Chief Electoral Officer)

In *Sauvé v. Canada (Chief Electoral Officer)* the language of "common sense" also plays a central role in the justices' articulation of what is required in order to demonstrably justify the breach of a constitutional right, this time in the context of section 1 of the Canadian Charter of Rights and Freedoms. In that case, the Supreme Court of Canada was asked to assess the constitutionality of part of the Canada Elections Act, which denied the vote to "[e]very person who is imprisoned in a correctional institution serving a sentence of two years or more."[132] This legislation was challenged by Richard Sauvé and other prisoners, who argued that the legislation violated their right to vote and their right to equality. On the question of the right to vote, protected by section 3 of the Charter, the government conceded that the legislation infringed this right, but it argued that this infringement was justified in a free and democratic society pursuant to section 1 of the Charter.[133] The government argued that the legislation was justified because it pursued the objectives of promoting civic responsibility and imposing appropriate punishment.[134]

Chief Justic Beverley McLachlin, writing for a majority of herself and four other justices, held that the legislation unjustifiably infringed the right to vote and was unconstitutional. She raised concerns about the "vague," "abstract," and "thinly based" nature of the rationales offered by the government, but she held that it was nonetheless "prudent" to proceed with the proportionality analysis.[135] McLachlin found that the legislation was not rationally connected to the government's stated objectives, that it did not minimally impair the right in question, and further that the detrimental effects of the legislation greatly outweighed any benefit that might flow from it.[136] Writing for himself and three other dissenting judges, Justice Charles Gonthier found that the government's evaluation of philosophical and policy issues merited deference and that the legislation did in fact meet the tests for justification.[137]

Both judgments feature prominent references to "common sense," particularly in relation to the question of whether the government adequately demonstrated the connection between the stated objectives and the means chosen to achieve them, as well as the approach that should be taken to the justification exercise in general. In the majority judgment, McLachlin writes, "The right to vote is fundamental to our democracy and the rule of law and cannot be lightly set aside. Limits on it require not deference, but careful examination.

This is not a matter of substituting the Court's philosophical preference for that of the legislature, but of ensuring that the legislature's proffered justification is supported by *logic and common sense*."[138] In this passage, McLachlin finds that it is part of the court's obligation to ensure that the government's proffered justification *does accord with common sense*. Unlike in other passages in this judgment and others, common sense is described as mandatory, not just supplementary or optional. Common sense is aligned with "logic" and contrasted with "philosophical preference." In other passages, McLachlin writes as though common sense can serve to *supplement* evidence in the justification process (and indeed, as a matter of legal doctrine, this appears to be the general approach).[139] But here, in this passage, "common sense" is invoked as part of what is required in order for the government to justify the breach of a right.

The majority and dissenting justices in *Sauvé* explicitly disagree about the *content* of common sense in relation to the rational connections alleged in this case. Specifically, while considering the government's claim that disenfranchisement formed a part of appropriate punishment, McLachlin finds that "[n]either the record nor common sense supports the claim that disenfranchisement deters crime or rehabilitates criminals."[140] In contrast, Gonthier finds that common sense does support a rational connection to both of the government's stated objectives:

> I support the analysis of the courts below: reason, logic and common sense, as well as extensive expert evidence support a conclusion that there is a rational connection between disenfranchising offenders incarcerated for serious crimes and the objectives of promoting civic responsibility and the rule of law and the enhancement of the general objectives of the penal sanction.[141]

> I share the view of the courts below that given that the objectives are largely symbolic, common sense dictates that social condemnation of criminal activity and a desire to promote civic responsibility are reflected in disenfranchisement of those who have committed serious crimes.[142]

In this respect, the treatment of common sense by both judgments in the *Sauvé* case again reflects Gramsci's fundamental observation that the content of common sense is much too heterogeneous and incoherent as a body of knowledge to meaningfully count as evidence of any given claim: one can always find both a proposition and its opposite in common sense. Common sense tells us that disenfranchisement can serve as a meaningful punishment, *and* common sense also tells us that this makes no sense. Faced with this problem, Thomas Reid might say that a claim about the connection between social condemnation of crime and disenfranchisement lies far beyond the jurisdiction of common sense knowledge. But Gramsci argues that common sense – our uncritical conception of the world – does include a wide range of things that might well include an approach to punishment and its relationship to civil rights. On the face of things, it is unclear how Gramsci's theory of common sense could guide legal judgment through this impasse created by two competing common sense claims. But a careful look at the aspect of common sense under consideration here provides a way through. Gramsci's approach to common sense also requires attention to the context of common sense claims and an analysis of how people come to hold the views they do. Unlike the judgments in *Chaoulli*, both judgments in *Sauvé* also offer some observations that speak to this issue.

For example, Gonthier goes on to identify the source of the disagreement about the content of common sense on this matter as resting with differing social and political philosophies.[143] He argues that the chief justice's rejection of the government's claims consists merely of a rejection of one reasonable philosophical view in favour of another, without offering supporting reasons for so doing.[144] Indeed, the heart of Gonthier's dissent is that, in many cases, the act of justification under section 1 must involve some appreciation of these underlying philosophical views. He argues that, "[i]n the case at bar, there is very little quantitative or empirical evidence either way. In such cases, the task of justification relates to the analysis of human motivation, the determination of values, and the understanding of underlying social or political philosophies – it truly is justification rather than measurement."[145]

Gonthier finds that the task of true justification in this sense, when the question seems to be about a fundamental philosophical perspective rather than evidence or expertise, should involve deference to the way that Parliament has approached the matter.[146] In this respect, Gonthier's judgment suggests a further element of Gramsci's common sense, which is the idea that common sense is not only a source of knowledge but also an entire conception of the world with political and philosophical content. Part of Gonthier's argument is about institutional competence and the question of who should be charged with resolving public debates about alternative conceptions of the world, and he opts to defer this exercise to the legislature. I think Gramsci would be unhappy with this outcome because of the resulting further political marginalization of prisoners in the context of a capitalist society. However, I also think Gramsci would agree with Gonthier's general assertion that these are choices with political and philosophical content.

In his discussion of "principled reasoning" in relation to *Sauvé*, legal scholar Graham Mayeda argues that McLachlin also sidesteps the question of alternative political theories, not by deferring to the legislature but by invoking "common sense" and focusing on the more pragmatic proportionality analysis.[147] Without principled engagement with the alternative philosophical frameworks at play, McLachlin's judgment lacks transparency, and the invocation of "common sense" allows judgment to proceed without scrutiny of the political and philosophical commitments at play.[148] This is a consequence at the heart of Gramsci's notions of common sense and hegemony. However, as Mayeda also notes, McLachlin does address some issues that flag the need for justification and "principled reasoning." These issues arise especially in relation to "common sense."[149]

Specifically, McLachlin addresses the possible reasons that might exist for disagreement about the content of common sense. Whereas Gonthier speaks generally about philosophical perspectives, McLachlin notes specifically the risk that "stereotypes" can engender: "[O]ne must be wary of stereotypes cloaked as common sense, and of substituting deference for the reasoned demonstration required by s. 1."[150] Here, McLachlin is more explicitly endorsing a form of critical review for common sense to test its adequacy against the norms of legal judgment. "Stereotypes," adopting the general definition offered by feminist legal scholar Denise Réaume, are "inaccurate generalizations about the attributes of members of a group that can usually be traced back to a time when social relations were based more overtly on contempt for the moral worth of the group."[151] On this view, for legal judgment, stereotypes are a problem not only because they may be wrong or misleading but also because they can reflect inequalities in existing social relations and can function to silence and oppress. Although the specific stereotypes at work in this case are not explicitly identified, one can imagine potential candidates, such as the idea that people in prison are inherently incapable of contributing to a democratic community or that people in prison are lesser citizens for whom the right to vote is not important or who must be taught civic responsibility in a punitive manner.[152]

The invocation of "common sense" as a possible conduit for "stereotypes" brings Gramsci's more critical perspective to bear on legal judgment in this case. At the same time, the language of "stereotypes" is actually quite limited as a way to articulate how "common sense" should be measured against "justice." For example, in her analysis of equality law and the concept of human dignity, Réaume points out that "[p]rejudice and stereotype are core cases of impugning the moral worth of others. Their eradication constitutes a necessary part of the landscape of equality. However, protection against them does not exhaust the notion of respect for human dignity."[153] Testing common sense for the presence of stereotypes may be an essential part of ensuring its legitimacy for legal judgment, but it is a far cry from the thoroughgoing and dialogical critique that Gramsci envisions in the "philosophy of praxis."[154] And the risks of adopting common sense in the absence of this richer critique were made manifest in the case of *Gosselin*.

Gosselin v. Quebec (Procureur général)

In chapter 2, focusing on the aspect of common sense that we see in Thomas Reid – common sense as common knowledge – the appearance of "common sense" in *Gosselin v. Quebec (Procureur général)* raised issues about false claims of universality and the rhetorical re-exclusion of marginalized peoples. Reid's perspective reveals the importance of common sense knowledge in grounding judgment and articulating a commitment to egalitarianism, but his approach provides little guidance once we identify significant conflicts within common sense knowledge that cannot be resolved with the simple reference to "self-evidence" that Reid imagined. In the context of *Gosselin*, we need Gramsci's perspective in order to develop criteria for accepting some common sense and rejecting other common sense, for distinguishing between "good sense" and what is just commonly believed. We need access to the aspect of common sense as a whole conception of the world that relates us to our communities. Looking again at the text referring to "common sense" reinforces the idea that we learn different things about legal judgment when reading with this new aspect of common sense in mind.

In *Gosselin* the language of "common sense" does not appear in the context of questions about government justification of the breach of a right. Rather, it appears in the context of the analysis of section 15 equality rights. However, in this case, McLachlin's majority judgment effectively imports some aspects of justification into the section 15 analysis, so once again the issue is in part about what is required to establish a connection between a government's proffered objective and the means it has chosen to achieve that objective.[155] In comparison with most of the judgments in *Chaoulli* and *Sauvé*, references to "common sense" in *Gosselin* create a stronger sense of confidence in the value of common sense. Here, McLachlin adopts the phrase "common sense" to describe the content of her own argument. In one passage, dealing with the impact of the impugned law, she writes, "*As a matter of common sense*, if a law is designed to promote the claimant's long-term autonomy and self-sufficiency, a reasonable person in the claimant's position would be less likely to view it as an assault on her inherent human dignity."[156]

McLachlin uses the language of "common sense" to articulate the basis of a substantive claim in the case, one that gives the government's proffered justification for the law significant leverage in the discrimination analysis. McLachlin also writes that the "legislator *is entitled* to proceed on informed general assumptions," where those assumptions are grounded in "common sense."[157] Compared with most of the judgments discussed above, these passages portray a general approach to common sense that is optimistic about its potential value. Perhaps the strongest contrast can be found in McLachlin's statement in *Chaoulli* that "[t]he task of the courts, on s. 7 issues as on others, is to evaluate the issue in the light, not just of common sense or theory, but of the evidence."[158]

But in *Gosselin*, as in *Sauvé*, McLachlin calls for caution in relying on "common sense" because of the risk that it might harbour "stereotypes." In *Sauvé* she cautions against "stereotypes cloaked as common sense,"[159] and in *Gosselin* she notes that the government's underlying "common sense" assumptions must not be based on "arbitrary and demeaning stereotypes."[160] This caution is merited in the context of both cases, which deal with groups of people who are often the subject of powerful and damaging stereotypes. Incarceration in federal prisons in Canada overlaps with social categories such as mental illness, race, aboriginality, and gender.[161] Low-income status overlaps with social categories such as gender, mental and physical disability, immigration status, and age.[162] All of these categories invoke relations of social inclusion and exclusion, relative power, and experiences of oppression.

In *Sauvé* this wariness of common sense and its potential to cloak stereotypes leads McLachlin to reject resort to common sense, whereas in *Gosselin* the majority judgment does not eschew but relies on common sense knowledge that is quite compromised by stereotypes.[163] For example, note again the passage about whether the law in question properly responded to the claimant's "actual needs and circumstance": "Logic and *common sense* support the legislature's decision to structure its social assistance programs to give young people, who have a greater potential for long-term insertion into the work force than older people, the incentive to participate in programs specifically designed to provide them with training and experience."[164] McLachlin writes that this conclusion does not rely on stereotypes because it corresponds to the "actual needs and circumstances" of young people and constitutes an "affirmation of their potential."[165] This finding constructs an understanding in which stereotypes are generalizations that are necessarily empirically false. Therefore, the common sense proposition at hand is found not to be a stereotype because it is empirically true.[166] This approach to the concept of stereotype merits further scrutiny, as I discuss below. But setting this concern aside, I note that it is also unclear whether this particular common sense proposition does, in fact, avoid untrue stereotypes.

For example, in her analysis of the case, equality scholar Gwen Brodsky argues that the challenged regulation is "manifestly based on the view that the under-thirty group of social assistance recipients needs to be coerced, through a highly punitive withdrawal of support, to make them seek employment opportunities."[167] By upholding the law and accepting the government's explanation of its purpose, the Supreme Court also endorses this stereotype: "The *Gosselin* decision itself perpetuates a negative stereotype of poor young adults. The claimants in *Gosselin* were viewed by the majority as resilient but lazy young adults with enormous, but untapped, human potential, who needed some tough love."[168] Addressing the tone of the judgment more generally, Natasha Kim and Tina Piper write: "In addition to failing to account for the simple realities of those living in poverty, the paternalistic undertones of [certain passages from the judgment] would seem to be based on underlying stereotypes of the poor and the young as being unemployed by choice, lack of motivation, or laziness. Clearly the majority did not intend to invoke stereotypes, but its subtle assumptions (combined with the lack of proof or discussion of their veracity) are reflective of the insidious discrimination faced by the poor in society generally."[169]

Thus there is a strong argument to be made that the invocation of "common sense" in the *Gosselin* case indeed facilitates the perpetuation of stereotypes.[170] Further, in this case, common sense worked to close down the discrimination claims of a marginalized and impoverished group in society. Gramsci's perspective highlights this effect of common sense and the need for critical review in order to make common sense a worthy foundation for knowledge, reasoning, and action.

With Gramsci's approach in mind, I want to make two further comments about the invocation of "common sense" in *Gosselin*. First, it seems clear that the concept of stereotype is inadequate to serve as the sole criterion for distinguishing liberatory from oppressive common sense, or for identifying "good sense," as Gramsci would say. The justice issues at stake in *Gosselin* involve concerns about poverty, sexism, age discrimination, and the obligations of the state in a liberal democracy; these issues include, but go far beyond, the question of whether the impugned regulation or the court's use of "common sense" advanced a stereotype of young adults as lazy. In particular, the concerns about justice in *Gosselin* remain active whether or not this stereotype is "true." This issue recalls the approach to "prejudice" that Thomas Reid employs, concerning himself with the epistemological risk of empirical error. But for Gramsci, the criteria for "good sense" are not only *empirical* criteria but also *political* criteria about the capacity for good sense to ground the judgment and action of whole groups of people – in other words, to allow them to understand their own social reality and to take up action in order to resist their oppression by others. In a similar vein, some legal scholars critique the court's reliance on the concept of stereotype as a benchmark for inequality precisely because injustices can occur in the absence of "untrue" generalizations.[171] Indeed, sometimes it is the state's attempts to pin down the exact "truth" of marginalized groups that is the source of injustice,[172] so our attention must reach beyond the risks of stereotypes.

Second, Gramsci's concern about the capacity of common sense to promote the interests of dominant groups is made manifest in *Gosselin* in a way that is clearer than in other cases. The differences between the outcomes of *Gosselin* and *Chaoulli* are particularly stark from this perspective. In *Chaoulli*, "common sense" is an insufficient basis for the government's claim that the public medical system must be protected from the effects of private insurance. This conclusion advances the interests of those who benefit most from the status quo, at the expense of the redistributive or transformative potential of the universal public medical insurance regime. In *Gosselin*, "common sense" *is* sufficient to uphold the government's claim that young adults on social assistance have greater employment opportunities than older adults and that a law providing incentives to join the labour force, even in the form of the threat of extreme poverty, would not infringe the dignity of a reasonable person. The judgment denies the rights claims of some of the most impoverished and marginalized people in our society. Thus, despite the identification of the need to distinguish legitimate from illegitimate common sense, in *Gosselin* this process of scrutiny fails to achieve what is needed in order to strengthen legal judgment for social justice.

The process of identifying "good sense" is dependent on the existence of a whole set of political conditions, enabling meaningful critical reflection by both more powerful and less powerful people. Gramsci's "philosophy of praxis" makes it possible to identify which elements of common sense are useful to political transformation and which are not. The most important part of this analysis – an understanding of power relations, including the ways that common sense upholds and maintains those relations – is largely absent from the judicial considerations of common sense in *Chaoulli*, *Sauvé*, and *Gosselin*. Thus the distinction between "common sense" and "stereotypes" offered by McLachlin in *Sauvé* and *Gosselin* hints at something important but stops before this distinction can be of much service. Without a process for the kind of ambitious self-reflection envisioned by Gramsci, set in the context of the right social conditions, nothing prevents McLachlin from embracing common sense claims that uphold the power of dominant groups and that continue to marginalize people in poverty.

CONCLUSION

The aspect of common sense that comes to light by reading Gramsci is the notion of common sense as a historically and politically constituted "conception of the world" that is constructed through heterogeneous social experiences and embedded in relations of power. Common sense serves, in part, to uphold the cultural domination of some groups by others and to maintain the political and economic relations that serve the interests of the powerful. However, common sense is also a necessary part of individual and collective life, and Gramsci advocates that attention be turned to the practices of critical reflection that can transform fragmentary and oppressive common sense into a coherent conception of the world that helps people to make sense of their experiences.[173]

Examining legal judgments that use the language of "common sense" through the lens provided by this aspect of common sense leads to certain conclusions about its role and meaning in legal judgment. As explicitly identified by a number of judges in the cases considered in this chapter, the fragmentary and incoherent nature of common sense makes it a highly suspect source of evidence in the context of legal judgment. We see contradictory claims all made in the name of common sense, and in Gramsci's view this is an inherent characteristic of common sense that makes it inappropriate as "proof" of anything in particular. There is a sense in which this characteristic of common sense could render uncertain or unknowable the necessary burden of proof in any given case; a judge may invoke "common sense" to uphold a finding, but doing so does nothing to structure the case that a litigant must meet.[174]

However, the problem with the incoherence of common sense is not just that its contents can self-contradict or that it might have any content in particular. Rather, this self-contradiction takes place in a specific context where some experiences and some kinds of knowledge are valued over others. Thus the problem with common sense is that it consists of knowledge that functions precisely to maintain existing power relations. In the context of legal cases concerned with adjudicating the rights of marginalized individuals and the evidence required to support a government's interference with those rights, Gramsci's perspective on common sense provides good reasons to be wary of common sense, not because it is empty of meaning but because its rich and persuasive meaning is imbued with unequal power relations.

This caution applies even more strongly when the case in question involves a proffered government justification for infringing the rights of historically marginalized people. Indeed, in the context of constitutional equality claims, Sheila McIntyre writes that "judicial complacency in invoking or accepting 'common sense' notions about historically marginalized, stigmatized or stereotyped groups amounts to bad judging."[175] Gramsci's approach explains why, *in this context*, legal judgment requires scrutiny of common sense. For Gramsci, the critique of common sense is an essential part of political transformation that aims to improve the lives of marginalized groups and to end disparities in wealth and power. For a conception of legal justice also motivated by these values, the critique of common sense in legal judgment is essential.

Gramsci's approach to common sense takes it to be embedded in our daily experiences as well as our membership in a multitude of social groups, especially those based on economic class. Common sense is not a discrete body of knowledge but is located in all kinds of knowledge and practices, with their attendant role in maintaining the hegemony of dominant groups. Further, common sense helps to structure the way that people see the world; nothing sits fully outside of its reach. This approach to common sense issues a major challenge to legal judgment because it contemplates that, insofar as they rely on or participate in common sense, all legal actors and institutions are implicated in the creation and replication of relations of power.

Gramsci proposes that common sense must be made the subject of criticism. He further argues that in order to do this in a full and meaningful way, certain political conditions must exist to enable the participation and self-reflection of all kinds of people. These political conditions and the "philosophy of praxis" are what make it possible to engage in the kind of self-reflection that has the potential to identify "good sense" and render common sense coherent and meaningful. I argue that just as the philosophy of praxis is necessary for the critique and transformation of common sense, a framework for critical self-reflection is necessary for the exercise of good legal judgment. The judgments considered in this chapter acknowledge the need for some reflection on the content and meaning of "common sense" in order to make it a useful or legitimate part of legal judgment.

Caution about "common sense" is raised in *Chaoulli*, and the need for criteria to test the legitimacy of common sense knowledge is proposed in *Sauvé* and *Gosselin*. The prospect of stereotyping is raised. However, these judgments contain very little guidance about what this practice of critique and reflection might look like. Although Gonthier argues in *Sauvé* that questions of justification may require substantive engagement with philosophy rather than weighing measurable facts, he defers the substance of this exercise to nonjudicial actors. The absence of a framework for critical self-reflection means that the question of problematic common sense is opened but not addressed, which makes it possible, for example, for McLachlin to rely on stereotypes about people on welfare while explicitly denying that she is so doing.[176] It also allows McLachlin and Major to avoid turning their critical attention to the ways that "common sense" exists in the context of other forms of knowledge, such as "science" and "evidence."

In the concluding chapter, I say more about what this kind of critical reflection might look like in legal judgment. Here, it is important to notice how radical Gramsci's demands are for the transformation of common sense and that it is likely these demands could never be faithfully fulfilled within the bounds of legal judgment in a capitalist, liberal democracy due to class-based inequalities generated by capitalism. However, Gramsci's writings do provide some starting points for thinking about how to structure the critique of common sense in legal judgment in a way that reflects the goals and spirit of his analysis. For example, in articulating how the philosophy of praxis will work, Gramsci relies heavily on educational metaphors; he argues that the relationship between philosophers and mass community members must be one in which each party is *both* a student and a teacher. Gramsci also notes the importance of individuals who have the knowledge and social role that enable them to help bridge gaps between community and elite conceptions of the world; these are the "organic intellectuals," whose interests and commitments lie with mass society but who have had the opportunity to develop their conception of the world into a useful framework for thought and action.

These strands in Gramsci stress the importance of integrating expert and nonexpert knowledges and of facilitating exchange between powerful and less powerful people. They suggest that legal judges should see their role, at least in part, as trained practitioners who should use their special knowledge but who must understand the needs and interests of ordinary people. Critical self-reflection about the invocation of "common sense" and the adequacy of any given common sense claim must come from a place of allegiance with marginalized groups and constant openness to critique.

Gramsci also leaves a number of significant unanswered questions when it comes to practices of critical reflection. In particular, there are outstanding questions about the way that this kind of critical reflection can or should take place in the context of legal judgment, which is highly structured and constrained by legal institutions and principles, as well as highly subjective, emerging from the knowledge and experiences of individual judges, who, by Gramsci's account, are also affected by the practices and interests of their own social groups. Gramsci's focus on reason and transparency leaves questions unanswered about the capacity of individuals to transform their thinking in the manner required. To address some of these issues, I turn in the next chapter to Hannah Arendt.

4

Hannah Arendt's Common Sense: Imagining Communities and the Basis of Valid Judgment

Queen Common-Sense takes the stage at London's Haymarket Theatre in 1736. We glance around for our guest, political theorist Hannah Arendt, arrived from the late twentieth century. She has chosen a seat in the front row, far stage right, where she can see into the wings if she turns her head slightly and where she can also watch the reactions of the other audience members. She observes the proceedings with interest.

> Oh! Traytor, thou hast murder'd Common-Sense.
> Farewel vain World! to Ignorance I give thee,
> Her leaden Sceptre shall henceforward rule.
> Now, Priest, indulge thy wild ambitious Thoughts,
> Men shall embrace thy Schemes, 'till thou hast drawn
> All Worship from the Sun upon thy self:
> Henceforth all things shall topsy turvy turn;
> Physick shall kill, and Law enslave the World:
> Cits shall turn Beaus, and taste Italian Songs,
> While Courtiers are Stock-jobbing in the City.
> Places, requiring Learning and great Parts,
> Henceforth shall all be husled in a Hat,
> And drawn by Men deficient in them both.
> Statesmen – but Oh! cold Death will let me say
> No more – and you must guess & cetera.
> [Dies.][1]

As Queen Common-Sense recites her dying speech, Arendt laughs. But there is a hint of knowing sadness in her eyes.

INTRODUCTION

This chapter engages with the third and last aspect of common sense that I use to build a more constructive representation of common sense in legal judgment, aiming to see common sense in new ways and evaluating those perspectives against the requirements of politically reflective and legitimate legal judgment. In this chapter, I explore the work of Hannah Arendt, whose use of the phrase "common sense" is part of a different discourse about the possibility and potential of human judgment and about the role of shared communities in contemporary society.

The work of identifying and exploring different aspects of common sense has unfolded in two stages so far. First, I looked at common sense from the perspective of Thomas Reid, who understands common sense as a kind of shared knowledge that arises from daily life and is equally accessible to all. Reid's common sense reveals elements of common sense that support democracy and hold us accountable for exercising our own judgment. At the same time, Reid's perspective also reveals elements of common sense that are vulnerable to capture by powerful groups, and it reveals the ways that common sense can rhetorically fortify the knowledge of dominant groups. Reid's perspective is insufficient to address these concerns adequately, so I shifted perspective to see the aspect of common sense revealed by Antonio Gramsci, who is concerned directly and explicitly with questions of power. From Gramsci's perspective, common sense is a socially constructed body of knowledge that we inherit through our membership in various communities. Common sense is a historically contingent framework that we use to understand and assess other kinds of knowledge. Gramsci's perspective reveals elements of common sense that are tied to social power and that work to replicate this power for dominant groups. We also see the potential for common sense to be the subject of critical reflection and to be transformed in a way that could allow all communities to more effectively make sense of their experiences. But Gramsci's perspective also leaves questions unanswered, especially about the capacity of individuals to engage in the kind of critique that Gramsci advocates and about the links between common sense and practices that reach beyond rational argument, such as judgment and emotion. To think through these questions, I change perspectives again in order to explore the aspect of common sense that is revealed by engaging with the writings of political theorist Hannah Arendt.

Hannah Arendt (1906–75) was born in Germany. In 1933 she was forced to leave Germany and moved to Paris, where she worked with Jewish refugee organizations. In 1941 she emigrated to the United States, where she became very active in many aspects of intellectual life. As a political theorist, she wrote and lectured on many themes, including totalitarianism, human rights, and modern society, and she is widely regarded as one of the most influential thinkers of the twentieth century.[2] In Arendt's writings, "common sense" is embedded in explorations of the human capacity for judgment and its practice in later twentieth-century Western society. Engagement with common sense is the way that judgment can become valid across a community. Common sense signifies the judgments of the people who make up a community as these judgments are imagined by an individual seeking to judge in a particular case. Consequently, common sense is not a static body of information that can be specified in advance but is part of a dialogical practice that helps both to identify and to generate shared beliefs and standards. Common sense and judgment are important for Arendt because of their connections to freedom and genuine political action. Thus the aspect of common sense that emerges from engagement with Hannah Arendt is that of common sense as part of the practice of judgment, where judgment is understood as an activity of the mind that is inherently connected to the sociability of human beings.

Arendt's perspective provides a point of contrast with both Reid and Gramsci, whose notions of common sense are more descriptive of an identifiable body of knowledge or method of reasoning. Gramsci envisions common sense as dynamic and changing from context to context, and even Reid identifies ways that our access to common sense can be improved. For Arendt, "common sense" refers to the common judgments of the diverse others who form a community. This community sense enables the practice of judgment, which in turn works to shape that very community. Thus the *process* of developing our common sense and engaging with it through judgment forms the heart of Arendt's approach. For Reid, everyone has the capacity to form judgments in accordance with common sense. For Gramsci, everyone has a common sense "conception of the world"[3] that shapes their thought and action. For Arendt, what pre-exists for everyone is the nascent capacity to judge as a member of a community.

Like the previous chapters on Reid and Gramsci, this chapter has two parts. In the first part, I describe Arendt's perspective on common sense in more detail. I focus on three themes: the role of common sense in determining the validity and assessing the quality of judgment, the relationship between common sense and the role of persuasion, and the way that common sense works not only to reflect but also to *constitute* communities through the choices we make about community boundaries and communicability. To accurately understand and describe Arendt's approach, I make reference to the context of her arguments and to the questions that she was trying to address as a political thinker. At the same time, I also use my own framework – concerned as it is with *legal* judgment and the social justice problem of poverty – to determine which aspects of her approach to elaborate and evaluate.

In the second part of this chapter, I explore Arendt's notion of common sense in the context of legal judgment. In this part, I ask what can be learned about legal judgment by thinking about common sense as Arendt does. I also make my own concerns about law and poverty the measures for evaluating the strength of Arendt's approach for understanding common sense in the context of legal judgment. In this endeavour, I choose for consideration texts involving the issue of judicial impartiality and the Supreme Court of Canada's use of the phrase "common sense" in relation to the concept of a "reasonable apprehension of bias." I discuss the case of *R. v. R.D.S.*,[4] which brings these two concepts together and which touches upon many of Arendt's concerns about community, validity, and impartiality. I also reread *Gosselin v. Quebec (Procureur général)* in light of the aspect of common sense that we see in Arendt.[5] Although the *Gosselin* case is not "about" the concept of judicial impartiality in a doctrinal sense, it is worth considering in relation to this concept because of the way that the various judgments invoke concepts like imagination and the proper role of judges in defending their findings.

Arendt's perspective on common sense demonstrates the great potential of this concept to facilitate good judgment. By working to identify and create the communities that are necessary not only for judgment but also for political action and human flourishing, Arendt's common sense creates links between the private act of judgment and the public, shared life of the community. Adopting this perspective on common sense shifts emphasis away from epistemology and toward communicability and persuasion as criteria for good judgment. And in this way, Arendt's common sense also creates a powerful connection between common sense and justice.[6] Taking this aspect of common sense seriously shows the potential for common sense to serve as a way to find practices of legal judgment that are capable of addressing injustices of poverty and marginalization.

ARENDT ON COMMON SENSE

Validity and Criteria for Good Judgment

Arendt's discussion of common sense is situated in the context of her writings on judgment. For Arendt, "common sense" refers to the judgments of the multiple others in communities, judgments to which we refer in our imaginations when we engage in the act of judging. Common sense is part of the practice of judgment. Arendt's explicit discussions of judgment as a human practice emerged near the end of her life, and she did not live to complete the full volume on this topic that she intended.[7] However, in a number of texts, most explicitly in her *Lectures on Kant's Political Philosophy*, Arendt sets out some elements of her perspective on judgment, why it is important, and what is at stake in our understanding of judgment. In the *Lectures*,

Arendt invokes Immanuel Kant's theory of aesthetic judgment as a framework for developing her approach to political judgment.[8] Her particular take on common sense is central to this account.

In this context, Arendt uses the word "judgment" to describe the distinct human faculty that makes possible the act of judging: one judges the morality of a practice or the beauty of a work of art. "Judgment" is also a noun: one passes judgment, or comes to a judgment, or shares a judgment. In this chapter, the multiple uses of the term "judgment" become particularly evident and the slippage between them particularly productive. If one is a judge in a court of law, one's practices of judgment, the content of one's judgments, and the written reasons for one's disposition of a legal dispute – a "judgment" – are all subject to scrutiny from a justice perspective. The practice of judging is a distinct human capacity, one that lies at the heart of political life. In this chapter, I engage more fully with the implications of understanding legal judgment as part of this larger category of human judgment.[9]

Judging involves the *evaluation* of a particular person or thing.[10] It might involve, for example, determining whether something is good or bad, right or wrong, beautiful or boring, meaningful or empty. Further, this evaluation is of a *particular* person or thing and does not simply involve the application of rules or established categories.[11] Arendt writes, "If you say, 'What a beautiful rose!' you do not arrive at this judgment by first saying, 'All roses are beautiful, this flower is a rose, hence this rose is beautiful.'"[12] Consequently, judgment is different from logical or other forms of purely rational thought; judgments cannot be arrived at by simple deduction or induction.[13] Rather, although it does not end there, judgment begins with a kind of experience of liking or not liking something, and in this way it shares some of the characteristics of aesthetic "taste" as understood by Kant.[14] This process of assessment always has an inherently subjective component that cannot be decontextualized or established as "true" in a universal sense.

At the same time, judgment is not the same as taste and is not solely concerned with subjective experiences of preference or pleasure. Indeed, Arendt argues that judgments make claims to validity that extend beyond the individual. Thus, when I say, "I like this novel," I am expressing my taste or preference, and I probably have no expectation that my statement reflects more than my subjective experience. But when I say, "This is a great novel," I am making a judgment. Although I do not understand myself to be expressing a universal truth, I am staking out a claim that the novel is "great" in some sense that extends beyond my personal preference. I believe that others would make the same judgment, and I am prepared to justify my judgment on those terms.[15]

Common sense lies at the heart of the practice of judgment through a process that Arendt calls "enlargement of mind" or "enlarged mentality."[16] The practice of enlarged mentality requires one to consider the perspectives of other judges in a community and to measure one's own (tentative, initial) judgment against theirs. Arendt describes the judgments of others, with which we engage when judging, as the "common sense" of the community.[17] She also uses the Latin phrase *sensus communis* or the English translation "community sense" when she wants to draw particular attention to the special way that she is using these words.[18] Arendt writes, "One's community sense makes it possible to enlarge one's mentality."[19] Developing an enlarged mentality is what allows us to move beyond our private feelings, beliefs, and idiosyncrasies so that we may come to a conclusion that is not just a statement of opinion but also a *judgment*.[20] A judgment is *valid* beyond my individual preferences *to the extent* that I have engaged with the judgments of others.[21] It is the process of reflection and judgment that characterizes Arendt's use of "common sense" and differentiates it from other uses, including Reid's and Gramsci's.[22]

There are two parts to the process of developing an "enlarged mentality" by engaging with common sense. The first part involves *imagination*. Here, I imagine or represent to myself what I know about the feelings and beliefs of others. I think about their views and try to imagine what my views would be in their place.[23] Arendt writes, "To think with an enlarged mentality means that one trains one's imagination to go visiting."[24]

The second part of engaging with common sense involves *reflection*.[25] Here, I reflect on my own private experience of liking or not liking something and try to think about whether others would agree. I imaginatively compare my ideas with the ideas of others and consider whether and how I could explain and justify my conclusions to them. I do not adopt the views of others uncritically; this would merely be substituting their idiosyncrasies for mine.[26] Rather, I think about what would be required to persuade others in my community that my judgment is right. Thus, according to Arendt, expressions of taste are transformed into judgments through *reflective* engagement with the common sense of a community.[27]

The importance of reflection in Arendt's notion of judgment means that the relationship between good judgment and common sense is not entirely straightforward. Arendt is clear that attention to common sense is not the same as deferring to an empirical social consensus on something, which could mean ratifying a consensus produced by prevailing power relations or unreflective popular opinion.[28] Engagement with common sense does not mean that I "count noses in order to arrive at what I think is right."[29] Nor is it about "an enormously enlarged empathy through which one can know what actually goes on in the mind of all others ... This would be too 'passive,' and might simply constitute replacing one's prejudices with the prejudices of others."[30] These passages suggest an essential critical distance between Arendtian judgment and the actual judgments of people in a community. The common sense of a community is part of a practice of judgment that necessarily includes acts of critical reflection, as well as attention to the boundaries of the community of judging others. Crucially for Arendt, sometimes good judgment will require one to judge against one's community.[31] Judgment relies on common sense, but sometimes true judgment – reflective and exercised with an enlarged mentality – will diverge from popular opinion or from tradition.[32]

The quality and validity of a person's judgments are determined by the nature of their engagement with the common sense of the community. Whereas the validity of a logical deduction or some other truth claim might be general or universal, the validity of a judgment is specific and context-dependent.[33] In particular, for Arendt, the validity of a judgment is specifically linked to the scope of the common sense that has been engaged. A judgment's "claims to validity can never extend further than the others in whose place the judging person has put himself for his considerations."[34] A judgment is valid across the community of judging others who share in the common sense that grounds that judgment.

Communication and Persuasion

Judgments can be communicated across a community of judging others who share a common sense; thus communication, common sense, and judgment are inherently linked.[35] In her discussion of reflective judgment, Arendt argues that "the criterion, then, [for judgment] is communicability, and the standard of deciding about it is common sense."[36] The idea of communicability and the related ideas of persuasion and intersubjectivity are important aspects of Arendt's notion of common sense.

This social character of judgment begins with Arendt's orientation of judgment outside of the self and toward common sense and the other members of a judging community. Some modes of thinking, such as logic and even some versions of moral reasoning, are directed to internal consistency and agreement with the self.[37] Further, once I discover, through independent thought, that something follows the rules of logic, this fact is established for any context; the truth of the matter "compels" agreement from others examining the same rules of logic. In contrast, when I make a judgment, I must orient my thinking to other people. Arendt states, "The power of judgment rests on a potential agreement with others, and the thinking process which is active in judging something is not, like the thought process of pure reasoning, a dialogue between me and myself, but finds itself always and primarily, even if I am quite alone in making up my mind, in an anticipated communication with others with whom I know I must finally come to some agreement."[38] Moreover, when claims about agreement are made, they are never "compelled" in the way that "truth" claims can be. No judgment is ever certain or final. Instead, judgment relies on *persuasion* to reach agreement.[39] Arendt writes, "[O]ne can never compel anyone to agree with one's judgments ... [O]ne can only 'woo' or 'court' the agreement of every-one else. And in this persuasive activity one actually appeals to the 'community sense.' In other words, when one judges, one judges as a member of a community."[40] The central role of persuasion in the practice of judgment is part of how judgment comes to be oriented so strongly toward the world and the actual communities that inhabit it rather than toward the abstract "self." If judgment requires that I consider how I might justify my judgment to others, I have to know something about who those others are, what their views might be, and what kinds of arguments they might find persuasive.[41]

Persuasion is about bringing others to see something in a new way, even if they might not have seen it that way before. Feminist political theorist and Arendt scholar Linda Zerilli writes,

> The ability to persuade depends upon the capacity to elicit criteria that speak to the particular case at hand and in relation to particular interlocutors. It is a rhetorical ability, fundamentally creative and imaginative, to project a word like *beautiful* or a phrase like *created equal* into a new context in ways that others can accept, not because they (necessarily) already agree with the projection (or would have to agree if they are thinking properly), but because they are brought to see something new, a different way of framing their responses to certain objects and events.[42]

To come to a valid judgment, I have to test my judgment against the collective judgments of the others in my community – against the common sense of that community. But to think about how I might justify a judgment to others in my community, there has to be a certain level of shared understanding that might allow me to communicate with others and potentially persuade them. Thus the process of identifying and reflecting on common sense actually requires considerable engagement with other people.[43]

This element of Arendt's common sense, which involves communication and persuasion, provokes questions about the nature of the "community" to which a judge should refer when engaging in reflective judgment. One way to approach these questions is with a distinction between "communicability" in the abstract and the actual "communications" that take place in reality.[44] Unlike some other approaches, such as Kant's, Arendt's account of common sense is rooted in an understanding of "community" as an actual, empirical community.[45] Arendt argues that communicability "obviously implies a community of men who can be addressed and who are listening and can be listened to."[46]

However, among interpreters of Arendt, there is debate about what exactly is required to critically engage with the common sense of real communities.[47] This debate is fuelled in part by the fact that Arendt's own writings are complex and ambiguous on this point.[48] On the one hand, Arendt does indicate that her notions of common sense and the enlarged mentality refer not to an abstract or universal "human" community but to concrete, specific communities in the real world. Take, for example, the passages quoted above that are about judging as a member of a community and that refer to a listening audience. Arendt also says that "this enlarged way of thinking, which as judgment knows how to transcend its own individual limitations ... cannot function in strict isolation or solitude; it needs the presence of others 'in whose place' it must think, whose perspectives it must take into consideration, and without whom it never has the opportunity to operate at all."[49]

On the other hand, Arendt also expresses a great deal of faith in the capacity of the imagination. For example, when describing Kant's own attempts at enlargement of mind purely through reading, she writes that "he – who never left Konigsberg – knew his way around both London and Italy."[50] Indeed, it is possible to read Arendt as saying that the imaginative representation of others is actually a *better* way of taking their perspective into account. For example, she writes,

> Suppose I look at a specific slum dwelling and I perceive in this particular building the general notion which it does not exhibit directly, the notion of poverty and misery. I arrive at this notion by representing to myself how I would feel if I had to live there, that is, I try to think in the place of the slum-dweller. The judgment I shall come up with will by no means necessarily be the

> same as that of the inhabitants, whom time and hopelessness may have dulled to the outrage of their condition, but it will become for my further judging of these matters an outstanding example to which I refer ... Furthermore, while I take into account others when judging, this does not mean that I conform in my judgment to those of others, I still speak with my own voice and I do not count noses in order to arrive at what I think is right. But my judgment is no longer subjective either.[51]

This passage emphasizes the essential critical distance that exists between the empirical common sense of a given community and the practice of reflective judgment. The passage also alludes to the potential for oppressive social conditions to interfere with someone's capacity to exercise judgment. It is also possible to interpret this passage as denying the value of the situated knowledge of marginalized people or even as saying that the common sense of marginalized people is best understood through an imaginative exercise of the privileged. Indeed, this passage could be read to support the view that marginalized people are, *by their very experience of marginalization*, precluded from contributing to a community of judgment. For feminists and social justice critics, such consequences would be deeply troubling and would seem to condemn common sense to an ongoing allegiance with the status quo. Indeed, the parallel to the invocation of "common sense" in *Gosselin* immediately springs to mind: by interpreting the law through her subjective experience of poverty rather than through the purported benevolent aims of the state, Louise Gosselin is excluded from the community of judgment. This is one of the dangers of common sense, one that has arisen in all of the theories considered so far, and interpreting Arendt in this way certainly allows her approach to fall into this same problem.

However, I argue that the most useful readings of Arendt are those focusing on common sense as a part of the process of developing an enlarged mentality, which always includes both an imaginative and a critical reflective component. I follow those interpreters of Arendt, including feminist interpreters, who take Arendt in a distinctly democratic direction by focusing on the complexity of the "common senses" to which we have access and on the contextualized processes of engagement with common sense.[52] For example, in her discussion of the requirements of the enlarged mentality, political and legal theorist Jennifer Nedelsky argues that it is crucial to attend to the complexity of social locations and to consider our relationships to each other and to our social conditions. This complexity allows us to see that we rely on a "variety of 'common senses' that are available to us from the different communities to which we belong."[53] Engagement with our different communities will provide us with different, and potentially contradictory, versions of common sense. Further, we may undertake more or less critical reflection about different aspects of our social context. For example, Nedelsky writes that "a person who is poor in a rich country such as Canada may feel that it is her fault that she is poor. Or she may have a carefully developed critique of the distribution of wealth, of the subsidy of corporations, and of the very limited extent to which Canada has a progressive income tax regime. Her standpoint on welfare reform, on corporate tax, and on whom to vote for will depend on the nature of her relation to her 'location' as a poor person."[54]

Thus, when we engage with the perspectives of others, we engage not with their unconsidered opinion or simply their social location but with a reflective consideration of all of the relevant perspectives.[55] We do not "count noses," as Arendt says, but we also do not simply disregard the views of marginalized people. Nedelsky stresses that we must approach all of this with an adequate dose of humility about the extent to which we can understand perspectives different from our own and that disregarding the views of marginalized peoples would transgress this requirement.[56] Here, focusing on the complexity of social location and intellectual humility allows Nedelsky to read Arendt's reflective judgment in a way that is compatible with feminist and social justice goals.

Nedelsky argues that relationships and dialogue are important aspects of developing judgment. In summarizing her own approach to judgment, Nedelsky writes that "Arendt says very little about the kind of experience it takes to be able to exercise the enlarged mentality. I think it is important to actually talk to people. Imagination is fine as long as it has a lot of real experience on which to build."[57] Crucially, Nedelsky argues that such "real experience must be characterized by openness, attentiveness, and receptivity."[58] These qualities are the conditions for identifying common sense that can form the basis for valid judgment.

Another way to approach this issue is to ask questions about what, exactly, must be shared between people in order to make possible the acts of imaginative "visiting" that Arendt describes. What must I understand about others to meaningfully imagine their perspectives or to think about what might persuade them in judgment? In her assessment of Arendt's approach, political theorist Iris Marion Young cautions against any interpretation that relies on the symmetry or interchangeability of individual subject positions.[59] Young argues that it is "neither possible nor morally desirable for persons engaged in moral interaction to adopt one another's standpoint."[60] Rather, Young argues, it is necessary for people to recognize the differences that characterize their experiences and locations, as well as to adopt a mode of respectful communication that does not presume sameness or symmetry between their positions. Young argues that the best way to take up Arendt's ideas is to fully respect the centrality of human plurality in Arendt's work and that this can be achieved only if we attend not only to the perspectives of others but also to the specific context in which they arise.[61] This process needs to account for the ways that individuals and communities are located in society and for the collective ways that our judgments are shaped. Young writes, "We make our moral and political judgments, then, not only by taking account of one another's interests and perspectives, but also by considering the collective social processes and relationships that lie between us and which we have come to know together by discussing the world."[62]

In locating common sense within a process of respectful dialogue, Young is able to show the links between reflective judgment and practices of deliberative democracy.[63] Similarly, Nedelsky focuses on the ways that the "enlarged mentality" is not a static, objective measure but part of a process in which one continuously attempts to expand one's horizons.[64] It is not that there is a predetermined level of "sharedness" that can or must be achieved but that there is an ongoing practice of reflection, challenge, and expansion. The common sense that can form the basis of good judgment need be understood not as a static body of knowledge but as something that grounds an ongoing process. Nedelsky writes, "One can expand the scope of one's mentality by acquiring a broader base of knowledge. One's common sense is a starting point because one cannot begin to put oneself in another's place without something that is shared. But one can build that common sense."[65] Common sense, as the collective judgment of a community, is always a work in progress and contributes to good judgment when it is part of an ongoing practice of communication and critical reflection.

The other thinkers considered in this book also raise related issues about the need to have a wide variety of social experiences in order to strengthen one's access to common sense. Gramsci's whole approach to common sense is focused on the connections between social experience and the content of common sense knowledge, as well as on the potential for transforming common sense through critical reflection. And, as noted previously, Reid also writes about avoiding prejudices by increasing the breadth of one's social experience: "Men judge other men by themselves, or by the small circle of their acquaintance ... It is commonly taken for granted, that this narrow way of judging of men is to be cured only by an extensive intercourse with men of different ranks, professions, and nations; and that the man whose acquaintance has been confined within a narrow circle, must have many prejudices and narrow notions, which a more extensive intercourse would have cured."[66]

However, it is here with Arendt that this practice of *developing* common sense takes on the most central role. Adopting the readings of Nedelsky and Young ties common sense to actual communities and actual communication; adequate engagement with common sense requires us to engage with real communities. We make our common sense better, and thereby increase our capacity for judgment, through a practice of ongoing reflection, dialogue, and critique. This insight is important from a feminist perspective because it has the potential to respond to feminist concerns about marginality and privilege. Focusing on common sense as part of a practice that links judgment and the community not only affects common sense but also affects the community, and it is this theme that I explore next.

Judgment and the Creation of Communities

Reflective engagement with common sense is a condition for good judgment; it is through common sense that a judge moves away from partiality and toward validity. Judgment is valid to the extent that the judge has engaged with the common sense of the relevant community. Thus the act of judging marks and circumscribes a community. Arendt says that common sense "fits us into a community."[67] In some respects, this hearkens back to Gramsci's idea of "good sense" and the way that it allows us to understand our lives in context. But there is another special relationship between Arendt's common sense and communities. Arendt writes,

> The difference between [a] judging insight and speculative thought lies in that the former has its roots in what we usually call common sense, which the latter constantly transcends. Common sense – which the French so suggestively call the "good sense," *le bon sens* – discloses to us the nature of the world insofar as it is a common world; we owe to it the fact that our strictly private and "subjective" five senses and their sensory data can adjust themselves to a nonsubjective and "objective" world which we have in common and share with others. Judging is one, if not the most, important activity in which this sharing-the-world-with-others comes to pass.[68]

Arendt argues that when people judge with reference to their shared common sense, they are making space for a "common world" and deciding what it will be like.[69] Common sense not only allows us to move beyond our purely subjective experiences but also "discloses to us the nature of the world insofar as it is a common world." Through the creation of shared space, engagement with common sense thus not only *relies* on communities but also works to *create* them.[70] Creating or recreating communities is what happens when we practise judgment.[71] In his essay on the relationship between law and reflective judgment in general, including consideration of Kant and Arendt, philosopher William Rasch emphasizes the way that reflective judgment conceives of common sense as part of judging practice rather than as a pre-existing set of knowledge. In reflective judgment, common sense is "retroactively posted as the supplement of judgment."[72] Summarizing the role of judgment in creating communities, Rasch writes, "A judgment is made and with it comes a challenge that others should make the same judgment. What emerges is a community, and not just one community, but a plurality of communities, each legitimizing its own decisions on the basis of a universality that can only be performed and never grounded. What emerges is the world as if it had always already existed."[73]

As part of the disclosure of common space, engagement with common sense is also about disclosure of the *self*. As Arendt says, "Wherever people judge the things of the world that are common to them, there is more implied in their judgments than these things. By his manner of judging, the person discloses to an extent also himself, what kind of person he is."[74] Or in Nedelsky's words, "As we judge, and communicate our judgments, we enable ourselves to be known."[75] When we judge through our engagement with common sense, we disclose some of our selves, and we make choices about the community of reference to which we are appealing. Arendt writes, "By communicating one's feelings, one's pleasures and disinterested delights, one tells one's *choices* and one chooses one's company."[76]

In her discussion of Arendt's theory of judgment and its relationship to freedom, Zerilli focuses on this community-building aspect of judgment and argues that this is the real significance of political judgment.[77] Arendt herself says, notably, that "common sense ... is the political sense par excellence."[78] This element of common sense, which involves judgment and disclosure, importantly goes beyond knowledge to involve acts of choice and political will. Nedelsky writes, "Knowing the possibility of change opens a path for change, but it does not simply bring it about."[79] We have to choose to judge, to act, to participate. Returning to the idea of judgment, Zerilli argues that political judgment is not about finding truth but about creating political space, and doing so involves not a contest of facts but political choices: "Every extension of a political concept always involves an imaginative opening up of the world."[80]

The political and community-creating aspects of common sense are tied to Arendt's political theory in general, especially her commitments to freedom, plurality, and a form of civic republicanism.[81] These commitments provide criteria for the choices we exercise in judgment. In explaining how this process works, Zerilli writes, "Understood as a *political* concept, plurality is something of which we need to take account when we decide what will count as part of our shared or common world. Judging is the activity that enables us to take account of plurality in this distinctly political sense."[82]

In this book, the role of common sense as part of the practice of judgment and as a way that communities are marked and created takes place not just in relation to political judgment but also in relation to legal judgment, which introduces some new themes and new criteria for judgment that require consideration. In this context, the values of plurality and diversity are still important, but attention must be paid to the specific conceptual and institutional requirements of law and legal reasoning. These requirements also generate criteria for the choices we make about good judgment and the boundaries of communities.

ARENDT'S COMMON SENSE IN LEGAL JUDGMENT: IMPARTIALITY, PERSUASION, AND PRACTICE

It is noteworthy that Arendt's approach to judgment and common sense is developed in the service of a theory of *political* judgment. There are important differences between political judgment and *legal* judgment, which is the subject of my inquiry. Arendt's own thoughts on the nature of legal judgment are complicated. Arendt was interested in law and legal judgment. For example, she famously chronicled the trial of the Nazi official Adolf Eichmann, who was tried and convicted of war crimes in Jerusalem in 1961.[83] She also provided commentary on the desegregation of schools in the United States.[84]

In contemporary scholarship, her work is being used to understand many aspects of law, including international law, human rights, and constitutionalism.[85] However, when writing about common sense and the practice of enlarged mentality, Arendt addresses practices of political judgment, not legal judgment. And although Arendt's idea of judgment can reach across different areas of life to include, for example, aesthetic judgment, moral judgment, or political judgment, Arendt herself did not think that the legal decisions of a court were a form of judgment in this sense.

Indeed, Arendt interpreters, including Jennifer Nedelsky and Ronald Beiner, conclude that Arendt did not intend to incorporate legal judgment into her analysis of reflective judgment.[86] Nedelsky writes, "Neither Arendt nor Kant thought that this special capacity for what Kant called reflective judgment was involved in law. Both saw legal judgments as determined by rules or principles, whereas one of the key characteristics of reflective judgments is that they cannot be determined by rules or concepts."[87] However, following scholars such as Nedelsky, I think it is nonetheless useful to apply Arendt's idea of common sense and judgment to legal judgment. Arendt's notion of common sense helps to address a number of important questions about legal judgment, as I discuss below. I also suggest that this extension or recontextualizing of Arendt's concept of judgment is consistent with her overriding concerns with freedom and human plurality. Summarizing her own position on this point, Nedelsky says,

> My own view is that one should have an open mind about the nature of judgment in all these different spheres and, indeed, about the nature of judgment in all the daily forms it takes: in the evaluation of character, of policy, of books, of arguments, of courses, colleagues, students, and exams. I think it is likely that all of these forms of judgment share a basic nature; they all pose the problem of making thoughtful, defensible judgments that cannot be determined by rules or concepts. It is also likely that there are interesting differences between judgments made by judges in court and those made by legislators or ordinary citizens in evaluating policy.[88]

Bringing Arendt's theory of common sense in judgment to the legal context challenges the idea that legal judgment is only, or even primarily, about the application of rules. Although the nature of legal judgment is the subject of all kinds of debate, most judges and commentators acknowledge that legal judges necessarily engage with their own subjective experiences, interests, and knowledges to some degree when making legal judgments.[89] Moreover, even in traditional terms, legal judgment is understood as intersubjective at least to some extent; for example, in addition to engaging with the written judgments that form the precedents for a case, judges in appeal courts often sit on panels and hear each other's lines of argument and forms of reasoning. Thus the line between legal and other forms of judgment, such as moral, political, or aesthetic judgment, should not be drawn too sharply.

However, once this element of subjectivity is brought into the picture, many theories of legal judgment have difficulty reconciling their accounts of legitimacy or validity with the presence of this subjectivity. In the context of some approaches, the influence of judicial subjectivity constitutes a threat to basic legal principles such as judicial impartiality or the rule against applying laws retroactively. For example, if reflective judgment were understood to mean that judges paid no heed to legal rules or precedents and instead simply did what they judged to be right (a mistaken interpretation, in my view), judges in a court of law would not be respecting their unique institutional role. Thus it can appear that we are faced with a choice between denying the human subjectivity of judges and abandoning legal judgment to the realm of arbitrariness and preference – a choice between a satisfying account of human practices and capabilities, on the one hand, and the core values of the rule of law, on the other.[90] Arendt's approach to judgment and the role of common sense within it creates a potential way through this impasse.

Adopting Arendt's approach to judgment for law situates legal judgment alongside other forms of judgment – moral, aesthetic, and political – as part of one more general human practice.[91] At the same time, Arendt's approach, which places common sense at the centre of judgment, requires that attention be paid to the specific context of law. Thus, while allowing us to see the ways that judgment is the same across various contexts, common sense also requires that we attend to the ways that judgment must be evaluated with reference to criteria that derive from a *particular* context. This contextual requirement exists because judgment is always oriented to the assessment of something particular. For example, Arendt writes, "How ... is one able to judge, to evaluate, an act as courageous? When judging, one says spontaneously, without any derivations from general rules, 'This man has courage.' If one were a Greek, one would have in 'the depths of one's mind' the example of Achilles present."[92] Thus the criteria for valid *legal* judgment will come, in part, from highly context-specific sources, including legal institutions, values, and principles. In the following sections of this chapter, I discuss one important concept for valid legal judgment: judicial impartiality.

In his discussion of Arendtian judgment and common law legal judgment, Graham Mayeda highlights some of the unique characteristics of legal judgment that must play a role for validity in this context.[93] Joining those interpreters who focus on and extend Arendt's less transcendental and more democratic aspects, Mayeda argues that the validity of common law legal judgment must in part derive from the attention of judges to the *particulars* of the dispute before them. These particulars include the individual parties as well as the specifics of how the case came before the court. He writes,

> To make Arendt's theory an acceptable theory of legal judgment, we must thus adapt it by deriving the normativity of impartiality, not from disinterest, but from the function of the judge as a person involved in an actual dispute ... What this points to is that the judge must consider the impact of her judgment and its effect both on the broader community (Kantian and Arendtian enlarged mentality) and on the parties. She must also take into account the specific parties before her. And because of the reciprocal relationship between the parties and this community, the judge must also consider the impact that the community norms and values have had on causing and framing the dispute.[94]

Mayeda's point about the importance of a specific, actual dispute in common law legal judgment directs attention to a further issue, namely the need to determine the proper community of reference for the common sense that should underlie a legal judgment. As Nedelsky notes, "By basing judgment in real community, Arendt invites the question that underlies so much jurisprudential and political debate: good judgment for and according to whom?"[95] When judges communicate their decisions, to what audience do they direct their reasons? What community or communities do they imagine when coming to a conclusion?

Several overlapping possibilities come to mind. Judges direct their reasons to the litigants in the case. Legal principles tell us that both parties should understand the reasons for the decision, and even the unsuccessful party should believe that a just procedure was followed to reach the decision.[96] Legal principles and institutions, such as the doctrine of precedent and the appellate court system, also mean that judges direct their reasons to the community of other judges and legal practitioners. Further, judges direct their reasons to a larger community, which might be the larger political community or the entire set of people who are bound by the law.[97]

Thinking about reflective *legal* judgment also draws attention to legal criteria of impartiality, equality, and justice. Mayeda, Nedelsky, and Young all argue that we must pay attention not only to the boundaries of the relevant communities but also to the relationships between them and to the social phenomena that shape those relationships. For example, Mayeda writes, "Thus while Arendt considers that the community of judgment consists of those who share our values and to whom we can communicate our judgments, from the point of view of legal judgment, the appropriate community of judgment must include the party or parties for whom the judgment is to be valid (and therefore, who will be affected by the judgment) *and who are actually or systematically excluded from the community because they may not share community values.*"[98] This attention to the relationships between communities and the characteristics of the specific common sense(s) they bring to bear on judgment is important in the context of legal judgment. One of the most influential communities of judgment in a legal case is the community of other judges and legal practitioners. Legal principles and institutions such as the doctrine of precedent, the appellate court system, and our understanding of judicial impartiality are part of what frames the community of judgment in this way; judges have to measure their judgments in part against how they think other judges would decide.[99]

However, the community of judges and other legal professionals is in fact very narrow in some respects. Indeed, the Canadian judiciary is overwhelmingly drawn from very particular groups – specifically white and middle-class men and some white and middle-class women.[100] It is the obligation of legal judges to make decisions that apply to society as a whole, but they come from only a small subset of that society. Nedelsky writes, "To understand judicial impartiality, we must ask who judges are, and with whom they imagine themselves to be in conversation as they make their judgments. Whom do they imagine persuading and on whom do they make claims of agreement? If their attention is turned to only a narrow group (white, middle-class males), then judges will surely remain imprisoned in their limited perspective."[101] Thus, if judges refer their imaginations only to the common sense of fellow judges, doing so impedes their ability to come to judgments that are valid across a wider part of Canadian society. Scrutinized through a feminist and anti-poverty lens, the problem of diversity (or the lack of it) becomes a problem of validity and thus of legitimacy. And Arendt's notion of common sense begins to speak directly to the requirements of justice and of practices for good legal judgment.

In this chapter, I have chosen to explore the strengths and weaknesses of Arendt's common sense in the context of the law on judicial impartiality. This is an area where there is a meaningful overlap between the specific, context-derived legal requirements of legitimate legal judgment and the requirements of validity as understood through Arendtian reflective judgment. Both invoke the notion of impartiality, and in both cases the language of "common sense" is important.

Judgments by the Supreme Court of Canada directly addressing judicial impartiality form a small but significant group of cases.[102] The phrase "common sense" is not a repeated trope in these cases. However, in 1997 the court handed down its complex decision in *R. v. R.D.S.*, which has played an important role in shaping Canadian law. In this case, "common sense" is invoked by the majority judgment and is referenced by a number of the other judgments. In the following sections, I explore Arendt's notion of common sense in relation to the invocation of "common sense" in the context of the law on judicial impartiality.

R. v. R.D.S.

R. v. R.D.S. is a case that is completely turned on its head when we give the phrase "common sense" the meaning that Arendt does. Judges working with Arendt's aspect of common sense would see very clearly not the potential for bias but the increased potential for validity when Arendtian common sense is shared between judges and the people bound by the law. Thus the *R.D.S.* case is a great example for exploring the constructive potential – as well as the daunting scope – of Arendt's notion of common sense and her theory of judgment as a way to think about legal judgment.

In the case of *R. v. R.D.S.*, the Supreme Court of Canada was called upon to review the law on judicial impartiality and its application to the conduct and verdict of a Youth Court judge in Nova Scotia. The defendant was a fifteen-year-old African Canadian boy who was arrested after allegedly interfering with the arrest of another youth. He was charged with offences related to interfering with a police officer in the course of his duties, including assaulting the police officer. At the trial, the accused and the police officer, who was white, provided the only testimony. Judge Corinne Sparks – herself a black woman living in Halifax – found that the testimony of the accused raised a reasonable doubt as to his guilt, and she acquitted him. In the course of her judgment, she made the following comments:

> The Crown says, well, why would the officer say that events occurred the way in which he has relayed them to the Court this morning. I am not saying that the Constable has misled the

> court, although police officers have been known to do that in the past. I am not saying that the officer overreacted, but certainly police officers do overreact, particularly when they are dealing with non-white groups. That to me indicates a state of mind right there that is questionable. I believe that probably the situation in this particular case is the case of a young police officer who overreacted. I do accept the evidence of [the defendant] that he was told to shut up or he would be under arrest. It seems to be in keeping with the prevalent attitude of the day.
>
> At any rate, based upon my comments and based upon all the evidence before the court I have no other choice but to acquit.[103]

The Crown alleged that Judge Sparks's comments raised doubts about her impartiality as an adjudicator, and these comments became the subject of appeals up to the Supreme Court of Canada.[104] The Supreme Court was divided in its judgment on this case. A majority decision, written by Justice Peter Cory, and the concurring reasons, written by Chief Justice Beverley McLachlin and Justice Claire L'Heureux-Dubé, found that Judge Sparks's conduct did not raise a reasonable apprehension of bias. A dissenting judgment by Justice John C. Major found that it did.

All of the judgments agree on the relevant legal test: it is the task of the reviewing court to determine whether the impugned words or conduct of the judge have raised a "reasonable apprehension of bias." This test for judicial impartiality was authoritatively stated by the Supreme Court in an earlier case in which it was found that "the apprehension of bias must be a reasonable one, held by reasonable and right-minded persons, applying themselves to the question and obtaining thereon the required information ... [The] test is 'what would an informed person, viewing the matter realistically and practically – and having thought the matter through – conclude.'"[105] The differences between the judgments in *R.D.S.* concern how the test for judicial impartiality should be applied in this case. Cory finds that Sparks's comments did not raise a reasonable apprehension of bias, although they were "unfortunate" and "close to the line" because they were insufficiently clear about the difference between "generalizations" about race and credibility, as contrasted with the individual facts of the case.[106] The dissenting justices found that this line had been fully crossed and that Sparks's comments indicated that her conclusions were drawn on the basis of generalizations for which there was no evidence in the case before her.[107] In contrast, McLachlin and L'Heureux-Dubé hold that Sparks's comments "reflect an entirely appropriate recognition of the facts in evidence in this case and of the context within which this case arose – a context known to Judge Sparks and to any well-informed member of the community."[108]

All of the judgments in *R.D.S.* reflect considerable engagement with the question of how legitimate, impartial legal judgment relates to social context and to the personal knowledge and experience of a judge. In his judgment, Cory specifically calls on the language of "common sense" to help articulate his view:

> It is the highly individualistic nature of a determination of credibility, and its dependence on intangibles such as demeanour and the manner of testifying, that leads to the well-established principle that appellate courts will generally defer to the trial judge's factual findings, particularly those pertaining to credibility ... However, it is also the individualistic nature of a determination of credibility that requires the judge, as trier of fact, to be particularly careful to be and to appear to be neutral. This obligation requires the judge to walk a delicate line. On one hand, the judge is obviously permitted to use common sense and wisdom gained from personal experience in observing and judging the trustworthiness of a particular witness on the basis of factors such as testimony and demeanour. On the other hand, the judge must avoid judging the credibility of the witness on the basis of generalizations or upon matters that were not in evidence.[109]

In this passage, "common sense" is set beside "wisdom gained from personal experience" as a legitimate basis on which to render judgment, including as to the credibility of witnesses. Cory contrasts this use of "common sense" with reliance on "generalizations," which might well raise a reasonable apprehension of bias.

The aspect of common sense that comes to light in Arendt's writings resonates with this passage and the *R.D.S.* case as a whole. First, the test for "reasonable apprehension of bias" itself contemplates the necessity for a kind of community knowledge similar to Arendt's notion of common sense. Knowledge of our fellow judges is essential when we are imagining how we might persuade or "woo" their agreement in judgment. In the law on judicial impartiality, knowledge of the community is essential in order to know what people in that community might perceive as biased. In elaborating on the test for reasonable apprehension of bias, Cory writes,

> This test ... contains a two-fold objective element: the person considering the alleged bias must be reasonable, and the apprehension of bias itself must also be reasonable in the circumstances of the case ... Further the reasonable person must be an informed person, with knowledge of all the relevant circumstances, including "the traditions of integrity and impartiality that form a part of the background and apprised also of the fact that impartiality is one of the duties the judges swear to uphold" ... To that I would add that the reasonable person should also be taken to be aware of the social reality that forms the background to a particular case, such as societal awareness and acknowledgement of the prevalence of racism or gender bias in a particular community.[110]

In further describing what is required for impartial judging in a diverse society, he writes,

> Canada is not an insular, homogeneous society. It is enriched by the presence and contributions of citizens of many different races, nationalities and ethnic origins. The multicultural nature of Canadian society has been recognized in s. 27 of the *Charter*. Section 27 provides that the *Charter* itself is to be interpreted in a manner that is consistent with the preservation and enhancement of the multicultural heritage of Canadians. Yet our judges must be particularly sensitive to the need not only to be fair but also

> to appear to all reasonable observers to be fair to all Canadians of every race, religion, nationality and ethnic origin. This is a far more difficult task in Canada than it would be in a homogeneous society. Remarks which would pass unnoticed in other societies could well raise a reasonable apprehension of bias in Canada.[111]

Seen through the lens of Arendt's theory of judgment and common sense, these passages can be understood to provide guidance on the nature and scope of the common sense with which a legal judgment must engage in order to render a valid judgment in Canadian law. For Cory, the relevant community is the entire political community of Canada, which he characterizes in the second passage as "multicultural." At the same time, in the first passage, Cory circumscribes the relevant community to include only those Canadians who are "reasonable" and "informed," including about the prevalence of racism in a given community. Thus it seems that, for Cory, legally relevant common sense must be structured by the legal requirements of reasonableness and community knowledge.

In their concurring reasons, McLachlin and L'Heureux-Dubé take this idea further and refer directly to an approach to judgment influenced by Arendt. In setting out their approach to impartiality, these justices refer to the concept of the "enlargement of mind," quoting Nedelsky's work on judging:

> Judicial inquiry into the factual, social and psychological context within which litigation arises is not unusual. Rather, a conscious, contextual inquiry has become an accepted step towards judicial impartiality. In that regard, Professor Jennifer Nedelsky's "Embodied Diversity and the Challenges to Law" ... offers the following comment:
>
> What makes it possible for us to genuinely judge, to move beyond our private idiosyncracies and preferences, is our capacity to achieve an "enlargement of mind." We do this by taking different perspectives into account. This is the path out of the blindness of our subjective private conditions. The more views we are

> able to take into account, the less likely we are to be locked into one perspective ... It is the capacity for "enlargement of mind" that makes autonomous, impartial judgment possible.[112]

Whereas Cory frames his approach to impartiality in terms of respecting "diversity" in the abstract, McLachlin and L'Heureux-Dubé talk more directly about the actual communities that are being referenced, including the local communities of which Judge Sparks was a member. This particular community context is one in which anti-black racism, including on the part of state actors, is a reality.[113]

Further, the reasonable person, from whose perspective apprehended bias is to be assessed, is someone who knows this reality. As McLachlin and L'Heureux-Dubé write,

> The reasonable person is not only a member of the Canadian community, but also, more specifically, is a member of the local communities in which the case at issue arose (in this case, the Nova Scotian and Halifax communities). Such a person must be taken to possess knowledge of the local population and its racial dynamics, including the existence in the community of a history of widespread and systemic discrimination against black and aboriginal people, and high profile clashes between the police and the visible minority population over policing issues ... The reasonable person must thus be deemed to be cognizant of the existence of racism in Halifax, Nova Scotia. It follows that judges may take notice of actual racism known to exist in a particular society.[114]

Thus, for McLachlin and L'Heureux-Dubé, the community of reference for generating the appropriate common sense includes people who are not only aware of the diversity of the Canadian population but are also connected directly with the local communities in question and know their history. Therefore, "as a member of the community, it was open to [Judge Sparks] to take into account the well-known presence of racism in that community and to evaluate the evidence as to what occurred against that background ... In alerting herself to the racial dynamic in the case, she was simply engaging in the process of contextualized judging which, in our view, was entirely proper and conducive to a fair and just resolution of the case before her."[115]

McLachlin and L'Heureux-Dubé also introduce a further criterion for the common sense that could form the basis for valid, impartial judgment in this case. They say that the reasonable person contemplated by the test for bias is someone who, "as a member of the Canadian community, is supportive of the principles of equality."[116] This criterion for circumscribing the relevant community of judgment is very valuable when assessing legal judgment against equality and social justice goals. Thus the common sense that should inform legal judgment must be structured by a commitment to the constitutional value of equality, and this criterion is grounded directly in the legal system itself.[117]

In some respects, the "common sense" invoked by Cory in this case reflects the aspects of common sense revealed in Reid and Gramsci: "common sense" refers to a body of shared knowledge, assumptions, generalizations, or perspectives that underlie legal judgments. Gramsci, more than the other two theorists, would be alive to the political context of *R.D.S.*, with its overlapping engagement with issues of race, class, age, and locality. But Arendt's aspect of common sense as part of an ongoing *practice* of reflection and judgment also comes to the surface.[118] For example, Cory invokes "common sense" in tandem with "wisdom gained from personal experience," but he goes on to insist that such common sense and wisdom be transformed with reference to reason and the knowledge of relevant communities. McLachlin and L'Heureux-Dubé introduce further criteria for engagement with common sense that are not about empirical reality but about political choice and legal values. By focusing on equality values, the judgment of McLachlin and L'Heureux-Dubé also brings a further element of Arendt's common sense into their notion of judicial impartiality, namely the requirement for *reflection* on one's own assumptions and on the consequences of those assumptions. If the relevant common sense must reflect equality values, background knowledge that is grounded in discrimination is illegitimate for legal judgment.

Arendt's ideas about the role of common sense in judgment thus help us to understand *how* the subjective experiences and knowledge of judges can work to enhance, rather than detract from, the impartiality of their judgments. This is so because a judge's personal experience can – as it did in *R.D.S.* – provide important access to the common sense of a relevant community. Engagement with the common sense of black residents of Halifax as a member of that community does not compromise the impartiality of the judge in this case but is *essential* in order for that judgment to have the requisite validity. Without engagement with *this* common sense, legal assessment of judicial bias would not be valid across that community. In this sense, Judge Sparks was quite possibly an ideally situated adjudicator, in contrast to other judges lacking a basis in this community's common sense. At the same time, judges whose common sense begins in other subjective experiences (e.g., judges who live with race privilege or who live in rural areas) are not powerless to remedy their partiality in this respect. A judge can *achieve* impartiality by seeking out the community sense that is needed to ground a valid judgment in any case. In their commentary on the *R.D.S.* case, the members of a forum of Canadian feminist legal scholars argue that this approach is reflected in the doctrinal findings of the majority and concurring judgments. They write, "One aspect of grounding legitimacy in the knowledge of the reasonable person in the community, and not the individual judge, is that it places responsibility on all judges, regardless of their gender, race, or ethnic background, to be sensitive to the operation of discriminatory effects of racialization in the fact determination process ... Grounding legitimacy in the knowledge of the community also ensures that one aspect of legitimacy is that knowledge of social context draws on empirical and other data available to the community."[119] Thus judges who seek to make impartial judgments that will be valid beyond their own subjective experiences, and valid across relevant communities, must engage with the common sense of those communities. Arendt's approach to common sense and to judgment thus generates an obligation on the part of legal judges to actively take steps to correct their own subjective partiality and, through the practice of engagement with common sense, to develop a practice of judgment that reflects an enlarged mentality.

The invocation of "common sense" in *R.D.S.* also provides a way to discuss the community-creating element of legal judgment and of common sense. The *R.D.S.* case is not only about determining whose common sense should count for the basis of valid legal judgment; it is also about determining the communities to whom the law speaks. The case rhetorically works to *create* communities by delineating who matters. In her commentary on *R.D.S.*, feminist critical race scholar Sherene Razack focuses on this aspect of the judgment, characterizing it as a "case about home."[120] She writes, "I propose to read *R.D.S. v. Her Majesty the Queen* as a ... moment of public education in Canada [similar to the O.J. Simpson case in the United States], when an official story, an agreed-upon public truth, is told. This public truth is also about race. It is the story that race does not matter *except under highly specific and limited circumstances*. The heroes of this story are innocent, white subjects ... If the official story is that there is no racism in Canada, then those who insist otherwise do not belong."[121]

Like Arendt's approach to common sense, Razack's analysis focuses on the practices of judgment and persuasion and on the ways that they work to create community and belonging. Razack's critique of the case is itself a compelling demonstration that legal judgment has this effect: she describes the "line" that separates "those who think race always matters from those who think it only matters, if at all, under highly limited circumstances involving specific individuals."[122] Razack shows how the legitimacy of the Supreme Court of Canada is undermined for people of colour when the court fails to comprehend their reality. Razack also shows that this failure goes far beyond the matter of accurate social facts, extending into the ways that legal judgment can affirm or deny membership in a community.[123]

Gosselin v. Quebec (Procureur général)

In *Gosselin v. Quebec (Procureur général)*, as in *R.D.S.*, the invocation of "common sense" has implications for understanding the role of the impartial legal judge and the boundaries of the communities to whom the judgment speaks. With Arendt's understanding of common sense in mind, the "common sense" invoked in *Gosselin* seems both more significant and more problematic from the perspective of justice. Recall that Chief Justice Beverley McLachlin writes, "*As a matter of common sense*, if a law is designed to promote the claimant's long-term autonomy and self-sufficiency, a reasonable person in the claimant's position would be less likely to view it as an assault on her inherent human dignity."[124]

When reading this passage in light of Gramsci's perspective on common sense, I said that it shows that sometimes "common sense" is invoked as a substantive ground upon which to base a legal judgment. McLachlin claims that common sense supports her conclusion. Seen through the lens provided by Reid, we also see that this common sense claim marks the boundary between reason and nonsense. But here, against the background of Arendt's approach to common sense, the rhetorical effect of this passage becomes more than a marker of rational debate; it becomes a marker of community.

A "reasonable person in the claimant's position" would come to a certain judgment about the welfare rules under consideration. Because she disagrees, Louise Gosselin herself is being unreasonable and not properly exercising her judgment. Further, because this judgment is a matter of common sense – the common sense that is appropriate for legal judgment in this case – Gosselin is set outside the community of people to whom the law should speak. The passage is a reiteration that Gosselin does not belong; her perspective is specifically contrary to common sense. Thus common sense works not only to determine the appropriate form and content of legal justification but also to create the community to which the law should be held accountable.

In her dissenting judgment, L'Heureux-Dubé also addresses this question of who will count as a member of the relevant community. She does not use the language of "common sense" in her judgment, but she engages with the majority argument on this point quite directly:

> [If we acknowledge that Gosselin's physical integrity was breached,] [t]he sole remaining question is whether a reasonable

person in Ms. Gosselin's position, apprised of all the circumstances, would perceive that her dignity had been threatened. The reasonable claimant would have been informed of the legislature's intention to help young people enter the marketplace. She would have been informed that those 30 and over have more difficulty changing careers, and that those under 30 run serious social and personal risks if they do not enter the job market in a timely manner. She would have been told that the long-term goal of the legislative scheme was to affirm her dignity.

The reasonable claimant would also likely have been a member of the 88.8 percent who were eligible for the programs and whose income did not rise to the levels available to all adults 30 years of age and over. Even if she wished to participate in training programs, she would have found that there were intervals between the completion of one program and the starting of another, during which the amount of her social assistance benefit would have plunged. The reasonable claimant would have made daily life choices in the face of an imminent and severe threat of poverty. The reasonable claimant would likely have suffered malnourishment. She might have turned to prostitution and crime to make ends meet. The reasonable claimant would have perceived that as a result of her deep poverty, she had been excluded from full participation in Canadian society. She would have perceived that her right to dignity was infringed as a sole consequence of being under 30 years of age, a factor over which, at any given moment, she had no control. While individuals may be able to strive to overcome the detriment imposed by merit-based distinctions, Ms. Gosselin was powerless to alter the single personal characteristic that the government's scheme made determinative for her level of benefits.

The reasonable claimant would have suffered, as Ms. Gosselin manifestly did suffer, from discrimination as a result of the impugned legislative distinction. I see no other conclusion but that Ms. Gosselin would have reasonably felt that she was being less valued as a member of society than people 30 and over and that she was being treated as less deserving of respect.[125]

The particular context of the legal claim and the experiences of a specific community are the appropriate markers for understanding the "reasonable claimant." Here, she is someone who has "made daily life choices in the face of an imminent and severe threat of poverty."

L'Heureux-Dubé also uses other language that engages an Arendtian understanding of common sense:

> As a result of [the impugned regulation], adults under 30 were uniquely exposed by the legislative scheme to the threat of living beneath what the government itself considered to be a subsistence level of income. Of those eligible to participate in the programs, 88.8 percent were unable to increase their benefits to the level payable to those 30 and over. Ms. Gosselin was exposed to the risk of severe poverty as a sole consequence of being under 30 years of age. Ms. Gosselin's psychological and physical integrity were breached. There is little question that living with the constant threat of poverty is psychologically harmful. There is no dispute that Ms. Gosselin lived at times below the government's own standard of bare subsistence. In 1987, the monthly cost of proper nourishment was $152. The guaranteed monthly payment to young adults was $170. *I cannot imagine* how it can be maintained that Ms. Gosselin's physical integrity was not breached.[126]

By placing Louise Gosselin outside the bounds of the community that participates in the relevant common sense, the majority judgment in this case further excludes poor and marginalized women rather than seizing an opportunity to include their views among those who count, or those who will find a "home" in Canadian law. The aspect of common sense revealed by Thomas Reid shows how "common sense" as invoked in *Gosselin* sets the boundaries of reasonable debate. The aspect revealed by Antonio Gramsci shows how "common sense" in *Gosselin* allows powerful social groups to benefit from how we allocate the burden of proof and how it enables hegemonic worldviews to maintain their hold on public discourse. But Arendt's aspect provides a way to see why common sense, *as part of a practice of judgment*, not only reflects injustices of sexism and poverty but also recreates them.

Because Arendt's common sense works to circumscribe and develop communities, it can be invoked to exclude and marginalize. But it can also be invoked to broaden, to include, and to diversify. Arendt's approach to common sense as a fundamental part of human judgment requires that we make choices about the membership of the communities we refer to when justifying our judgments. Judgment is always a normative, evaluative exercise.[127] In legal judgment, those choices can be guided or "disciplined" by legal principles such as equality.[128] In the concluding chapter, I take some further steps toward developing criteria that could be used to guide how legal judges engage with common sense.

CONCLUSION

The aspect of common sense that is made visible by reading Arendt situates common sense as a central part of the human practice of judgment. Engagement with common sense, as part of a process of imaginative representation and critical reflection, is what enables one to make judgments that are valid across some greater community. Common sense is related to communicability, persuasion, and the disclosure of oneself to others. Engagement with common sense, through judgment, opens up space for communication and generates community.

In the context of legal judgment, Arendt's approach to common sense has direct consequences for how the role of the judge should be understood; when legal judgment is understood as a form of reflective judgment, the duty of impartiality is fulfilled not by attempting to limit one's thinking to the application of rules but by attempting to achieve an enlarged mentality through engagement with relevant communities. Arendt's common sense signals an ongoing practice that is rooted in subjective experience and transformed through critical reflection. For these reasons, Arendt's perspective has the potential to be productive for developing practices of judgment that have the capacity to address the injustices of poverty and social marginalization. Arendt's common sense calls on judges to think critically about whether their judgment is valid for the right communities and about whether the criteria that guide their judgment are justifiable.

As with the critical reflection advocated by Gramsci, which enables one to turn common sense into "good sense," the critical reflection required to practice genuine Arendtian judgment is very demanding, particularly when questions of social inequality arise. This is a context where critical reflection poses the most challenges as well as the place where it is most needed to achieve validity. Engagement with common sense is partly about disclosure of the self and about willingness to reflect on the extent to which one's subjective experiences can be generalized to others. However, as the above discussion of *R.D.S.* and *Gosselin* demonstrates, core legal principles such as the principle of judicial impartiality provide points of contact with this approach and show that although Arendt's approach is demanding, it is not impossible.[129]

Arendt's perspective on common sense is also productive in the context of legal judgment because of its focus on the way that common sense works to mark and create communities. The rhetorical effects of a legal judgment are especially important when understood in this light, and Arendt's common sense provides a way to comprehend how legal judgment both reflects and generates multiple communities. Arendt's aspect of common sense thus provides resources we can use to address the question "common to whom?" when this question becomes important in legal judgment. This aspect of common sense also helps to explain why this question is so important: it is not only about the accuracy of the information courts use in their judgments but also about political claims of membership and inclusion.

In their own ways, all three of the theorists considered here place a high value on the knowledge and sense of "the people." For Reid, this valuation leads to the view that we should allow common sense to benefit from a presumption of reliability and that the appropriate posture toward common sense is one of intellectual humility. For Gramsci, presumptions about the reliability of common sense are deeply suspect, not only from a philosophical perspective but also from a political perspective. Gramsci asks that we be much more specific and critical when thinking about who "common" people are. Arendt's aspect of common sense prompts us to return to the reason for Reid's reluctance to overthrow common sense, namely that when people hold a belief, they do so for a reason or because it serves some valuable purpose in their life and, further, that we can ask what that purpose is. Taking an Arendtian approach and demanding attention to particular context, we can look at the invocation of "common sense" in legal judgment and ask whether it serves the purpose it purports to serve there, guided by the political and legal values in which we choose to ground our judgment.

Arendt's aspect of common sense also prompts a return to Gramsci's critique of common sense. Although Arendtian judgment provides openings for common sense to facilitate justice and equality, Arendt herself does not provide the criteria needed to achieve this outcome. Gramsci's worries about common sense and hegemony, and indeed Arendt's own ambiguity on these issues, reaffirm the need for an analysis of power and inequality. Feminist and social justice perspectives are essential in order to structure the choices that must be made in the exercise of reflective judgment. Incorporating these perspectives makes it possible to move from common sense in judgment to common sense and justice.

5

Conclusion: Common Sense for Good Legal Judgment

At the end of Henry Fielding's satire *Pasquin*, the ghost of Queen Common-Sense laments that, with her death, the world will be ruled by Queen Ignorance, aided by the unchecked power of Law, Religion, and Science. But, she promises, the world will always be haunted by Common-Sense. In many respects, all legal judgments are haunted by common sense; it sits in the background to frame judgment, or to ground assumptions, or to circumscribe reflective reasoning. But, in some cases, a judge writes the words "common sense" in the reasons for judgment, and Queen Common-Sense reappears in person. In this book, I have explored these appearances of "common sense" in legal judgment. I have asked what is learned and what is challenged when we observe Queen Common-Sense from the perspectives provided by Thomas Reid, Antonio Gramsci, and Hannah Arendt.

Taking all three of these perspectives into account creates a richer and more productive understanding of common sense. It becomes possible to see different aspects of common sense. Common sense is a kind of shared knowledge. Common sense is a philosophical frame that is inherited from our social history. And common sense is part of the practice of judgment, which makes demands on our political values. Taken together, these aspects of common sense do not form a complete or coherent representation of the concept.[1] Rather, the juxtaposition of these three aspects reveals the multiplicity of layers and uses that characterize any truly meaningful piece of language. Just as Gramsci claims about the content of common sense, the *concept* of common sense itself has a complex intellectual history and contains contradictory as well as mutually reinforcing components. The usefulness and meaningfulness of the phrase "common sense," as with all language, are not impeded by the impossibility of a singular definition but are made richer. The purpose of creating what Ludwig Wittgenstein calls a "perspicuous representation" is thus not to answer questions about meaning definitively but to open up avenues for consideration and debate.[2]

The value of this critical opening is that it enables better ways of thinking about and using common sense in legal judgment – ways that have the potential to make legal judgment more sensitive to the demands of equality and social justice. In chapter 1, I argued that legal discourse is, to some extent, captive to a picture of common sense as a type of shared knowledge. I said that this captivity is facilitated partly by the nature of common sense itself as a concept that eludes critique and circumscribes debate. This captivity allows common sense to function in an unexamined and problematic (but also powerful) way in legal judgments about poverty. While held captive in this way, we invoke "common sense" without full appreciation of its power to oppress and marginalize, but we also invoke "common sense" without allowing it to transform our judgment in a progressive and inclusive way.

The exploration of common sense presented here breaks down our captivity to a particular point of view, allowing discourse about common sense and legal judgment to address a much wider range of issues that are relevant to justice, including issues arising from feminist and anti-poverty demands about justice. Doing so enables us to ask not only whether common sense knowledge is appropriately "common" but also how common sense relates to rules and expertise, how it relates to power, and what communities are reflected and generated by its invocation.

At the most general level, this richer representation of common sense makes it clear that subjecting common sense to scrutiny from the perspective of equality and social justice means more than restricting its use. That is, the response is not simply one of blanket condemnation of recourse to common sense. All three aspects of common sense do reveal significant potential for common sense to compromise the quality and legitimacy of legal judgment in the context of poverty and marginalization. But they also show that reliance on common sense can sometimes require a type of reasoning or practice of judgment that actually demands robust consideration of issues that relate to poverty and social justice, such as marginalization in public discourse, the political history of knowledge, and the valuation of different types of reasoning. Thus the best practices of legal judgment will *actively engage* with common sense, neither relying on it unreflectively nor excluding it wholly by abandoning it as merely an artifact of oppressive ideology.[3]

Each of the three aspects of common sense explored in this book generates criteria that can be used to assess a legal judge's engagement with common sense. In the remainder of this chapter, I pull together these criteria and expand on what they mean for legal judgment specifically. In the following sections, I first describe how each aspect of common sense configures an image of the legal judge. Second, I explore some of the criteria for evaluating the use of common sense in legal judgment that emerge from the representation of common sense created by consideration of all three aspects. Finally, I return a final time to the case of *Gosselin v. Quebec (Procureur général)* and the issue of poverty as a concern for justice and legal judgment.[4]

THE ROLE OF THE JUDGE

Reid, Gramsci, and Arendt each present a particular view about what constitutes good judgment and about how common sense fits into judgment. Each aspect of common sense also contains implicit or explicit notions that speak to the proper role of judges as part of a particular institution in a particular context. For example, in the context of Gramsci's work, it is important to consider whether any of his exhortations for good judgment could be achieved by people operating as part of the state in a capitalist democracy. When asking about the "role of the judge," all of these insights are valuable. However, it is interesting that when writing about common sense, in particular, each thinker also describes a certain distinctive figure whose characteristics disclose a special relationship between good judgment and common sense. In each case, these special figures bear some relationship to the individual thinker him or herself: for Reid, it is the educated person who speaks on behalf of common sense; for Gramsci, it is the organic intellectual; and for Arendt, it is the critical, thinking person who exercises an enlarged mentality. These special figures can also be used to help think through how the role of the legal judge is best understood when it comes to common sense.

The Educated Representative of Common Sense

The special figure who emerges from Reid's perspective on common sense is, in a sense, Reid himself: an educated representative of common sense. Although the idea of an "expert" or "specialist" in common sense is possibly paradoxical – and, as philosopher John Coates observes, definitely odd – it also reflects some of what Reid and his fellow members of the Wise Club had in mind when they championed the knowledge of ordinary people.[5] As Sophia Rosenfeld writes, "[T]he defense of this distinctive epistemology [in which common sense is privileged] produced in eighteenth-century Aberdeen the phenomenon of a new and lasting social type: the educated avatar of common sense who has no choice but to define himself (and only considerably later, herself) as a spokesman for the truths already established by masses of ordinary people."[6]

In her discussion of the political history of common sense and its relationship to democracy, Rosenfeld argues that this figure – "the educated avatar of common sense" – continues to play a role in democratic politics, an arena in which discussants in political debates are very likely to justify their positions at least in part on the basis of common sense. In that context, the figure of the educated representative of common sense is presented as the ideal person for exercising political judgment. But what of legal judgment? When this special figure is considered as a model for the person exercising legal judgment – the judge – the conceptual and institutional requirements of legal judgment come into play. In a liberal democracy like Canada, which is the legal context that forms the context for my exploration, judges are bound by precedent, by their duty to act impartially, and by their constitutional role. Thus embodying common sense is not enough; judges must also carry their special expertise in law into their judging practices.

But Reid's representative of common sense, who exercises good judgment, who gives credence to the knowledge that ordinary people already share, and who values daily life as a source for legitimate knowledge, does provide some interesting criteria for thinking about the role of a judge. Reid's theory of common sense places a high value on the knowledge of ordinary people and opposes the intervention of expert knowledge or systems of rules where those interventions might interfere with the thoughtful exercise of judgment. These are postures that can be adopted by judges of law, just as much as by judges of any matter. As a legal judge, the avatar of common sense would place a burden of proof on propositions contradicting the content of that knowledge. This common sense legal judge would also be alive to the boundaries of "real" common sense in order to restrict the influence of "prejudices" that might mislead or undermine the proper exercise of good judgment. Judges who approach their role in a way that requires the representation of the knowledge of ordinary people bring Reid's egalitarianism into the heart of legal judgment. On many matters (but certainly not all), what is already known in the community should be respected, not overturned by the presumptuous opinions of experts.

At the same time, Reid's avatar of common sense is insufficient as a model for the legal judge. This model insists on the value of knowledge held by ordinary people but is grounded in the assumption that all such ordinary knowledge is the same and that all legitimate common sense will be shared universally. On the one hand, this assumption limits what can count as common sense knowledge to a very narrow list of items (e.g., the existence of physical objects). On the other hand, it also invites a much wider range of things to be treated with the same approach, privileging what is already widely believed by nonexperts (e.g., how to determine when a witness is telling the truth). Reid's discussion of prejudice, which considers the risk that real common sense could be undermined by undue deference to authority or by reliance on unjustified analogies, demonstrates an understanding that common sense is not always a solid and unchallengeable body of knowledge. But Reid's worries about prejudice still leave us with questions about what a judge should do when presented with competing claims about common sense or when common sense claims seem problematic not because they are wrong but because they are tied to injustice. Further, Reid's avatar of common sense is bold in the face of distracting or elitist claims to superior knowledge but carries no record of his or her own history. How does Reid's common sense figure acquire common sense? To whom is this figure's judgment accountable? Reid himself, after all, was a member of a small class of educated and wealthy men who lived in a fairly insular town, yet his explicit aim was to discover universal principles of common sense. These outstanding questions show why the avatar of common sense cannot be a complete model for the good judge.

The Organic Intellectual

The second aspect of common sense studied in this book configures a different personage who has a special relationship to common sense and to good judgment: Gramsci's organic intellectual. Like Reid's avatar of common sense, the organic intellectual contains elements of education and connections to ordinary people. In a sense, both figures embody the knowledge and experience of a community. But Gramsci's organic intellectual does not simply speak for the common sense of the community. Rather, the organic intellectual embodies a process of critical self-reflection and transformation, in which the common beliefs of a community become *good sense* and thereby work toward the transformation of society. Gramsci's approach to common sense focuses on the processes that allow common sense to emerge and on the processes that are needed to challenge the hegemony of dominant worldviews and replace them with common sense that is capable of supporting equality and the liberation of oppressed peoples.

As a model for the *legal* judge, Gramsci's organic intellectual contemplates the enormous challenges associated with evaluating legal justice in a liberal democratic state in terms of the justice of liberation and equality that was the goal of Gramsci's political theory. There are fundamental ways that legal judges are manifestly *not* the "new" intellectuals that Gramsci thinks can critique hegemonic common sense and support political transformation; indeed, in many respects, they are the epitome of "traditional intellectuals," who claim objectivity and historical continuity but who are in fact captured by the hegemonic perspectives of the dominant group.[7] At the same time, there are at least two important ways that the figure of the organic intellectual can be important for legal judgment. First, Gramsci seems to have a particular optimism about the potential for expert practitioners to develop into organic intellectuals; he mentions engineers and architects as examples of people who must acquire a nuanced and abstract knowledge, while not losing touch with the physical reality in which their work will take place.[8] Gramsci suggests that organic intellectuals should approach their task, to some extent, as though they are expert practitioners of philosophy.[9] In general, the difference between the engineer and the philosopher is that although most people do not have much (or any) knowledge about building, everyone does have some knowledge about philosophy (for most people, in the form of common sense).[10] Therefore, what is required to make someone an "expert" in philosophy is not necessarily the acquisition of special knowledge but the opportunity to make one's knowledge more formalized and coherent. Organic philosophers gain their knowledge from everyday life, and they work to make it critical through the "philosophy of praxis."[11] Like engineers and architects, lawyers and legal judges do have specialized knowledge and can be understood as experts in a certain kind of practice. Their expertise sets them apart from other members of the community, but their necessary connections to the practical application of their ideas can help to keep them from becoming isolated or from acting as traditional intellectuals in an unproblematic way. Further, since law, like philosophy, contains connections to communities and to common sense, legal judges can use their status as practitioners to foster and develop those connections and thereby fulfil a role that is more like that of an organic intellectual.

Second, the figure of the organic intellectual provides an aspirational model for the practice of critical reflection and for the transformative potential of intellectual activity that genuinely engages with the needs of marginalized people. Gramsci argues that the relationship between organic intellectuals and "the masses" should be a mutually transformative one, analogous to a student-teacher relationship. For legal judges to adopt this relationship as a model for their own practices of reflection, and as a model for how judges should relate to the people in their communities, challenges judges to think carefully about the origin of their knowledge and about how it relates to legitimacy, democracy, institutional capacity, and justice at the broadest level. Although judges do not, for the most part, come from subaltern social groups themselves, the model of the organic intellectual still provides a valuable way to think about how practical experience and elite knowledges can be understood in order to generate positive intellectual transformation and political change. David Schneiderman's critique of *Gosselin* shows the tendency of the Supreme Court of Canada to follow behind the dominant common sense in Canadian society; Gramsci's approach shows how the court might, instead, lead the way.

The Judging Person Engaged with the Community Sense

Gramsci's description of organic intellectuals provides a compelling model for a legal judge. But it provides few details about how an individual judge might go about the practice of critical reflection that can transform "common sense" into "good sense." A third special common sense figure arises from the aspect of common sense that emerges in the work of Hannah Arendt. This figure is the judging person who practices "enlargement of mind" through engagement with common sense.[12] Arendt herself seems to offer Immanuel Kant as an example of such a person, observing that "he – who never left Konigsberg – knew his way around both London and Italy."[13] In this book, with the assistance of theorists such as Jennifer Nedelsky and Iris Marion Young, I have adopted Arendt's approach to enrich the model of the thinking, engaged judge for feminist and social justice purposes. For this special figure, access to common sense is constituted through engagement with actual communities and through scrutiny of one's imaginative acts from the perspective of justice and equality.

Arendt's model of the imaginative and reflective judge also displays a notable capacity and willingness to reflect on one's own views. The reflective judge is the opposite of the unthinking individual, who Arendt sees as such an enormous threat to political life. As in many aspects of her thought, Arendt values freedom and action, and she critiques any tendency to complacency, passivity, or deference. Arendt's figure of the imaginative, reflective judge provides an extremely useful model for the role of the legal judge: it calls for a form of impartiality in which judges may be required to actively seek out the information they need in order to identify and engage with the communities affected by the law.

It is important to notice that all three of these special figures – the avatar of common sense, the organic intellectual, and the reflective judge – emerge specifically through each theorist's engagement with common sense. These models become visible only because of the relationship between judgment and common sense specifically, reaffirming the importance of this concept and the need to examine it from the perspective of equality and justice.

CRITERIA FOR THE USE OF COMMON SENSE IN LEGAL JUDGMENT

The richer representation of common sense described in this book includes analysis of three aspects. Based on this methodology, it is not possible to extract from these three aspects a complete or objective understanding of common sense. However, it is notable that several criteria for the use of common sense in good judgment reappear, in different forms, in more than one of the aspects. These criteria are not formulaic rules; I do not suggest that it is possible to develop a checklist that, once completed, produces good legal judgment. Quite the contrary. My discussion of common sense in good legal judgment focuses on practices that are complex, even confounding, and that thus require judges to engage with all components of themselves as human beings in multiple communities. My discussion of criteria emerges from my treatment of legal judgment as a form of human judgment in general and reflects my insistence (following scholars such as Nedelsky) that embracing the subjective, reflective elements of human judgment does not abandon legal judgment to the realm of arbitrariness, idiosyncratic preference, or bare political interest. It is possible to have touchstones and ideals for developing practices that work toward good legal judgment, practices that are better or worse as far as common sense is concerned.

In this section, I describe three criteria for the use of common sense in legal judgment. Although it will always be necessary for judges to approach their task with openness and flexibility, attention to these three criteria will be essential to the understanding and use of common sense in legal judgment in the service of social justice. Properly made common sense claims should work toward fulfilling the requirements of good judgment, and, in this section, I explore in more detail what it means for common sense claims to be *properly made* in legal judgment.

In earlier parts of this book, I have attempted to pay careful attention to the actual texts under review (both scholarly and legal) and to show that the three aspects of common sense that emerge from these texts are quite distinct. The goal of these earlier chapters has been to consider the apparent conundrum of common sense – as both self-evident and inscrutable – by exploring it from three distinct perspectives. In this concluding chapter, I talk about common sense in general terms, sometimes allowing slippages between the different aspects. Having started to notice the different ways that common sense can be used and understood, it is necessary to see what happens when all of these issues are returned together to the context of legal judgment.

Intellectual Humility and Critical Self-reflection

Attention to multiple aspects of common sense reveals the significance of self-reflection as part of good judgment. This self-reflection takes different forms and has different meanings for each aspect of common sense, but it continually reappears. For all three thinkers, the self-reflection that is called for by common sense finds value in an attitude of intellectual humility. For Reid, commitment to common sense challenges the hubris involved in rejecting outright the legitimacy of the knowledge that ordinary people rely on every day. For Gramsci, thinking about common sense forces one to see the connections between beliefs, politics, and history and thus to reject any attempt to view one's own knowledge as transcendent or universal. And for Arendt, the essential role of common sense in judgment is what transforms subjective, idiosyncratic preferences into justifiable and valid judgments; we must always be aware that our untested private beliefs are never enough, on their own, to ground valid judgment. All three thinkers find some value in other modes of reasoning, including abstract philosophizing and purely introspective rational thought. But *good judgment* does not need a posture of comprehensive rationality, the universal application of a framework, or the quest for some ground upon which I can say that my knowledge is true for everyone and true everywhere. Instead, good judgment requires careful attention to the limits of my own experience and to the specificity of the derivation of my own knowledge, as well as the capacity to listen to the views of others.[14]

Beyond this general starting point of humility and openness, all three perspectives also require that the legitimate invocation of "common sense" involve acts of critical self-reflection. The different aspects of common sense assign a different scope and significance to this self-reflection, but the theme is reiterated across the different perspectives. For example, Reid points to the need to check one's common sense knowledge for signs of prejudices, and he insists that one must never treat one's common sense as infallible. Gramsci calls for an enormously demanding form of self-reflection that makes known the connections between so-called common sense and the hegemony of powerful social groups; he calls on everyone to think about whether and how common sense can help us to make sense of our own interests and experiences. Arendt's writings on common sense and the enlarged mentality introduce another form of critical self-reflection, in which good judgment requires judges to actively test their beliefs against the common sense of a community of other judging people.

Thus intellectual humility and critical self-reflection can be adopted as conditions for the use of common sense in judgment. These might be adopted just as a general intellectual approach, but they can also guide interpretation of specific legal concepts. For example, a commitment to common sense, understood adequately, provides a certain lens for understanding what is required by judicial impartiality. The use of common sense can support the impartiality of a legal judgment if the reference to "common sense" prompts the judge to engage in critical self-reflection and to consider the value and relevance of community knowledge that is offered or implied by others. For good legal judgment, we need impartiality that is informed by common sense based on intellectual humility and critical self-reflection.

Humility and self-reflection are especially important in legal judgment when judges are asked to decide on questions involving poverty, inequality, and marginalization. As mentioned in earlier sections, Canadian judges are drawn largely (although not entirely) from the most privileged social groups in Canadian society. Further, the role of a judge itself grants certain forms of privilege and social power. As a group, the people who are judges in Canada rarely have experience with living in poverty and are most likely to have social and community lives that are isolated from people who do. Their knowledge of poverty is likely to be abstract and incomplete at best. Thus intellectual humility and an openness to new perspectives are necessary.

Moreover, as Gramsci demonstrates, through the concept of hegemony, that which seems the most natural or the least problematic from the perspective of dominant groups can sometimes turn out to be the thing that merits the greatest scrutiny. Importantly, it can be easiest to be sure of yourself when you are standing in a position of power. Since, like Gramsci (and informed by a host of feminist theorists), I take the position that such unequal power relations are intimately related to justice and injustice, the certainty of those in power is worthy of critical attention. Thus the kind of humility required for common sense to work in favour of good legal judgment is not only intellectual but also political; it requires acts of political will for privileged individuals to question their most certain or their most comfortable assumptions.

Political Justification and Accountability

Common sense demands intellectual humility and, further, asks for caution in overturning the knowledge of any community. At the same time, common sense calls on judges to be bold in their thorough exercise of human judgment; it does not permit the abdication of judgment to a system of rules or the opinion of an expert. Common sense requires judges to acknowledge that they are making choices with political consequences and that the consequences of these choices must be justified and transparently accounted for. The unavoidability of political claims, and the need to justify those claims, is part of what is revealed through my "perspicuous representation" of common sense.

For Reid's aspect of common sense, this theme of judgment and justification emerges in a nascent way through his juxtaposition of common sense with philosophical "systems" and expertise. Undue deference to the opinions of experts permits and indeed encourages people to hold beliefs without exercising judgment. Reid does not explicitly recognize the political nature of common sense claims, but he does insist that people exercise judgment independently and with attention to the consequences. It is genuine human judgment – not reference to rules – that has the potential to allow people to develop meaningful knowledge of the world. The exercise of judgment is necessary in order to think clearly about accountability; the people who judge are accountable for the judgments they render.

Gramsci takes this question of accountability much further, explicitly pointing to the political consequences of certain bodies of knowledge and philosophical outlooks, including common sense. Gramsci asks *whose* common sense is at work in a given judgment and whether the content of common sense knowledge is capable of supporting the kind of political transformation that he seeks. Gramsci shows us that common sense is infused with political choice and reveals the need for justification. Making a common sense claim is a claim about good knowledge, about shared knowledge, and thus must be justified. For Gramsci, this justification is always political. In Arendt's aspect of common sense, the exercise of justification is at the heart of what she means by "common sense." "Common sense" or the "community sense" is the basis for judgment, which always involves the practice of imaginatively justifying a judgment to a community of others. Thus common sense claims are importantly related to questions of political choice and the justification of those choices.

Although each theorist envisions different kinds of methods and criteria for holding judges accountable and for testing the justification of their choices, in each case, a good invocation of "common sense" requires a sort of bravery and commitment, a willingness to put oneself on the line for one's judgment. Arendt understands this process as disclosure of the self to others, and she puts it at the centre of the act of judgment and engagement with common sense. Bravery and self-disclosure might seem to be in tension with the idea of intellectual humility, but both arise from self-reflection. Critical self-reflection will ask me to think carefully about my invocation of "common sense" and about the grounds on which I can justify that invocation. Having made a choice, I communicate my judgment and my reasons to others and accept responsibility for that judgment.

The related acts of political choice and political justification are challenging and even provocative when used to guide the invocation of "common sense" in legal judgment. With this approach, the use of common sense in legal judgment can strengthen the quality of that judgment when it facilitates meaningful justification of the political choices that are always part of judging practice. Meaningful justification can enhance transparency and legitimacy.[15] Invoking "common sense" requires judges to reflect on and make choices about the political consequences of the knowledge and framework they are endorsing. So, for example, when a judge says that the irrelevance of the timing of disclosure for the credibility of a child's account of abuse is a matter of *common sense*, this is not (or not only) an empirical claim but (also) a political and legal claim about what knowledge should form the basis of legal judgment; here, the judge is making a political choice to privilege the value of equality and the perspective of children. By this invocation of "common sense," the judge orients the exercise of justification toward those political values; what must be justified is not so much the empirical claim about the timing of disclosure as the valuation of children's testimony in the context of their vulnerability and inequality. A different choice about the use of common sense might, for example, privilege the value of the adversarial trial process by allowing debate on absolutely any matter.

As this example shows, these choices are complex and it is by no means obvious how to draw the link between a political or legal value and a particular judgment. However, what is clear is that reliance on common sense (or refusal to rely on it) does involve the exercise of political will.[16] A question immediately arises: on what basis can judges exercise political will and still respect the goals and limitations of their institutional role? It is clear, for example, that legal judges cannot base their judgment on a personal ideological preference. Various strands of legal theory have sought to answer this question in different ways. All of these traditions have something useful to say about the complex process of legal judgment (and, indeed, about the act of judgment in any context). However, I argue that the component of judgment that is subjective, calling on the political and other commitments of a legal judge, is unavoidable because it lies at the heart of the practice of judgment, not at its periphery. But, as Arendt demonstrates, the necessary subjective component of judgment is not a reason to despair about the validity or legitimacy of judgment.

Here, the value of having a "perspicuous representation" of common sense becomes evident. If common sense is understood too narrowly, perhaps only as a form of community knowledge, it is less clear how common sense can meet the challenges of impartial judgment. However, if it is understood that common sense can also refer to philosophical outlook and the collective component of the judging process, common sense becomes a very useful idea for thinking about impartiality. Common sense can provide a way to understand how human particularity and subjectivity can work to make judgment better and more legitimate instead of less so. If, as Arendt suggests, invoking "common sense" in judgment requires attention to the knowledge of a relevant collective of judging others, this requirement breaks down partiality in judgment and actively builds impartiality and reflective validity.

Thus, when judges in a court of law invoke "common sense" with attention to intellectual humility and reflective political choice, the quality of their judgment can be enhanced, and the potential for addressing social injustices is strengthened. This book focuses on increasing the number, form, and character of the questions that can be asked about common sense and legal judgment. But this should not leave readers with the idea that the concept of common sense is so complex or dynamic that it can provide no guidance. Indeed, I suggest that very central and established legal principles provide considerable resources for guiding the exercise of political will that attends this kind of complex judging practice.

In particular, the constitutional value of equality, codified in section 15 of the Canadian Charter of Rights and Freedoms, provides a reason for judges to exercise their political will in favour of marginalized communities, in favour of knowledge arising from marginalized experiences, and in favour of legal outcomes that reduce rather than replicate or enhance social inequality. As explored in chapter 4, the concepts of judicial impartiality and reasonable apprehension of bias also provide doctrinal support for exercising judgment in a manner that pushes toward equality. These laws and doctrines are resources for grounding legitimate legal judgment from within the legal system.

However, focusing on common sense shows that an act of political will, of political choice (and the attendant justification of that choice), is inescapable. Concepts like equality and impartiality are valuable and show how we can find criteria for good judgment that are securely moored in the legal system. But ultimately the way that these concepts are understood and deployed will always require acts of judgment and justification. Exercise and invocation of "common sense," fully understood, requires attention to the fact that judgment does require these acts of political will that must be justified and for which the judge is held accountable.[17] Common sense does not permit us to point to a system of rules or to escape the fact that judgment can never be completely certain; instead, it holds us accountable for what, in the end, must always be a politically grounded choice. This idea has appeared in numerous places in this book. It appears in relation to my adoption of a methodology that works toward making something useful (rather than true or certain). It appears in relation to Justice Charles Gonthier's finding that the justification exercise under section 1 of the Charter will at least sometimes be impossible as an exercise of "measurement" and will instead truly be about "justification." And it appears in relation to Arendt's idea of self-disclosure as part of the practice of judgment.

My insistence on the importance of acts of will as part of the practice of judgment is informed by the feminist thinkers whose writings motivate this study and assist in interpreting my research materials.[18] It is persuasively summarized by philosopher Naomi Scheman:

> Justification is not less so for being fallible: it is, in fact, demonstrated openness to demonstrable fallibility that marks true justification. The demand for something that would put an end to the process, some bedrock that would ground it, is a demand for the dismantling of what actually makes justification work. Arguing that the demand is for the impossible, while conceding that without it justification is ungrounded, lets one off the hook when it comes to being responsible for what makes justification come to an end (or seem to) when it does, and for creating the conditions under which it could come to a better one.[19]

In this passage, Scheman interprets and expands on Ludwig Wittgenstein's methodological ideas, in which the justification of a theoretical approach ultimately ends with a political choice, not an empirical truth. I have adopted this methodolgocial approach in this book. However, I am also arguing here that the unavoidability of political claims and justification is part of what has been revealed about common sense and legal judgment in the substantive part of the book. Different choices can be made: judges *can* come to other conclusions, and legal judgments *can* be made differently.

A compelling demonstration of this variation can be found in the global emergence of projects focused on the writing of alternative judgments, including the Women's Court of Canada, the UK Feminist Judgments Project, the Australian Feminist Judgments Project, the Northern/Irish Feminist Judgments Project, and the Mainstreaming

Diversity Project for the European Court of Human Rights.[20] These projects undertake to rewrite the legal histories of their jurisdictions in a way that centres rather than marginalizes the rights of women and other groups, and they thus demonstrate the contingency of legal judgments that oppress or discriminate.[21] As exercises in exploring practices of good judgment, these projects touch a number of themes that emerge in relation to common sense. First, it is notable that among the rewritten, feminist judgments, a large number do not alter the outcome of the case.[22] The concern is with *practices* of judgment, with the reasoning processes in which the judges engaged to come to a conclusion. This concern is reflected in an essay introducing the Women's Court of Canada by legal scholar Diana Majury: "We wanted to go beyond critique to offer a fully articulated alternative. We wanted to see if, within the limits of a judicial decision, we could say what we wanted to say, what we believe should be said, what must be said. In this process, we are no longer offering a perspective or an argument or even an analysis; we are giving a judgment."[23] Second, all of the projects highlight the goal of disrupting existing jurisprudence by demonstrating that, even within the constraints of existing precedents and judicial conventions, *judgment can be practised differently*. There is nothing necessary or obvious about the practices of judgment that currently dominate in our courts. In a way, the alternative judgment projects seek to free us from captivity to a certain picture of legal judgment by demonstrating the contingency of that picture. This also liberates us to consider how common sense might be used as part of an alternative, progressive judging practice that attends to questions of inequality and the injustices of marginalization.

Finally, the alternative judgment projects also engage with the question of subjective identity in judgment. The Northern/Irish Feminist Judgments Project in particular is very explicit about this goal: it seeks to inaugurate "a fresh dialogue on gender, judicial power, and national identity within Ireland."[24] It engages the issue of identity by thinking not only about the identities of legal judges but also about how practices of judgment work to create the identities of people bound by the law.[25] Judging can be practised differently.

Attention to Rhetorical Effects and the Creation of Communities

All of the aspects of common sense explored here reveal its enormous rhetorical significance, capturing the powerful ways that the phrase "common sense" is used in communication and persuasion. "Common sense" is invoked to draw lines around rational debate, around the norms and values of the reasonable person, and around the communities that count in any given context. It not only reflects these boundaries but also works to enforce and even create them. Invoking "common sense" can persuade and alienate, include and exclude. For common sense to be used in the service of good legal judgment, this rhetorical power must also be used thoughtfully, and judges should be attuned to its effects and accountable for its consequences.

Among the rhetorical objectives of a written legal judgment is the persuasion of the community at large that justice has been done. When judges address this objective, they reveal the boundaries of the community that "counts" in this respect. The people who are referenced, appealed to, or persuaded by the judgment are members of the community to which the judgment is addressed. They are the people whose sense of justice the judgment tries to meet. When the phrase "common sense" appears in a judgment, different communities are drawn, reinforced, or erased, depending on the context and the way that "common sense" is invoked. For example, in *Vetrovec v. The Queen*, "common sense" seems to reference a community of undifferentiated nonexperts or "ordinary" Canadians, all capable of making judgments about credibility. In *R.D.S.* "common sense" is used to describe what is known by the members of a particular community who share, among other things, the values enshrined in the Charter. These are the communities of people to whom the judges direct their words, whose perspectives matter, and who are among those ultimately bound by the judgment issued by the court.

In Reid's approach to common sense, the rhetorical power of the concept comes from its normative universality and from the way that common sense marks what should be known by every reasonable person. According to Reid, claims contrary to what every reasonable person knows from everyday life are properly subject to heavy scrutiny and even ridicule. There is an egalitarian impulse at the heart of this approach that can provide some guidance for judges exercising their rhetorical options. Most strongly, Reid's approach reminds judges that ordinary people matter and that the tools of communication and persuasion that judges choose to engage will affect how the law is positioned in relation to those people.

When it comes to identifying the right community that a legal judge must address, Gramsci provides much more specific answers: justice requires that subaltern peoples be empowered to overturn the political structures that oppress them, so those subaltern peoples are the ones whose views and interests must be considered for common sense to be transformed into "good sense." Although this specific vision of socialist emancipation may be far removed from the task and situation of legal judges in a liberal democracy, it does provide some guidance about how legal judges should think about the communities bound by that law and the rhetoric used to address them. Claims about common sense are important rhetorically and politically and can either support or subvert the political freedom of any group; the choice must be made with reflection and knowledge of the relevant history.

The aspect of common sense that emerges from Arendt's writings speaks even more directly to the rhetorical consequences of invoking "common sense." Arendt argues explicitly that engaging with common sense not only reflects and affects certain communities but also constitutes those communities. It matters a great deal who our imagined communities are. All three theorists suggest that judgment is improved by diverse social discourse. Reid argues that a wider circle of exchange decreases the risk of prejudicial reasoning through reliance on inappropriate analogies. Gramsci argues that the common sense of intellectual elites and the common sense of the masses must be brought into meaningful conversation with each other. And Arendt shows how there is a substantive link between our communities of judgment and the reflective validity of our judgments.

In the context of practices of legal judgment, there are a number of ways that this diverse social discourse, or validity-enhancing reflection, might be made stronger. The first is the diversity of the imagined communities. This diversity includes, crucially, that of the judiciary itself. It also includes the diversity of the legal profession as a whole because the members of this profession form an important community of reference for legal judgment.[26] But, moreover, Arendt's approach to common sense and judgment shows that it is important to think beyond this community to the other communities that are created and maintained through the practice of legal judgment. Importantly, both Gramsci and Arendt suggest that our common sense, and thus our judgment, cannot be made better *just* by widening the scope of our social discourse per se. Diversity can play its role in strengthening judgment only under certain conditions that allow marginalized voices to be heard and critical reflection to take place. We need a framework of respect, equality, and accountability for these things to happen in political judgment or in legal judgment.[27]

When legal judgments address social marginalization, claims about common sense can work to actively exclude and silence, reducing the space for a community in the public sphere. Alternatively, the public proclamation of "common sense" that has reflectively engaged with the judgments of a marginalized group does more than affect the outcome of the judgment; it also supports the life of the community. Through such critical engagement, we move closer to justice both because the judgment becomes more valid and because community life becomes more inclusive.

POVERTY AND *GOSSELIN V. QUEBEC (PROCUREUR GÉNÉRAL)*

Throughout this book, the case of *Gosselin v. Quebec (Procureur général)* has served as a touchstone for exploring the intersection of common sense, legal judgment, and the injustices of poverty in Canada. It is a case in which the invocation of "common sense" by the majority of the justices of the Supreme Court of Canada compromises the quality of legal judgment as practised in that case. That is because, in a context of overlapping inequality based on poverty, gender, and age, "common sense" is invoked to reify the perspectives of the privileged, to reinforce the marginalization of young women in poverty, to legitimize stereotypes, and to reject the claimant's arguments as lying outside the realm of reasonable debate. Taking a broad view, these are all legitimate uses of the phrase "common sense," and they draw on a number of the aspects studied in this book. But in the context of law, where judgment is measured by its capacity to effect justice, these invocations of "common sense" undermine the legitimacy, validity, and quality of *legal judgment*. Of course, this claim is grounded in political commitments that privilege certain values (e.g., equality and inclusion) over others (e.g., deference to legislative decisions or some forms of individual liberty). It has been an overarching claim in this book that such judgments, and the obligation to be held accountable for them, are always at work when "common sense" is invoked.

I have argued throughout this book that the invocation of "common sense" in *Gosselin* compromises the quality of that judgment in many different ways. In their imaginative rewriting of the *Gosselin* case, the Women's Court of Canada also identifies problems with the language of "common sense" in that case. The judgment, co-authored by Gwen Brodsky, Rachel Cox, Shelagh Day, and Kate Stephenson, contrasts the majority's assessment of the claimant's experience on the basis of "common sense" with the "objective reality" of her circumstances:

> Also unconvincing is the view of the Supreme Court of Canada that the government's intention of integrating young people into the workforce militates against a finding of discrimination. McLachlin C.J. explained her conclusion by claiming that the intention of the legislator was a positive one. She wrote: "As a matter of common sense, if a law is designed to promote the claimant's long-term autonomy and self-sufficiency, a reasonable person in the claimant's position would be less likely to view it as an assault on her inherent human dignity" (Gosselin SCC, at para 27). Given the objective reality of the impoverished circumstances of people trying to survive on the reduced rate, this is deeply troubling.[28]

The judgment also notes the way that common sense facilitates the operation of stereotyping in that case:

> The Supreme Court of Canada majority treated the government's claimed positive intention for the scheme as though it were determinative. Yet it is well established in human rights and Charter equality rights law that good intentions do not justify discriminatory effects. As early as 1985, in the landmark case of Ontario (Human Rights Commission) v. Simpson-Sears Ltd. (O'Malley), [1985] 2 S.C.R. 536, the Supreme Court of Canada held that a well-intended policy could have discriminatory effects and that proof of adverse effects is sufficient to ground a claim of discrimination. In this case, however, the majority of the Supreme Court of Canada treated the government's positive intention as though it were the equivalent of positive outcomes and used it to negate the very harm that was the grounding of Louise Gosselin's section 15 claim. The majority decision provides a demonstration of how insidious stereotypes can be – a stereotype can be so accepted in society that it is invisible even to conscientious judges.[29]

Thus the Women's Court of Canada writers identify some of the ways that common sense can undermine practices of good judgment. By their act of reimagining the judgment, they also work to relativize the judgment itself, opening our minds to other possibilities. But their treatment leaves "common sense" itself relatively untouched. Like other critics of the *Gosselin* case, their (trenchant and appropriate) critique of the invocation of "common sense" leads them to set it aside. They do not use the phrase "common sense" in their own judgment.

Although I endorse their critique, my aim differs from that of the writers of the Women's Court of Canada. The focus of my challenge is our captivity to a picture of common sense. Working through my "perspicuous representation" has led to the view that "common sense," *properly invoked*, can be a tool for *good* legal judgment. When "common sense" is invoked in accordance with the three criteria described above – in the spirit of intellectual humility, through open political justification, and with attention to the boundaries of communities – its potential as a resource for good legal judgment is made manifest.

What would have been the consequences if the Women's Court of Canada *had* invoked "common sense" in this way? How could its members have achieved this? What difference would it have made? In this book, I have argued that what is required to make common sense a progressive concept for strengthening legal judgment is a dynamic, even confounding, approach that maintains a constant openness and attends to complex social phenomena of politics and rhetoric. As Nedelsky argues in relation to the development of Arendt's "enlarged mentality,"[30] this is an endeavour that is indeed an *exercise* or a *practice*; it takes concerted effort and is never easy.[31] Without diminishing the demanding nature of this undertaking, I also want to suggest that it is not impossibly difficult to engage with common sense in this way – to respond to the criteria of intellectual humility, political accountability, and attention to communities. As an invitation to think through these issues, I offer a series of passages invoking "common sense" that could have been part of a feminist, anti-poverty judgment in the *Gosselin* case. These passages engage with different aspects of common sense: as shared knowledge, as a "conception of the world,"[32] as a part of judgment. Some of these invocations of "common sense" would be mutually contradictory in a single judgment, whereas others might be used together.

1. "There is no social scientific evidence needed to support the claim that individuals attempting to survive on less than $200 per month will experience the harms of destitution. It is a matter of common sense."
2. "The government's claim that a proffered well-meaning objective will mitigate the harms of poverty and discrimination belies common sense and is approached with caution."
3. "Ms. Gosselin's evidence, placed in the context of the common sense of her community, provides valuable insights into the effects of the impugned legislation."
4. "The government's argument advancing the value of 'incentives' in moving young adults from welfare to

paid employment seems to be supported by certain forms of 'common sense.' However, this perspective excludes important justice considerations and is therefore partial and inadequate as the 'common sense' of this court."

5. "The law must be interpreted in accordance with the common sense held not by a few but by all communities bound by the law."

Each of these passages engages a different aspect of common sense and takes up different concerns for legal judgment, including the quality of evidence, the identities of the communities bound by the law, and the assignment of burdens of proof. All of them are problematic in their own ways, but they suggest the possibilities that exist when common sense is understood in a complex and nuanced way.

COMMON SENSE FOR GOOD LEGAL JUDGMENT AND THE TRANSFORMATION OF LORD LAW

To say that common sense is conservative, or majoritarian, or works to close down debate is to point to real issues that will always be significant for questions of justice. However, to relinquish the idea of common sense is to leave practices of judgment without a powerful and positive tool for grappling with community, with subjectivity, and with the significance of daily life.

Common sense draws boundaries, to be sure, and a judge must always be ready to defend those boundaries as appropriate for the context, but this exercise can be productive as well as dangerous. Common sense can be ideal for covering over our most centrally held assumptions, but once a judge is compelled to reflect on this power, it can direct attention to the political consequences of those assumptions and their appropriateness (or not) for the legal judgment at hand. And common sense brings with it revaluation of everyday, nonexpert knowledge, which might reify a dominant perspective or simply rein in the scope of a judgment to those things we are competent to truly, genuinely judge in a responsible way.

Without common sense, we lose the ability to take on the exasperated voice of the ordinary person encountering obfuscating bureaucracy or oppressive discourses of expertise; we lose the ability to insist that meaningful communicability and shared experience should be essential bases for judgment; and we lose a powerful way of making the democratic claim that everyone's knowledge can be valuable and is worthy of critical reflection when it is called upon.

The judgment in *Gosselin* that a young woman living in poverty in a Canadian city experiences no infringement of her legal rights because "common sense" insists that her dignity is intact or because her government made a "common sense" decision to reduce welfare rolls with harsh incentives is not only a mistaken interpretation of Canadian law. It is not only a misrepresentation of the facts involved in that case. It is not only a politically charged rejection of social and economic rights. It is also, importantly, an affront to common sense. It represents a failure to respect and represent the valid knowledge of the community that lives under the law, a failure to take responsibility for the political choices underlying the judgment, and a failure to appreciate the rhetorical consequences of endorsing an unreflective and oppressive view of people in poverty. Instead, it is necessary to develop practices of judgment that are attuned to the rhetorical effects of common sense, that foster accountability, that are based on knowledge of relevant communities, that constitute communities in accordance with who is governed by the law, and that demonstrate acts of critical imagination. This is the common sense that can challenge the injustices of poverty.

In *Pasquin*, Lord Law refuses to remain in the court of Queen Common-Sense; he does not want merely to *serve* Common-Sense. Although in the play this decision leads him to treason, I suggest that Law is fundamentally right in that resistance. But I also suggest that this need not be the end of the story for Queen Common-Sense and Lord Law. What might happen if Lord Law were to leave the Royal Court and take up a position on the bench of a common law court? As a legal judge, Lord Law might become convinced to see common sense not just as a constraint on the power of law to serve its own interests but also as a complex source of wisdom. Following the untimely demise of Queen Common-Sense, her ghost promises to haunt the world forever. This book suggests that there are specific ways that Queen Common-Sense should haunt Lord Law. Common-Sense should pull Law away from the Royal Court and into the community, where Law can start to see the diversity of the world and the possibilities for justice.

Notes

INTRODUCTION

1 Kant, *Prolegomena*, 7. For one discussion of this passage, see Lemos, *Common Sense*, 67–9. Kant's writings about common sense go beyond this passage, and in other contexts "common sense" takes on very different meanings. Hannah Arendt draws on Kant's theory of judgment in her discussion of common sense, which is the subject of chapter 4.

2 Quoted in Maher, "Common Sense and Law," 600.

3 Henry Fielding is well known as a playwright and novelist but also as a barrister and magistrate who helped to form what some consider to be the first modern police force in eighteenth-century London, England. His overlapping contributions in law and literature make his reflections on common sense a particularly intriguing source for this book. See Allen, "Henry Fielding."

4 In this book, I discuss legal judgment as a form of the larger human practice of judgment. To reflect this approach, when referring to judges in a court of law, I sometimes use the (unconventional) term "legal judge" to distinguish this person from other kinds of judges who are making judgments, for example, about art or politics. I discuss this approach further in chapter 1.

5 My understanding of justice is significantly informed by the work of Nancy Fraser. See Fraser, *Scales of Justice*; Fraser and Honneth, *Redistribution or Recognition?*; Fraser, "What's Critical?"; Fraser, "Mapping the Feminist Imagination"; and Fraser, "Rethinking the Public Sphere."

6 For a discussion of the normative aspects of legal forms, see Rundle, *Forms Liberate*; and Fuller, "Positivism and Fidelity to Law."

7 In taking this approach, I adopt the view that questions of knowledge and evidence are ultimately about political accountability. For an example of how this approach can structure questions about justice, see Zerilli, "Doing without Knowing."

8 *Gosselin v. Quebec (Procureur général)*, 2002 SCC 84, [2002] 4 SCR 429.

9 Ibid., para. 7.

10 Ibid., paras 27, 44, 56.

11 For example, both sides of the dispute cited evidence showing that young adults in Quebec had a very high rate of unemployment. The claimant relied on this evidence to demonstrate the vulnerability of young adults to unemployment and poverty. In contrast, the government relied on this evidence as the basis for its legislative response, which, it said, was aimed at providing incentives to help young people find employment. See ibid., paras 39–40, 235, 240.

12 Gosselin's testimony contributed to the evidence before the court about the stressful and oppressive experiences of poverty and about the resulting survival strategies of young women in particular. See National Association of Women and the Law, *Factum of the Intervenor*.

13 Kant, *Prolegomena*, 7.

14 Quoted in Maher, "Common Sense and Law," 600.

15 One striking example was the famous (or infamous) invocation of "common sense" by Conservative Ontario premier Mike Harris, who characterized his political platform as the "Common Sense Revolution" when he ran for office in the 1990s. Harris called on "common sense" in opposition to government spending on social welfare programs. See Conservative Party of Ontario, "Common Sense Revolution."

16 In this book, I use the word "justice" to describe the benchmark for my normative evaluations. In my view, the concept of justice includes elements having to do with material well-being and the distribution of economic resources in society. Where I wish to draw attention to these elements of justice, I also use the phrase "social justice."

17 Wittgenstein describes his method as the generation of a "perspicuous representation" of language: "A main source of our failure to understand is that we do not *command a clear view* of the use of our words. – Our grammar is lacking in this sort of perspicuity. A

perspicuous representation produces just that understanding which consists in 'seeing connexions.'" Wittgenstein, *Philosophical Investigations*, sec. 122, emphasis in original.

18 Throughout this book, I treat the phrase "common sense" as an instance of language that has different meanings and uses in different contexts. For the most part, I write directly about common sense without quotation marks, but I urge readers to think about this phrase as an instance of language that appears in different social contexts and practices, as well as to suspend their judgment about whether "common sense" can be understood as a coherent concept or idea.

19 Gramsci, *Prison Notebooks*, 9.

20 Ibid., 328.

CHAPTER ONE

1 The Haymarket Theatre is in London, England. Built in 1720, it is one of the oldest London playhouses still in use.

2 Here, and at the beginning of the following chapters on Thomas Reid, Antonio Gramsci, and Hannah Arendt, I offer a short fictional vignette in which each of these thinkers attends a performance of Henry Fielding's satire *Pasquin*, about the life and death of Queen Common-Sense. These imaginative exercises speculate about what these thinkers might have thought, or felt, or done while watching this production. Their purpose is to invite the reader to begin to play with the notion of perspective and with the idea of looking at one thing from multiple points of view. This idea is at the heart of the methodology described in this chapter and employed in the following chapters. I hope these vignettes also provoke the reader to think critically about whether such acts of imagination are legitimate or fruitful and, if so, in what way.

3 Fielding, *Pasquin*, act 4, scene 1.

4 Geertz, "Common Sense as a Cultural System," 75.

5 Parret, "Common Sense in Philosophy."

6 Throughout this book, I approach legal judgment as one form of a larger human practice of judgment. This approach understands legal, political, and aesthetic judgment to share certain characteristics, even as they differ in important ways. See Nedelsky, "Communities of

Judgment." This approach also explains why I talk about "judgment" rather than "adjudication" or "decision making."

7 Questions of form and substance overlap for legal judgment, but in this book, I address the issue of good judgment from a practice or procedural perspective. For an example of how theorists can explore legal principles like impartiality as general criteria for practices of good legal judgment, see Boyle and MacCrimmon, "To Serve the Cause."

8 Canadian Judicial Council, *Ethical Principles*, principle 5, comment 2.

9 Allen, "Common Sense"; Maher, "Common Sense and Law"; Riddell, "Common Law."

10 This idea is widely discussed from many perspectives. For three different approaches, see Carter, "Do Courts Decide?"; MacCrimmon, "Fact Determination"; and Zuckerman, "Law, Fact or Justice?"

11 Allen, "Common Sense," 1428.

12 *R. v. D.D.*, 2000 SCC 43, [2000] 2 SCR 275.

13 *R. v. Lifchus*, [1997] 3 SCR 320, 150 DLR (4th) 733.

14 *Snell v. Farrell*, [1990] 2 SCR 311, 72 DLR (4th) 289.

15 Schneiderman, "Common Sense and the Charter." In this piece, Schneiderman explores the role that the invocation of "common sense" has played in judicial interpretation of the Canadian Charter of Rights and Freedoms. He argues that "common sense" often has the function of "conferring legitimacy on dominant accounts of the social world." Ibid., 14.

16 *Chaoulli v. Quebec (Attorney General)*, 2005 SCC 35, [2005] 1 SCR 791.

17 *RJR-MacDonald Inc. v. Canada (Attorney General)*, [1995] 3 SCR 199, 127 DLR (4th) 1.

18 *MacDonald v. MacDonald*, [1976] 2 SCR 259, 1975 CanLII 28 (SCC).

19 *R. v. Walle*, 2012 SCC 41, [2012] 2 SCR 438.

20 *Gosselin v. Quebec (Procureur général)*, 2002 SCC 84, [2002] 4 SCR 429.

21 Other important Supreme Court of Canada judgments that engage with the problem of poverty include *Eldridge v. British Columbia (Attorney General)*, [1997] 3 SCR 624, 151 DLR (4th) 577; *Baker v. Canada*, [1999] 2 SCR 817, 174 DLR (4th) 193; *New Brunswick (Minister of Health and Community Services) v. G.(J.)*, [1999] 3 SCR 46, 177 DLR (4th) 124; and *Lovelace v. Ontario*, 2000 SCC 37, [2000] 1 SCR 950.

22 Other cases in which the Supreme Court of Canada has addressed some aspect of a provincial welfare regime are *Alden v. Gaglardi et al.*, [1973] SCR 199, 1972 CanLII 140 (SCC) (re. exclusion of individuals whose need is a result of a strike or lockout) and *Finlay v. Canada (Minister of Finance)*, [1993] 1 SCR 1080, 101 DLR (4th) 567 (re. deduction from social assistance payments to recover overpayments). Other cases dealing with the legal context of welfare regimes include *Tranchemontagne v. Ontario (Director, Disability Support Program)*, 2006 SCC 14, [2006] 1 SCR 513 (re. jurisdiction of social assistance tribunal to consider human rights issues) and *Quebec (Attorney General) v. Canada*, 2011 SCC 11, [2011] 1 SCR 368 (re. obligation of federal government to share costs of programs).

23 There is a broader problem with the application of oppressive dominant norms and stereotyping in cases dealing with poverty. See Jackman, "Reality Checks"; Mosher, "Shrinking of the Public"; Mosher, "Managing the Disentitlement"; Mossman, "Choices and Commitments"; and Young, "Rights."

24 *Gosselin*, para. 9. Section 7 of the Charter reads, "Everyone has the right to life, liberty and security of the person and the right not to be deprived thereof except in accordance with the principles of fundamental justice." Section 15(1) reads, "Every individual is equal before and under the law and has the right to the equal protection and equal benefit of the law without discrimination and, in particular, without discrimination based on race, national or ethnic origin, colour, religion, sex, age or mental or physical disability." Canadian Charter of Rights and Freedoms, Part 1 of the Constitution Act, 1982, being Schedule B to the Canada Act 1982 (UK), 1982, c. 11.

25 For a detailed description of the various judgments, see Brodsky, "*Gosselin*."

26 *Gosselin*, para. 19. From a doctrinal perspective, subsequent jurisprudence has destabilized the notion of dignity as central to an assessment of discrimination. See *Quebec (Attorney General) v. A.*, 2013 SCC 5, [2013] 1 SCR 61. For a discussion of the relationship between dignity and equality, see Réaume, "Dignity, Equality and Comparison."

27 *Quebec (Attorney General) v. A.*, paras 26, 27, 41, 42.

28 Ibid., paras 42, 44.

29 Ibid., para. 44.

30 See National Association of Women and the Law, *Factum of the Intervenor*.
31 *Gosselin*, para. 130.
32 As a matter of constitutional doctrine, it is noteworthy that all of these passages relate to the analysis of section 15 equality rights.
33 *Gosselin*, para. 27, emphasis added.
34 Ibid., para. 44, emphasis added.
35 Ibid., para. 56, emphasis added.
36 Brodsky, "*Gosselin*"; Schneiderman, "Social Rights"; Jackman, "Reality Checks"; Kim and Piper, "*Gosselin v. Quebec*"; McIntyre, "Supreme Court and Section 15." For example, Gwen Brodsky critiques the majority's assessment of the evidence on the grounds that the judgment accepted the negative stereotypes of young people on social assistance that had framed the legislation in the first place. Brodsky argues that mischaracterization of the facts in the case allows the majority to endorse idealized and formal notions of autonomy and freedom, which are, in reality, not realizable without adequate support to meet basic needs. In this way, the majority undermines rather than enhances the equality and autonomy of poor women and other marginalized people. Brodsky, "*Gosselin*."
37 Schneiderman, "Social Rights."
38 Ibid.
39 Ibid., 68.
40 McIntyre, "Supreme Court and Section 15," 764. It is interesting to note the similarities between this comment and the passage by Kant cited at the beginning of the Introduction.
41 McIntyre, "Studied Ignorance."
42 Kim and Piper, "*Gosselin v. Quebec*," 780.
43 Victoria Anti-Poverty Coalition, "Gosselin Decision."
44 See United Nations Economic and Social Council, "Substantive Issues."
45 Statistics Canada's low-income cut-offs indicate those households who spend about 20 per cent more of their income meeting their basic needs than the average household. The Market Basic Measure identifies households whose income is insufficient to purchase a certain collection of goods. By both types of measures, about 10 per cent of Canadians are low-income. See Canadian Council on Social

Development, "Economic Security"; and Human Resources and Skills Development Canada, *Low Income in Canada*.

46 Canada Without Poverty, http://www.cwp-csp.ca, quotation accessed 20 July 2013, no longer online.

47 For example, a study by the Canadian Centre for Policy Alternatives found that approximately 40 per cent of Indigenous children in Canada are poor. See Macdonald and Wilson, *Poverty or Prosperity*; and Canadian Council on Social Development, "Economic Security." For more statistics and discussion, see Young, "Introduction."

48 The poverty experienced by Indigenous individuals and communities in Canada is complex and goes far beyond questions of legal judgment as practised by Canadian state courts; it relates to practices of colonialism, including dispossession of land, disruption of traditional economies, and discriminatory treatment by the state. See Cannon and Sunseri, *Racism, Colonialism, and Indigeneity*, part 6; and Palmater, "Stretched beyond Human Limits." The Centre for Policy Alternatives released a report in 2013 finding that 40 per cent of Indigenous children live in poverty. See Macdonald and Wilson, *Poverty or Prosperity*.

49 Canadian Centre for Policy Alternatives, "Fact Sheets on Women's Poverty."

50 McInturff, "Closing Canada's Gender Gap."

51 Brodsky et al., "Human Rights Denied."

52 In one study, women within three years of leaving an abusive relationship were twenty times more likely to access food banks than the general population. Canadian Centre for Policy Alternatives, "Fact Sheets on Women's Poverty," 6.

53 For a foundational account of how different forms of oppression can be understood as "intersecting" in individual bodies and communities, see Crenshaw, "Mapping the Margins."

54 *Falkiner v. Ontario (Director of Income Maintenance, Ministry of Community & Social Services)* (2002), 212 DLR (4th) 633, 59 OR (3d) 481 (ON ca).

55 *R. v. Hamilton*, [2003] 8 CR (6th) 215, 172 CCC (3d) 114 (ON Sup Ct J).

56 *R. v. Banks*, [2007] 275 DLR (4th) 640, 84 OR (3d) 1 (ON CA); *Federated Anti-Poverty Groups of* BC *v. Vancouver (City)*, 2002 BCSC 105, [2002] 40 Admin LR (3d) 159.

57 That legal regimes and outcomes can have an affect in survival situations was tragically made evident in the case of Kimberly Rogers, a woman who was found dead in her apartment in Sudbury, Ontario, on 9 August 2001. At the time of her death, Rogers was eight months pregnant and confined to her residence following a conviction for welfare fraud related to her receipt of student loans while on welfare. Her conviction had also resulted in an automatic suspension of her welfare benefits. For a detailed collection of inquest documents and media reports surrounding this case, see Justice with Dignity, "Remember Kimberly Rogers."

58 For general discussion of the significance of a representative judiciary, see Devlin, MacKay, and Kim, "Reducing the Democratic Deficit"; Graycar, "Gender of Judgments"; Nedelsky, "Judgment, Diversity"; and Wilson, "Will Women Judges?"

59 Omatsu, "Fiction of Judicial Impartiality." Of the 100 judges appointed by the federal government between 2010 and 2012, 98 were white. Makin, "Of 100 New."

60 As of 2013, of the 1,180 judges of all Canadian courts, 364 were women (approximately 31 per cent). Gill and Shaw, "Representing Canada on the Bench."

61 For recent explorations in the Canadian context, see the essays in Young et al., eds, *Poverty*; and in Rodgers and McIntyre, eds, *Supreme Court of Canada*.

62 Scheingold, *Politics of Rights*; Williams, *Alchemy*.

63 Bakan, *Just Words*.

64 Jackman, "Protection of Welfare Rights"; Petter, "Wealthcare."

65 Arbour, "'Freedom from Want'"; Wiseman, "Competence Concerns"; Gibbon, "Social Rights"; Wiseman, "Charter and Poverty."

66 Faraday, Denike, and Stephenson, eds, *Making Equality Rights Real*; Gavigan, "Poverty Law"; Mosher, "Shrinking of the Public"; Dua and Robertson, eds, *Scratching the Surface*.

67 Parret, "Common Sense in Philosophy."

68 In this vein, some writers argue that common sense does not have any particular content but describes a kind of naive realism about the world. See Forguson, *Common Sense*; and Allen, "Common Sense."

69 Tracing the intellectual history of common sense in the natural law tradition, Frits van Holthoon describes how these two strands of common sense come together in that tradition. Holthoon, "Common

Sense and Natural Law." It is also essential to note how these two aspects are related. See MacCrimmon, "What Is 'Common'?"

70 Recent philosophical, political, and historical writings on common sense include Rosenfeld, *Common Sense*; Snir, "Experts of Common Sense"; Holthoon and Olson, "Common Sense"; and Parret, "Common Sense in Philosophy."

71 Rosenfeld, *Common Sense*, 23.

72 Ibid.

73 Ibid.

74 Ibid.

75 Ibid., 3.

76 Ibid., 9.

77 Frits van Holthoon argues that the natural law tradition has incorporated many aspects of common sense. Holthoon, "Common Sense and Natural Law."

78 Boyd, "Some Postmodernist Challenges"; Hunt, "Ideology of Law."

79 Purvis and Hunt, "Discourse, Ideology."

80 Valverde, *Law's Dream*.

81 Riddell, "Common Law and Common Sense," 995, emphasis added.

82 Ibid., 996.

83 Finkel, *Commonsense Justice*.

84 Ibid.

85 Ibid., 95.

86 Allen, "Common Sense," 1426.

87 Ibid., 1431.

88 Howard, *Death of Common Sense*.

89 Ibid., 11.

90 Ibid., 118.

91 MacCrimmon, "What Is 'Common'?" 1444.

92 Ibid., 1442.

93 Ibid., 1443–4.

94 Ibid., 1446.

95 Maher, "Common Sense and Law."

96 Salter, "Common Sense," 213.

97 Maher, "Common Sense and Law," 600.

98 Salter, "Common Sense," 212.

99 This language comes from section 38 of *Philosophical Investigations*, a book that forms an important part of Wittgenstein's later

philosophy. Section 38 says, "A picture held us captive. And we could not get outside it, for it lay in our language and language seemed to repeat it to us inexorably." See also Wittgenstein, *On Certainty.*

100 Schneiderman, "Social Rights."

101 Wittegenstein's use of the word "aspect" is related to a larger engagement with visual metaphors and interpretive approaches. Wittgenstein talks about "seeing," "noticing an aspect," and "pictures" as important methodological strategies, and he makes use of visual diagrams in his work. See, for example, Wittegenstein, *Philosophical Investigations*, 165–6.

102 For a discussion of the methodology of "perspicuous representation" as practised by Wittgenstein, see Baker, "Philosophical Investigations." For examples of scholars who have adopted or modified the method to address questions of justice and politics, see Heyes, ed., *Grammar of Politics*.

103 Chakrabarty, *Provincializing Europe*.

104 Wittgenstein, *Philosophical Investigations*, sec. 66.

105 *Vetrovec v. The Queen*, [1982] 1 SCR 811, 136 DLR (3d) 89.

106 *R. v. Khela*, 2009 SCC 4, [2009] 1 SCR 104.

107 Charles Taylor argues that broader understanding arises "in comparisons or contrasts, which let the other be." Taylor, "Comparison, History, Truth," 152.

108 Finkel, *Commonsense Justice*.

109 Gramsci, *Prison Notebooks*.

110 In the introduction to Gramsci's chapter on the "Study of Philosophy," Hoare and Nowell Smith write, "Essential to Gramsci's approach is the notion that an intellectual revolution is not performed by simply confronting one philosophy with another. It is not just the ideas that require to be confronted but the social forces behind them and, more directly, the ideology these forces have generated and which has become part of what Gramsci calls 'common sense.' This last term is used by Gramsci to mean the uncritical and largely unconscious way of perceiving and understanding the world that has become 'common' in any given epoch. (Correspondingly he uses the phrase 'good sense' to mean the practical, but not necessarily rational or scientific attitude that in English is usually called common sense.)" Ibid., 322.

111 Arendt, *Lectures*, 66.

112 Ibid., 70–1.

113 Havercroft, "On Seeing Liberty As," 157.

114 David Owen writes that "it is vital that we can call a picture into question in order to assess its *value*, that is, its capacity to guide our judgments and activity such that we can make sense of ourselves as agents, in the ways that matter to us." Owen, "Genealogy," 84–5, emphasis in original. Texts in which feminist scholars draw on Wittgenstein to work toward related goals include Heyes, ed., *Grammar of Politics*; Scheman, "Forms of Life"; and Zerilli, "Doing without Knowing."

115 Fraser, "What's Critical?" 31.

116 For another discussion of "what is at stake," see Taylor, "Overcoming Epistemology."

CHAPTER TWO

1 Fielding, *Pasquin*, act 4, scene 2.

2 Ibid., act 5, scene 1.

3 Wittgenstein, *Philosophical Investigations*, sec. 66.

4 As noted in chapter 1, Wittgenstein uses the word "picture" to describe a worldview or frame of reference that provides the background against which we use and understand things. See Wittgenstein, *Philosophical Investigations*, sec. 115.

5 *Vetrovec v. The Queen*, [1982] 1 SCR 811, 136 DLR (3d) 89; *R. v. D.D.*, 2000 SCC 43, [2000] 2 SCR 275.

6 Reid, *Essays*, 46.

7 For general information about Reid's life and work, see Yaffe and Nichols, "Thomas Reid."

8 Broadie, *Scottish Enlightenment*.

9 Rosenfeld, *Common Sense*, 63.

10 Ibid., 65.

11 Ibid., 65–6.

12 Ibid., 67.

13 Ibid.

14 Ibid., 67–9.

15 For commentary on Reid's philosophy of common sense, see Boulter, *Rediscovery*; Coates, *Claims of Common Sense*; Houston, *Thomas Reid*; Lemos, *Common Sense*; Marcil-Lacoste, *Claude Buffier*; Snir,

"Experts of Common Sense"; Wolterstorff, *Thomas Reid*; and Wolterstorff, "Reid on Common Sense."

16 There are interesting methodological issues arising from Reid's choice to defer an explicit definition of this key term until far into his second book. Philosopher Louise Marcil-Lacoste argues that Reid was not so much *describing* a common sense philosophy as *demonstrating* how one would work. Marcil-Lacoste, *Claude Buffier*, 76–9.

17 Reid, *Essays*, 423.

18 Ibid.

19 Ibid., 424.

20 Reid's ideas about the connection between common language and common sense greatly influenced later thinkers. See Austin, *How to Do Things*; and Moore, "Defense of Common Sense."

21 Wolterstorff, "Reid on Common Sense," 77.

22 Ibid., 216: "The skeptic who preoccupied Reid was a foundationalist of the classically modern sort who tried to lay on the philosopher the obligation to use the deliverances of reason and of introspection to assess the reliability of all other belief-forming faculties. To fail to devote oneself to this task of critique is to defect from the high calling of the philosopher to live the life of reason; it is to live as the herd lives."

23 Lemos, *Common Sense*, 5.

24 There are two strands of thought about common sense in Reid. Nicholas Wolterstorff describes the two strands in these terms: "Sometimes he thinks of the principles of common sense as first principles of our reasoning; at other times he thinks of them as things taken for granted in the living of our everyday lives." Wolterstorff, "Reid on Common Sense," 82. Noah Lemos writes that Reid appears to be saying that sometimes common sense knowledge has "positive epistemic value" and that other times it is merely "irresistible." Lemos, *Common Sense*, 22. The distinction between these two strands in Reid does not play a role in this chapter because both strands speak to common sense as part of judgment. I discuss the ways that Reid's writings address both normative and empirical commonality for common sense knowledge in the following section.

25 Reid, *Essays*, 480.

26 Reid's description of the task and social role of the philosopher has quite radical elements in the sense that he rejects the "high calling" of the philosopher in favour of the idea that philosophers base their

thinking on exactly the same common sense beliefs that ground everyone's everyday activity. Wolterstorff, "Reid on Common Sense."

27 Reid, *Essays*, 46.

28 Wolterstorff, "Reid on Common Sense," 96. For an exploration of how Reid's understanding of the relationship between common sense and philosophy relates to democratic politics, see Snir, "Experts of Common Sense."

29 Reid, *Inquiry*, 19.

30 Reid, *Essays*, 528.

31 Ibid., 529.

32 This idea of a burden of proof is often invoked by philosophers defending common sense. See Lemos, *Common Sense*; Moore, "Defense of Common Sense"; and Boulter, *Rediscovery*.

33 Reid, *Essays*, 41.

34 Ibid., 409. Note that here Reid is relying on a notion of belief in which there is a fairly transparent correspondence between one's beliefs and one's actions. This notion of belief contrasts with the views of other theorists who appear in this book, especially Gramsci.

35 Ibid., 482.

36 Ibid., 427.

37 Coates, *Claims of Common Sense*.

38 Ibid., 15; Reid, *Essays*, 452.

39 Reid, *Inquiry*, 18.

40 As noted earlier, Reid scholars sometimes identify two strands in Reid's writings about the possible epistemic value of common sense propositions: whether we can say that common sense is really "true" and whether we simply have no option but to believe it. Again, this distinction, whether it appears in Reid or his interpreters, does not play a role in this book because the connections to judgment and daily life remain the same. Noah Lemos argues that the strand in Reid that identifies some "positive epistemic value" for common sense beliefs is what distinguishes Reid from Wittgenstein, who is not interested in claiming that common sense is "true" in that way. Lemos, *Common Sense*, 1, 6, 16, 20, 21, 22.

41 Reid, *Essays*, 41. Note again an interesting foreshadowing of Wittgenstein; indeed, what Reid is proposing here might be similar to the method of "perspicuous representation" I am pursuing, in which I explore different aspects of common sense.

42 Ibid. In rejecting this line of reasoning, Reid shares something with many thinkers, many of whom might roughly be described as anti-foundationalist (including Wittgenstein), who take some version of the view that our beliefs and actions are not ultimately grounded in some rationally defensible belief but in practices and ways of life.

43 See Wolterstorff, "Reid on Common Sense."

44 Reid, *Essays*, 528–9.

45 Ibid., 528. On the obligation to seek out the truth rather than defer to others, Reid also writes, "[T]here are many more who may be called mere beggars with regard to their opinions. Through laziness and indifference about truth, they leave to others the drudgery of digging for this commodity." Ibid., 529.

46 Ibid., 433. Despite Reid's identification of male, adult persons with certain mental capacities as the model for human experience, his claims about common sense are about true universality.

47 Ibid., 461.

48 Ibid.

49 Sophia Rosenfeld argues that this caveat is related to Reid's religious views and his need to preserve the particular tenets of his faith. Rosenfeld, *Common Sense*, 80.

50 Reid, *Essays*, 461.

51 Rosenfeld, *Common Sense*, 61.

52 Reid, *Essays*, 462. This view relates to the strand in Reid in which common sense principles are those things that we must necessarily rely on in daily life: "[W]hen an opinion is so necessary in the conduct of life, that without the belief of it, a man must be led into a thousand absurdities in practice, such an opinion, when we can give no other reason for it, may safely be taken for a first principle." Ibid., 467.

53 Ibid., 39.

54 Ibid., 424.

55 The social or intersubjective elements of Reid's philosophy in general have many implications for thinking about law. See Roberts, "Legal Positivism."

56 Rosenfeld, *Common Sense*, 63–7.

57 Reid, *Essays*, 477.

58 Ibid.

59 Ibid., 460.

60 Ibid., 47.
61 Ibid., 527.
62 Ibid., 528.
63 Ibid., 529.
64 Ibid., 528.
65 Ibid., 529.
66 Ibid., 530.
67 Arendt, *Lectures*, 42.
68 Reid, *Essays*, 42, emphasis in original.
69 Ibid., 42–3, emphasis in original.
70 Ibid., 464.
71 Ibid.
72 Ibid., 497.
73 Ibid., 461.
74 Ibid., 463.
75 Ibid., 462. For a discussion of Reid's style and rhetoric, including his use of ridicule and analogy, see Houston, *Thomas Reid*.
76 Wollstonecraft, *Vindication*. For a discussion of the social and scholarly reception of Wollstonecraft's works, see Falco, ed., *Feminist Interpretations*.
77 Consider, as one example, the media treatment of prominent US political leader Hillary Clinton. Jamieson and Gabbatt, "'You Don't Fit the Image.'" For a general discussion, see MacIvor, *Women and Politics*.
78 Reid, *Essays*, 462.
79 Ibid., 39.
80 Ibid., 462.
81 Ibid.
82 Ibid., 463.
83 Coates, *Claims of Common Sense*, 17.
84 For more general discussions of how Reid's philosophy might be applied to legal theory, see Roberts, "Legal Positivism"; and Holthoon, "Common Sense and Natural Law."
85 *R. v. Marquard*, [1993] 4 SCR 223, 108 DLR (4th) 47, para. 49.
86 For a general discussion of the complexity of credibility assessment, see Morrison and Comeau, "Judging Credibility." For more critical perspectives on the task of credibility assessment and fact determination in general, see Boyle and MacCrimmon, "To Serve the Cause"; and Thompson, "Common Sense."

87 Thompson, "Common Sense," 124. Thompson provides a nuanced discussion of the role of common sense in judicial assessments of credibility at the trial level.

88 *Vetrovec*, 818, 824.

89 Ibid., 822, 831.

90 Law Reform Commission of Canada, *Report on Evidence*.

91 *Vetrovec*, 826, emphasis added.

92 Ibid., 831–2.

93 Ibid., 832.

94 Reid says that anyone who is competent enough to be "held to account for his actions" is capable of exercising common sense judgment. Further, Reid identifies an obligation to exercise such judgment. Reid, *Essays*, 426, 528.

95 Finkel, *Commonsense Justice*; Howard, *Death of Common Sense*.

96 In a compelling example, Finkel cites studies showing that people find it much easier to say they are in favour of the death penalty than to actually impose one in an individual case. Finkel, *Commonsense Justice*, 39.

97 Williams, *Alchemy*.

98 Ibid., 148.

99 Ibid., 147.

100 Ibid., 149.

101 Ibid. This conclusion is reached by different means by other writers, including Scheingold, *Politics of Rights*.

102 Williams, *Alchemy*, 159.

103 Ibid., 149. See also Matsuda, "When the First Quail Calls."

104 Ibid., 11.

105 In jurisprudence subsequent to *Vetrovec*, the Supreme Court of Canada has continued to work out the balance of legal rules and common sense for the assessment of credibility and the law on corroboration. See *Khela*.

106 *D.D.*, para. 18.

107 Ibid., paras 4–7.

108 For one perspective on how common sense and expert evidence relate for the assessment of credibility, see Norris and Edwardh, "Myths." For an excellent critical assessment of the Supreme Court of Canada's resort to expert evidence for this purpose and others, see Cunliffe, "Without Fear or Favour?"

109 *D.D.*, paras 65–6.
110 Ibid., paras 24, 42.
111 Ibid., para. 18, underlining in original, emphasis added.
112 Ibid., para. 31.
113 Ibid., para. 25, emphasis added.
114 Reid, *Essays*, 433. Reid also says, "When judgment is ripe, there are many things in which we are incompetent judges. In such matters, it is most reasonable to rely upon the judgment of those whom we believe to be competent and disinterested." Ibid., 528.
115 For example, see the way Reid frames the "first principles" of his own work. Ibid., 41.
116 Bala, "Double Victims." For a discussion of "racial common sense" as a nonexpert method of fact determination and how it buttresses white privilege in the law, see Gotanda, "'Common Sense' of Race."
117 *R. v. Mohan*, [1994] 2 SCR 9, 114 DLR (4th) 419.
118 Reid, *Essays*, 453.
119 Berger, "Trial by Metaphor"; White, "Law as Rhetoric."
120 Rosenfeld, *Common Sense*, 15.
121 Maroney, "Emotional Common Sense," 914.
122 The contrast between common sense knowledge and expertise in this judgment also speaks to the ways that other frameworks for evaluation (e.g., science), although they may also be problematic, tend to provide more openings for challenge than does common sense because they contemplate questions and answers rather than single assertions. See ibid.
123 Reid, *Essays*, 529.
124 *Gosselin v. Quebec (Procureur général)*, 2002 SCC 84, [2002] 4 SCR 429, para. 27.
125 Ibid., para. 44, emphasis added.
126 Ibid., para. 56, emphasis added.
127 Maroney, "Emotional Common Sense."
128 In chapter 4, I engage with the work of political theorist Hannah Arendt to say more about how common sense works to identify and create communities.
129 Reid, *Essays*, 518.
130 Wittgenstein, *Philosophical Investigations*, sec. 122.

CHAPTER THREE

1 Fielding, *Pasquin*, act 5, scene 1.
2 Ibid., act 4, scene 1.
3 Wittgenstein, *Philosophical Investigations*, sec. 66.
4 Gramsci, *Prison Notebooks*, 9.
5 Ibid., passim.
6 Ibid., xviii.
7 Ibid.
8 Ibid., 12.
9 Ibid., 232.
10 *Chaoulli v. Quebec (Attorney General)*, 2005 SCC 35, [2005] 1 SCR 791; *Sauvé v. Canada (Chief Electoral Officer)*, 2002 SCC 68, [2002] 3 SCR 519.
11 *Gosselin v. Quebec (Procureur général)*, 2002 SCC 84, [2002] 4 SCR 429.
12 Gramsci, *Prison Notebooks*, 9, 323.
13 Ibid., 323. Gramsci also writes that there is a sense in which "[a]ll men are intellectuals." Ibid., 9.
14 Ibid., 9. Like Reid, Gramsci argues that common sense is possessed virtually universally: "[I]t is not possible to conceive of any man who is not also a philosopher, who doesn't think, because thought is proper to man as such, or at least to any man who is not a pathological cretin." Ibid., 347.
15 Robinson, "Towards an Intellectual Reformation," 472.
16 Gramsci, *Prison Notebooks*, 9.
17 Ibid., 323.
18 Ibid., 326.
19 Ibid.
20 Ibid., 324.
21 Ibid.
22 Ibid., 325.
23 Ibid., 324.
24 Gramsci's comments are therefore addressed to the concrete political context of his time and to common sense in a twentieth-century capitalist society. At the same time, Gramsci's arguments about common sense encourage us to think more broadly about the connections between politics and knowledge, and thus they have important

commonalities with arguments by Michel Foucault. See Foucault, *Power/Knowledge.*

25 For a detailed discussion of Gramsci's theory of hegemony, see Femia, *Gramsci's Political Thought.*

26 Examples of engagement with the concept of hegemony in law include Hunt, "Ideology of Law"; Lazarus-Black and Hirsch, *Contested States*; and Litowitz, "Gramsci, Hegemony."

27 Gramsci, *Prison Notebooks*, 12.

28 Translators Hoare and Nowell Smith point out that in these works, Gramsci treated many traditional Marxist terms with "substitution or circumlocution" to avoid drawing the attention of prison censors. Thus the word "class" never appears in the *Prison Notebooks*. Instead Gramsci refers to "social groups," "dominant" groups, and "subaltern" groups. Ibid., xi–xiv. In some contexts, it is clear that Gramsci is really talking about economic classes in a Marxist sense. However, Gramsci's approach as a whole, including his approach to common sense, is nuanced and creative and therefore amenable to extension into analysis of other kinds of social categories and forms of inequality.

29 Gramsci saw around him the hegemony of oppressive capitalist ideas, and he was centrally concerned with examining and challenging such ideas. Gramsci also envisioned that progressive or liberating ideas (e.g., communist ideas heralding a classless society) could possibly become hegemonic through political change. Therefore, in a way, the hegemony of certain ideas can be either liberating or oppressive, depending on the content of the ideas and their relationship to existing political conditions. However, Gramsci's approach to the philosophy of praxis demonstrates that he did not envision that liberation would come simply by reversing the position of dominant and subaltern groups; he sought *transformation* of common sense and of political life. Rupert, "Globalising Common Sense," 186.

30 See Femia, "Hegemony and Consciousness."

31 For example, Gramsci's idea of hegemony and the internalization of unjust social relations informed the work of the Frankfurt School. See Femia, *Gramsci's Political Thought*, 35. Douglas Litowitz further points out that "[m]any of the ideas associated with Gramsci and the Frankfurt School found their way into the writings of thinkers associated with the Critical Legal Studies movement." Litowitz, "Gramsci, Hegemony," 532.

32 Rupert, "Globalising Common Sense," 185.
33 Litowitz, "Gramsci, Hegemony," 515. Litowitz also quotes Terry Eagleton, who writes, "How do we combat a power which has become the 'common sense' of a whole social order, rather than one which is widely perceived as alien and oppressive?" Ibid., 542.
34 Gramsci, *Prison Notebooks*, 326–7.
35 Rupert, "Globalising Common Sense," 185.
36 For example, see Gramsci, *Prison Notebooks*, 330.
37 Ibid., 326. See also ibid., 419.
38 Ibid., 327. Itay Snir also explores the political and epistemological consequences of this tension. Snir, "'Not Just One.'"
39 Rupert, "Globalising Common Sense," 185.
40 For a nuanced discussion of the idea of false consciousness in the context of feminist scholarship, poverty, and law, see Matsuda, "Pragmatism Modified."
41 Gramsci, *Prison Notebooks*, 327.
42 Ibid., 333; Reid, *Essays*, 46.
43 Reid explicitly thought that patterns of common sense beliefs among social groups were evidence of prejudices and a failure of individuals to think for themselves. Reid, *Essays*, 528.
44 Gramsci, *Prison Notebooks*, 324; Ives, *Language and Hegemony*, 79; Robinson, "Towards an Intellectual Reformation," 472.
45 Gramsci, *Prison Notebooks*, 333.
46 Ibid., 419.
47 Ibid., 324.
48 Ibid., 420.
49 Ibid., 427. See chapter 2.
50 Maroney, "Emotional Common Sense," 858.
51 Gramsci, *Prison Notebooks*, 422.
52 Ibid., 423.
53 Ibid., 323; Robinson, "Towards an Intellectual Reformation," 477.
54 Gramsci, *Prison Notebooks*, 331.
55 See Ives, *Language and Hegemony*, 79.
56 Robinson, "Towards an Intellectual Reformation," 469–70.
57 Ibid., 470.
58 Gramsci, *Prison Notebooks*, 395.
59 Robinson, "Towards an Intellectual Reformation," 470.
60 Nun, "Elements for a Theory."

61 Ibid., 204.
62 Ibid.
63 Ibid., 207.
64 Ibid.
65 See comments about human nature as "process" and "becoming." Gramsci, *Prison Notebooks*, 355–9.
66 Ibid., 424.
67 I do not wish to overstate any disagreement between Robinson and Nun, both of whom take the fundamental position that Gramsci calls for a critique of common sense.
68 Rupert, "Globalising Common Sense," 185. This passage by Rupert is also reminiscent of how Michel Foucault conceives of power, which also supports the notion that common sense may have some positive or productive value in creating (alternative, subaltern) meaning. Foucault, *Power/Knowledge*.
69 Gramsci, *Prison Notebooks*, 328.
70 Robinson, "Towards an Intellectual Reformation," 479.
71 In their discussion of neoliberalism and Gramscian common sense, Stuart Hall and Alan O'Shea argue that engagement with "good sense" is essential in order to challenge the dominance of neoliberal discourses in contemporary society. Hall and O'Shea, "Common-Sense Neoliberalism."
72 Gramsci, *Prison Notebooks*, 348, 420.
73 Ibid., 348.
74 Ibid.
75 Ibid., 331–3.
76 Ibid., 328.
77 Ibid., 324.
78 Ibid., 327.
79 Gramsci writes, "School is the instrument through which intellectuals of various levels are elaborated." Ibid., 10. See also ibid., 341, 350.
80 Ibid., 28.
81 Ibid., 35–6.
82 Ibid., 435.
83 Ibid., 339.
84 Ibid., 340.
85 Ibid., 339–40.

86 Ibid., 232. Peter Ives argues that Gramsci's approach to language, both in the substance of his arguments and in his methodology, reveals an approach to meaning similar to that found in Wittgenstein's *Philosophical Investigations*. Further, Ives argues that this approach to language is important for Gramsci's political objectives. On Gramsci's refusal to coin new terms, he writes, "Just as he does not want rural peasants to adopt a language imposed on them from somewhere else, he does not want readers to adopt a new set of terms that are defined outside of their usage." Ives, *Language and Hegemony*, 65.
87 Gramsci, *Prison Notebooks*, 330–1.
88 Ibid., 330.
89 Ibid., 232–3. Note Gramsci's use of quotation marks around "simple."
90 Thinking about political transformation in pedagogical terms is central to Marxist discourse in general. For example, in his "Theses on Feuerbach," Marx writes, "The materialist doctrine that men are products of circumstances and upbringing, and that, therefore, changed men are products of changed circumstances and changed upbringing, forgets that it is men who change circumstances and that the educator must himself be educated. Hence this doctrine is bound to divide society into two parts, one of which is superior to society. The coincidence of the changing of circumstances and of human activity or self-change [Selbstveränderung] can be conceived and rationally understood only as revolutionary practice." In Marx and Engels, *German Ideology*, 121. See also Gramsci, *Prison Notebooks*, 350.
91 Gramsci, *Prison Notebooks*, 351.
92 Ibid., 9.
93 Ibid., 8.
94 Ibid., 7.
95 Ibid., 5–6.
96 Ibid., 5.
97 Ibid., 7–8.
98 Ibid., 10. Gramsci writes that the philosopher "Croce in particular feels himself closely linked to Aristotle and Plato, but he does not conceal his links with senators Agnelli and Benni, and it is precisely here that one can discern the most significant character of Croce's philosophy." Ibid., 8.
99 Ibid., 13.
100 Ibid., 11.

101 Political philosopher Joseph Femia notes that Gramsci's ideas about organic intellectuals and other communist elites also help to generate his views on the proper role for political parties. Femia writes, "Thus, Gramsci's concept of hegemony provides the basis for a theory of the revolutionary party. For it falls upon an organized elite of professional revolutionaries and communist intellectuals to instil in the masses the 'critical self-consciousness' which will enable them to overthrow the existing order and develop a morally integrated society based on proletarian, collective principles." Femia, *Gramsci's Political Thought*, 56.

102 Gramsci, *Prison Notebooks*, 9.

103 Gramsci's approach is situated in a Marxist tradition in which questions of epistemology are inherently linked to specific political structures and social location. For example, drawing on nineteenth-century philsopher Georg Hegel's master-slave dialectic, Karl Marx argues in his early writings that the position of the proletariat is unique since its members are the class in "radical chains" and that their potential for insight arises from this particular political location. This approach is also important for feminist "standpoint" epistemology. Marx, *Critique*, 141; Hartsock, "Feminist Standpoint." In this book, I bracket the question of whether subaltern social groups are specially or uniquely positioned to possess certain kinds of knowledge. Instead, I focus on Gramsci's argument that social location and community are relevant (or even essential) for developing common sense and thus that the common sense of different communities will be, indeed, different. Therefore, I suggest, the way that we approach common sense will have political as well as epistemological consequences, and we should be held to account for both kinds of choices.

104 Gramsci, *Prison Notebooks*, 10.

105 Rupert, "Globalising Common Sense," 186, emphasis in original.

106 Section 1 guarantees the rights and freedoms set out in the Charter "subject only to such reasonable limits prescribed by law as can be demonstrably justified in a free and democratic society." This provision sets out the circumstances under which the state can justify the infringement of a Charter right, thus making the infringing law constitutional. Pursuant to section 7, laws that interfere with an individual's "life," "liberty," or "security of the person" must accord with the "principles of fundamental justice" to pass constitutional muster. The

section 7 analysis is not, doctrinally speaking, about *justification* because at this stage a court would be asking whether there is an infringement of a Charter right to begin with. However, the analysis used to determine whether a law is "in accordance with the principles of fundamental justice" and the analysis used to determine whether a law is "demonstrably justified in a free and democratic society" are conceptually similar in several ways. Both modes of analysis require investigation into the relationship between individual rights and broader social objectives, and both acknowledge the evidentiary burden carried by the state to show that an interference with individual rights is constitutionally acceptable. In this book, I use the language of "justification" broadly to capture this balancing under both sections 1 and 7.

107 Choudhry, "So What?"

108 *Harper v. Canada (Attorney General)*, 2004 SCC 33, [2004] 1 SCR 827, para. 79. Examples include the connection between tobacco advertising and tobacco addiction in *RJR-MacDonald Inc. v. Canada (Attorney General)*, [1995] 3 SCR 199, 127 DLR (4th) 1; the connection between pornography and violence against women in *R. v. Butler*, [1992] 1 SCR 452, 89 DLR (4th) 449; and the connection between the publication of election results and the behaviour of voters in *R. v. Bryan*, 2007 SCC 12, [2007] 1 SCR 527.

109 See Schneiderman, "Common Sense and the Charter," 7–8.

110 Wittgenstein, *Philosophical Investigations*, sec. 66.

111 *Chaoulli*, para. 3.

112 Zeliotis and Chaoulli were found not to have sufficient interest in the issues at hand to undertake the litigation as private parties. However, they were granted public interest standing to proceed with the challenge. Ibid., paras 186–9.

113 Justice Marie Deschamps did not address section 7 of the Canadian Charter. Chief Justice Beverley McLachlin and Justice John C. Major found that both life and security of the person were engaged. Ibid., para. 124. Justices Ian Binnie and Louis LeBel found, "Like our colleagues McLachlin C.J. and Major J., we accept the trial judge's conclusion that in *some* circumstances *some* Quebeckers may have their life or 'security of the person' put at risk by the prohibition against private health insurance." Ibid., para. 191, original emphasis.

114 Ibid., paras 101–2.

115 Ibid., para. 102.
116 Ibid., para. 161.
117 Flood and Xavier, "Health Care Rights."
118 Canadian Charter of Rights and Freedoms, sec. 7. See *Chaoulli*, para. 109.
119 *Chaoulli*, paras 136–9, 168, 214.
120 For an older, but still useful, discussion of these issues, see Morgan, "Proof of Facts." For a more recent analysis of the justification context in particular, see Choudhry, "So What?"
121 *Chaoulli*, paras 136–7.
122 Ibid., paras 138–9.
123 Ibid., para. 152.
124 Ibid., para. 150, emphasis added.
125 Ibid., para. 168.
126 Ibid., para. 214. Between the two parts of the quoted passage, this paragraph recites at length the expert credentials of government witnesses, which I reproduce here to demonstrate both the content and rhetorical effect of the passage: "The experts heard by the trial court included Mr. Claude Castonguay, who was Quebec's Minister of Health in 1970 (the [translation] 'father of Quebec health insurance') and who chaired the Commission of Inquiry on Health and Social Welfare, as well as a number of other public health experts, including Dr. Fernand Turcotte, a professor of medicine at Laval University, who holds degrees from the University of Montreal and Harvard and has been certified by the Royal College of Physicians and Surgeons of Canada as a specialist in community medicine; Dr. Howard Bergman, Chief of the Division of Geriatric Medicine at Montreal's Jewish General Hospital, Director of the Division of Geriatric Medicine and a professor in the departments of Internal Medicine and Family Medicine at McGill University, a fellow of the American Geriatrics Society and an associate professor at the University of Montreal in the department of health administration; Dr. Charles J. Wright, a physician specialized in surgery, Director of the Centre for Clinical Epidemiology & Evaluation at the Vancouver Hospital & Health Sciences Centre, and a faculty member of the University of British Columbia and of the British Columbia Office of Health Technology Assessment; Professor Jean-Louis Denis, a community health doctor of the University of Montreal's [translation] 'health services

organization'; Professor Theodore R. Marmor, a professor of public policy and management and of political science at Yale University, who holds a PhD from Harvard University in politics and history and is a graduate research fellow at Oxford; and Dr. J. Edwin Coffey, a graduate of McGill University in medicine who specializes in obstetrics and gynecology, a fellow of the Royal College of Physicians and Surgeons of Canada and of the American College of Obstetricians and Gynecologists, and a former associate professor in the McGill University Faculty of Medicine."

127 The recitation of expert qualifications also harkens back to Reid's idea that common sense is a type of knowledge that can be contrasted with expert knowledge.

128 Choudhry, "So What?" 533.

129 Petter, "Wealthcare."

130 For example, McLachlin and Major invoke the interests of "the vast majority of Canadians (middle-income and low-income earners)" to support the idea that private medical insurance should be allowed, as only the wealthiest Canadians can afford to pay for private medical care out of pocket. *Chaoulli*, para. 137. At the same time, the majority judgment does not identify the commitment to needs-based (as opposed to wealth-based) access to healthcare as a primary rationale for the legislation and for the public healthcare system as a whole. Thus the judgment is able to align the interests of "the vast majority of Canadians" with access to private insurance, instead of access to public healthcare, and thereby find the legislation arbitrary.

131 Flood and Xavier, *Health Care Rights*, 3.

132 *Sauvé*, para. 2.

133 Ibid., para. 6.

134 Ibid., para. 19.

135 Ibid., paras 22–6.

136 Ibid., paras 53, 56, 62.

137 Ibid., paras 66–7.

138 Ibid., para. 9, emphasis added.

139 Ibid., para. 18.

140 Ibid., para. 49.

141 Ibid., para. 157.

142 Ibid., para. 159.

143 Ibid.

144 Ibid., paras 100, 157.
145 Ibid., para. 90. See also ibid., paras 91, 93.
146 Ibid., para. 101.
147 Mayeda, "Between Principle and Pragmatism."
148 Mayeda writes, "In reading *Sauvé II*, one cannot understand the normative basis for rejecting the government's explicit or implicit goals. Chief Justice McLachlin does not reject the goals of enhancing civic responsibility, respect for law and imposing additional punishment on prisoners put forward by the government. Instead, she dismisses them as vague and symbolic goals that belie the government's real, unstated objectives. But the Court never explains what these unstated objectives are or why they are illegitimate. At the very least, one could have expected the Court to explain the principled arguments for and against allowing prisoners to vote and explaining why the principles that favour denying such a vote are unjustifiable based on cogent reasons acceptable in the contemporary public forum." Ibid., 54.
149 Ibid., 51.
150 *Sauvé*, para. 18.
151 Réaume, "Dignity, Equality and Second Generation," 286.
152 McLachlin does note the "crisis" of the disproportionate incarceration of Aboriginal peoples in relation to the proportionality analysis. *Sauvé*, para. 60.
153 Réaume, "Dignity, Equality and Second Generation," 286.
154 For further discussion of the limitations of the concept of stereotypes in equality law, see Young, "Unequal to the Task."
155 Brodsky, "*Gosselin*."
156 *Gosselin*, para. 27, emphasis added.
157 Ibid., para. 56, emphasis added.
158 *Chaoulli*, para. 150.
159 *Sauvé*, para. 18.
160 *Gosselin*, para. 27.
161 Dauvergne, "Adult Correctional Statistics."
162 Collin and Jensen, "Statistical Profile."
163 Critical race legal scholar Neil Gotanda argues that common sense about race operates to perpetuate racism, including when it functions as an evidentiary methodology in a courtroom. Gotanda, "'Common Sense' of Race."
164 *Gosselin*, para. 44, emphasis added.

165 Ibid., para. 42.
166 See Young, "Unequal to the Task," 192–3.
167 Brodsky, "*Gosselin*," 205.
168 Ibid., 207. Note that the plural "claimants" in this quotation refers to the fact that the *Gosselin* case was framed as a class action lawsuit.
169 Kim and Piper, "*Gosselin v. Quebec*," 777.
170 Through the notion of hegemony, Gramsci shows us how such stereotypical views would come to be held not only by members of dominant classes but also by others, including people of the middle and working classes and even people living in poverty.
171 For example, see Young, "Unequal to the Task."
172 Michel Foucault argues much more broadly that power and knowledge are inherently linked; the study, classification, and interpretation of people can work to constitute and facilitate oppression. For example, see Foucault, *History of Sexuality*.
173 Gramsci expected that organic intellectuals from subaltern groups, such as unionists, feminist scholars, artists, and journalists, would lead the way in this process. Gramsci, *Prison Notebooks*, 14–16, 340.
174 McIntyre, "Supreme Court and Section 15," 744–5.
175 Ibid., 764.
176 Ibid., 760.

CHAPTER FOUR

1 Fielding, *Pasquin*, act 5, scene 1.
2 D'Entreves, "Hannah Arendt."
3 Gramsci, *Prison Notebooks*, 9.
4 *R. v. S.(R.D.)*, [1997] 3 SCR 484, 151 DLR (4th) 193 [*R.D.S.*].
5 *Gosselin v. Quebec (Procureur général)*, 2002 SCC 84, [2002] 4 SCR 429.
6 Pitkin, "Justice."
7 Nedelsky, "Communities of Judgment," 247.
8 Arendt's appropriation of Kant is controversial. It is addressed in this book only to the extent that questions about Arendt's reliance on Kant are linked to larger questions about her own theory of judgment. See Beiner, "Rereading Hannah"; Garsten, *Saving Persuasion*, 101; and Norris, "Arendt, Kant."

9 Arendt, "Crisis in Culture."
10 Arendt, *Lectures*, 66.
11 Ibid., 13. Ronald Beiner summarizes this aspect of Arendt's interpretation of judgment when he writes, "[T]his is what judgment means: to size up the unique particular that stands before one, rather than trying to subsume it under some universal scheme or interpretation of a pregiven set of categories." Beiner, "Rereading Hannah," 99.
12 Arendt, *Lectures*, 13.
13 Ibid., 4.
14 Ibid., 15, 66. Focusing on the link between aesthetic judgment and other forms of judgment, such as moral or political judgment, is the subject of considerable debate. For example, see Ferguson, *Politics of Judgment*, which explores the advantages of this approach, and Kateb, "Judgment of Arendt," which focuses on the risks of characterizing political judgment as fundamentally aesthetic.
15 Nedelsky describes a number of examples of reflective judgment and their relationship to the common sense of various communities. For example, in relation to the common sense of the feminist community, she provides a sustained exploration of reaching a judgment about the fashion choice to wear high-heeled shoes. Nedelsky uses this example to explore those aspects of judgment that are about politics, autonomy, self-knowledge, and community building. See Nedelsky, "Reciprocal Relation," 36–7.
16 Arendt, *Lectures*, 42–3.
17 Ibid., 66, 69.
18 Ibid., 71–2. Kant rejected resort to "common sense" when understood to mean simply the views of ordinary people, and he specifically criticized Reid for so doing. When describing judgment, Kant instead used the Latin phrase *sensus communis*. Arendt, too, uses this language, as well as the English translation "community sense," but as noted here, she also uses the English phrase "common sense." See summary in ibid., 72.
19 Ibid., 73.
20 Ibid., 72.
21 Note the way that Arendt's approach begins to collapse the distinction between "judgment" and "valid judgment" since a judgment that fails to critically engage with common sense is not just a poor or invalid judgment; it is not really a judgment at all. In a sense, this view

is reminiscent of Reid's insistence that following a philosophical "system" or set of rules does not really count as "judgment."

22 In this regard, Arendt is following Kant.

23 Arendt provides little detail about what precisely is required for this act of imagination. However, it is significant that for Arendt there are important differences between imagining someone else's views and imagining my own views in another's place. Nedelsky, "Reciprocal Relation," 54. Further, interpreters differ about how best to understand Arendt's notion of imagination and about how best to extend or critique this idea. For example, see Zerilli, "Toward a Feminist Theory"; Zerilli, "Response to Thiele"; and Thiele, "Judging Hannah Arendt."

24 Arendt, *Lectures*, 43. Arendt also says that the role of the imagination is to provide examples for judgment. Ibid., 80.

25 Ibid., 66.

26 Ibid., 43.

27 Ibid., 69, 72.

28 Ibid., 43.

29 Unpublished lecture by Arendt, quoted in Beiner, "Hannah Arendt on Judging," 107.

30 Arendt, *Lectures*, 43.

31 This aspect of judgment is essential for Arendt and is part of her thinking on the Holocaust and the trial of Adolf Eichmann. In that context, Arendt's focus was on the problem of thoughtlessness as opposed to reflective judgment. Arendt, *Eichmann*. See also Bilsky, "When Actor and Spectator."

32 Nedelsky, "Reciprocal Relation," 45.

33 Arendt describes this as "exemplary" validity. Arendt, *Lectures*, 76. Jerome Kohn, speaking specifically about Kant, notes that reflective judgment has "exemplary" rather than "apodictic" validity. Kohn, "Reflecting on Judgment," 271. Nedelsky notes that for Kant our common sense is based on universal cognitive capacities, making genuine judgments universally valid. For Arendt, judgment is connected to actual communities. Nedelsky, "Communities of Judgment," 250–1.

34 Arendt, "Crisis in Culture," 20.

35 For an exploration of how these three concepts relate in Arendt's thought, see Nedelsky, "Communities of Judgment."

36 Arendt, *Lectures*, 69.

37 Kant's categorical imperative has this characteristic. See Arendt, "Crisis in Culture," 19.

38 Arendt, *Lectures*, 20.

39 Gramsci's approach to common sense is also about persuasion in the sense that he recognizes the need to engage people on all levels so that they can come to understand the disconnect between dominant common sense and the reality of their lives.

40 Arendt, *Lectures*, 72. The persuasive as opposed to compulsory or coercive nature of judgment is important for Arendt because these are characteristics important for the sphere of political exchange that is the target of her analysis.

41 Garsten, *Saving Persuasion*.

42 Zerilli, "'We Feel Our Freedom,'" 171.

43 The idea of persuasion and rhetoric, including the role of common sense, has a long and rich history as a topic of philosophical and political conversation. In the context of my study, it is noteworthy that advocates of rhetoric and the art of persuasion as legitimate political speech connect good judgment with communities in a similar way that "common sense" does. Advocating for the value of rhetoric also opens many of the same concerns about power imbalances and conservatism. For example, see Garsten, *Saving Persuasion*; and Aune, "Review of *Saving Persuasion*."

44 Garsten, *Saving Persuasion*, 102.

45 Nedelsky, "Communities of Judgment," 265. This interpretation allows Arendt to address some of the concerns about power and context that are central to Gramsci's account. For a critique of this interpretation of Arendt, see Degryse, "Sensus communis."

46 Arendt, *Lectures*, 40. It is noteworthy that this is one of the fronts on which Arendt's appropriation of Kant is most controversial. For my purposes, it is sufficient to note that Arendt, regardless of whether her interpretation of Kant is a good one, prefers a formulation in which the community of reference is a real and empirical one, not a universal, abstract, or transcendent one. On this theme, Arendt's use of masculine pronouns to describe the scope of a community is worthy of interrogation.

47 Young, "Asymmetrical Reciprocity"; Benhabib, "Judgment."

48 Nedelsky, "Reciprocal Relation," 54.

49 Arendt, "Crisis in Culture," 20.

50 Arendt, *Lectures*, 44.

51 Unpublished lecture by Arendt, cited in Beiner, "Hannah Arendt on Judging," 107.

52 It is important to note that Arendt's body of work as a whole is deeply ambiguous when it comes to questions about gender, justice, and feminism as well as social justice and poverty. Arendt's own theories contain a number of concepts and approaches that are problematic from a feminist perspective, such as a form of public-private divide, devaluation of the physical body, and women's labour in the household. For example, consider Arendt's action-work-labour hierarchy and the sharp distinction between the social and the political in her book *The Human Condition*. At the same time, some feminists have found Arendt's work both substantively and methodologically useful. For discussion of these issues, see Honig, ed., *Feminist Interpretations*; and Pitkin, *Attack of the Blob*.

53 Nedelsky, "Reciprocal Relation," 45.

54 Ibid., 42.

55 Ibid. This approach would contrast with, for example, a simplistic version of "standpoint feminism."

56 Ibid., 43.

57 Ibid., 54.

58 Ibid.

59 Young, "Asymmetrical Reciprocity."

60 Ibid., 206.

61 Ibid., 223. Arendt's notion of plurality is also ambiguously situated in relation to feminism and social justice. For Arendt, respect for human plurality is extremely important. Human plurality relates to "the fact that men, not Man, live on the earth and inhabit the world." Plurality is the condition of human action "because we are all the same, that is, human, in such a way that nobody is ever the same as anyone else who ever lived, lives, or will live." Arendt, *Human Condition*, 7–8. But her idea of plurality is an individual one, and her focus is not on equality but on freedom. For one discussion of how this affects her take on law, see Bohman, "Moral Costs."

62 Young, "Asymmetrical Reciprocity," 225.

63 Seyla Benhabib takes a similar approach in her engagement with Arendt as a way to think about politics and public space. Benhabib, "Judgment."

64 Nedelsky, "Communities of Judgment," 265.
65 Ibid., 265.
66 Reid, *Essays*, 530.
67 Arendt, *Lectures*, 70.
68 Arendt, "Crisis in Culture," 20–1.
69 Ibid., 22. See also Zerilli, "'We Feel Our Freedom,'" 179.
70 Nedelsky, "Reciprocal Relation," 44. See also Snir, "Bringing Plurality Together."
71 Kohn, "Reflecting on Judgment."
72 Rasch, "Judgment," 102.
73 Ibid., 102–3.
74 Arendt, "Crisis in Culture," 22.
75 Nedelsky, "Reciprocal Relation," 43.
76 Arendt, *Lectures*, 74, emphasis in original.
77 Zerilli, "'We Feel Our Freedom'"; Zerilli, "Toward a Feminist Theory."
78 Cited in Thiele, "Judging Hannah Arendt," 707.
79 Nedelsky, "Reciprocal Relation," 51.
80 Zerilli, "'We Feel Our Freedom,'" 181. For a debate between feminist political theorist Linda Zerilli and political scientist Leslie Paul Thiele about the extent to which Arendt's judgment is all about creating openness and freedom as opposed to finding persuasive narratives/examples based on common sense, see ibid.; Thiele, "Judging Hannah Arendt"; and Zerilli, "Toward a Feminist Theory."
81 These major themes appear throughout Arendt's work, but all play an important role in her book *The Human Condition*.
82 Zerilli, "'We Feel Our Freedom,'" 165, emphasis in original.
83 Arendt, *Eichmann*.
84 Arendt, "Reflections on Little Rock." For critical discussion of Arendt's controversial essay "Reflections on Little Rock" and reactions to it, see Bohman, "Moral Costs." Bohman focuses on the ways that this essay reflects Arendt's commitment to her notion of plurality.
85 For example, see the essays in Goldoni and McCorkindale, eds, *Hannah Arendt and the Law*.
86 Beiner and Nedelsky, "Introduction," xii.
87 Nedelsky, "Communities of Judgment," 248.
88 Ibid. Nedelsky has explored the usefulness of Arendt's theory of judgment for law in a number of her texts, including "Embodied

Diversity," "Communities of Judgment," "Judgment, Diversity," *Law's Relations*, and "Reciprocal Relation."

89 For example, in their discussion of judicial impartiality in *R.D.S.* (discussed below), the majority of the Supreme Court of Canada, citing the Canadian Judicial Council with approval, wrote, "The requirement for neutrality does not require judges to discount the very life experiences that may so well qualify them to preside over disputes. It has been observed that the duty to be impartial 'does not mean that a judge does not, or cannot bring to the bench many existing sympathies, antipathies or attitudes. There is no human being who is not the product of every social experience, every process of education, and every human contact with those with whom we share the planet. Indeed, even if it were possible, a judge free of this heritage of past experience would probably lack the very qualities of humanity required of a judge. Rather, the wisdom required of a judge is to recognize, consciously allow for, and perhaps to question, all the baggage of past attitudes and sympathies that fellow citizens are free to carry, untested, to the grave. True impartiality does not require that the judge have no sympathies or opinions; it requires that the judge nevertheless be free to entertain and act upon different points of view with an open mind.'" *R.D.S.*, para. 119, quoting Canadian Judicial Council, *Commentaries on Judicial Conduct*, 12.

90 Nedelsky argues that "[l]aw, in particular, needs an articulation of the nature of judgment, with its irreducible element of subjectivity, that can sustain the core values of the rule of law." Nedelsky, "Communities of Judgment," 247. Nedelsky also discusses how this apparent dilemma of judicial subjectivity arises in the context of debates about diversity on the bench. Nedelsky, "Judgment, Diversity," 113. See also Webber, "Judicial Ethic."

91 Scholars who discuss the idea that legal decision making should be understood as a form of reflective judgment also engage with Kant directly, as well as with thinkers in the rhetorical tradition, such as Giambattista Vico. See Edlin, "Kant and the Common Law"; Kohn, "Reflecting on Judgment"; Mootz, "Vico and Imagination"; Meyer, "Between Reason and Power"; and Rasch, "Judgment." For an approach that frames law as a form of rhetoric itself, see White, "Law as Rhetoric." For a feminist analysis of how the rhetorical strategies at

play in a courtroom relate to experiences of oppression, see White, "Subordination."

92 Arendt, *Lectures*, 84.

93 Mayeda, "Uncommonly Common."

94 Ibid., 121.

95 Nedelsky, "Communities of Judgment," 251.

96 Berger, "Trial by Metaphor."

97 The way different communities are situated with respect to law can also be related to legitimacy using theoretical frameworks other than judgment. For a relational account of legitimate authority, drawing on theories of authority and legal pluralism, see Roughan, *Authorities*.

98 Mayeda, "Uncommonly Common," 122, emphasis added. Here, Mayeda draws attention to the fact that people who are legally members of the political community may nonetheless be excluded from the community of judgment to whom a legal judgment is addressed.

99 Nedelsky, "Judgment, Diversity," 114; Edlin, "Kant and the Common Law," 440–1.

100 Omatsu, "Fiction of Judicial Impartiality."

101 Nedelsky, "Embodied Diversity," 107–8.

102 A leading case in this area is *Committee for Justice and Liberty et al. v. National Energy Board et al.*, [1978] 1 SCR 369, 1976 CanLII 2 (SCC).

103 Ibid., para. 53.

104 It is rare for allegations of judicial bias to receive this level of judicial review, including when judges with race privilege make much more deeply problematic comments. See Razack, "*R.D.S.*"

105 *R.D.S.*, para. 111.

106 For discussion of the issue of "generalizations" in legal judgment and in this case in particular, see Boyle et al., "*R. v. R.D.S.*"

107 *R.D.S.*, paras 6–10.

108 Ibid., para. 30.

109 Ibid., paras 128–9.

110 Ibid., para. 111, underlining in original.

111 Ibid., para. 95.

112 Ibid., para. 42.

113 The reality of anti-black racism in Canada, and in Toronto specifically, was the subject of judicial notice in *R. v. Parks* (1993), 24 CR (4th) 81,

65 OAC 122 (ON CA), leave to appeal refused by *R. v. Parks*, [1994] 1 SCR x.

114 *R.D.S.*, para. 47.

115 Ibid., paras 56, 59.

116 Ibid., para. 48.

117 See the useful discussion of this issue in Boyle et al., "*R. v. R.D.S.*"

118 Reflecting this focus on process as essential to judicial impartiality, Mayeda argues that impartiality comes "from ensuring that judges engage with principles that the community and the particular litigants in the case would recognize as valid. Impartiality derives from the *process* of engaging with principle, not from the espousal of any particular principle." Mayeda, "Between Principle and Pragmatism," 47.

119 Boyle et al., "*R. v. R.D.S.*," 188–9. Other feminist scholars also take the view that the best understanding of judicial impartiality generates a positive obligation to seek out knowledge, especially when the judge is situated in a position of relative privilege. For example, see Boyle and MacCrimmon, "To Serve the Cause"; Feldthusen, "Gender Wars"; Hughes, "New Direction?"; Omatsu, "Fiction of Judicial Impartiality"; and McIntyre, "Studied Ignorance."

120 Razack, "*R.D.S.*"

121 Ibid., 282–3, emphasis in original.

122 Ibid., 284. Schneiderman also notes the rhetorical power of courts to "certify reality" through their invocation of "common sense." Schneiderman, "Common Sense and the Charter," 7.

123 Razack describes how these discourses work to create identity on a more individual level. She writes, "Without gambling Chinese and emotional Black women partial to their own people and biased against white police officers, there would be no reasonable and impartial white men." She also notes the way that these ideas are rooted at a deep emotional level. Razack, "*R.D.S.*," 286, 292.

124 *Gosselin*, para. 27, emphasis added.

125 Ibid., paras 131–3.

126 Ibid., para. 130, emphasis added.

127 In his discussion of law and reflective judgment, Rasch summarizes the practice of judgment in this way: "As a judge, one decides a case with a sidelong glance at the way one assumes another judge would also decide. The other judge in question is an empirically real judge, not an ideal construct (for that would duplicate the gesture of

subsumption that Schmitt aims to avoid), but we do not determine what that other judge would do by polling the other's opinion. In asserting that our decision would also have been made by another practicing judge, we are not engaged in a sociological or a mass-psychological exercise ... Rather, our act re-mains normative." Rasch, "Judgment," 101.

128 Boyle and MacCrimmon, "To Serve the Cause."

129 For a different discussion of how complex judging practices are already practised, see Cossman and Schneiderman, "Beyond Intersecting Rights."

CHAPTER FIVE

1 Gordon Baker writes that "there is clearly no commitment whatever to the idea that perspicuous representations must be (even roughly) additive ... There is no more reason to suppose that perspicuous representations are additive than to claim that the successive seeing of two different visual aspects in the duck-rabbit diagram can be combined into a single visual experience of seeing both aspects at once." Baker, "Philosophical Investigations," 7.

2 Wittgenstein, *Philosophical Investigations*, sec. 122.

3 Demonstrating the need to engage with, rather than reject, the language of "common sense," Boaventura de Sousa Santos calls for a "new legal common sense" in his work on law and globalization. Santos, *Toward a New Legal*.

4 *Gosselin v. Quebec (Procureur général)*, 2002 SCC 84, [2002] 4 SCR 429.

5 Coates, *Claims of Common Sense*, 17. In a lecture at the Faculty of Law, University of British Columbia, Justice Lynn Smith also invoked the idea that judges might think of themselves as "experts in common sense" and the possibility that such expertise might require judges to critically reflect on and actively develop their common sense. Smith, "What Can Judges Know?" See also Snir, "Experts of Common Sense."

6 Rosenfeld, *Common Sense*, 62.

7 Gramsci, *Prison Notebooks*, 5–8.

8 Ibid., 347. It is interesting to note that Arendt also describes the legal

profession as sitting somewhere between theory and practice: "For Kant, the 'middle term' that links and provides a transition from theory to practice is judgment; he had in mind the practitioner – for example, the doctor or lawyer, who first learns theory and then practices medicine or law, and whose practice consists in applying the rules he has learned to particular cases." Arendt, *Lectures*, 36.

9 Gramsci, *Prison Notebooks*, 347.

10 Ibid.

11 Ibid., 232.

12 Arendt, *Lectures*, 42.

13 Ibid., 44.

14 The notion of intellectual humility can be related directly to power. For example, Davina Cooper argues that people with the capacity to exercise power can choose to decline to do so. Cooper, *Challenging Diversity*, 80.

15 Mayeda argues that legal judgment can be made more transparent through engagement with "principled reasoning," which does engage with politics. For example, in relation to *Sauvé*, he argues that McLachlin's refusal to engage directly with the political questions at hand reduced the transparency of that judgment. Mayeda, "Between Principle and Pragmatism," 54.

16 Mayeda argues that the invocation of "common sense" can actually be a sign that a judge has specifically declined to engage in this kind of political reasoning. Ibid., 46. Overall, Mayeda's description of "principled reasoning" fits well with the conclusions in this book; the contrast lies with the fact that I focus on the ways that common sense can be part of that project rather than lying outside it.

17 Legal scholar Jean-François Gaudreault-DesBiens argues that judges must sometimes decide between alternative understandings of history. He writes, "Choices, often hard ones, underlie the constitution of historical memory." Gaudreault-DesBiens, "Quebec Secession," 798.

18 Linda Zerilli argues that the difficulty with some political-theoretical problems (e.g., those surrounding the category "woman") is not about knowledge or information but about "a problem of the will." Zerilli, "Doing without Knowing," 143.

19 Scheman, "Introduction," 20.

20 Brems, *Diversity*; Hunter, McGlynn, and Rackley, *Feminist Judgments*; University of Queensland, "Australian Feminist Judgments Project"; Majury, "Introducing the Women's Court."

21 For example, the Women's Court of Canada describes itself in the following terms: "The Women's Court of Canada is an innovative project bringing together academics, activists, and litigators in order literally to rewrite the Canadian Charter of Rights and Freedoms equality jurisprudence. Taking inspiration from Oscar Wilde, who once said 'the only duty we owe to history is to rewrite it,' the Women's Court operates as a virtual court, and 'reconsiders' leading equality decisions. The Women's Court renders alternative decisions as a means of articulating fresh conceptions of substantive equality." Women's Court of Canada, "Women's Court of Canada," 1.

22 Cochran, "Notes on 'Judicial Edgework.'"

23 Majury, "Introducing the Women's Court," 10.

24 Northern/Irish Feminist Judgments Project, http://www.feministjudging.ie.

25 Cochran, "Notes on 'Judicial Edgework.'"

26 Nedelsky points out that the diversity of the bench begins with the diversity of law schools, and it is beginning with law school that legal practitioners begin to "practise" the act of judging by justifying their conclusions to legal colleagues. Nedelsky, "Embodied Diversity," 108.

27 Nedelsky, "Reciprocal Relation," 54.

28 Brodsky et al., "*Gosselin*," 212.

29 Ibid., 213.

30 Arendt, *Lectures*, 43.

31 Nedelsky, "Communities of Judgment," 265.

32 Gramsci, *Prison Notebooks*, 9.

Bibliography

LEGISLATION

Canadian Charter of Rights and Freedoms, Part 1 of the Constitution Act, 1982, being Schedule B of the Canada Act, 1982 (UK), c. 11.

CASES

Alden v. Gaglardi et al., [1973] SCR 199, 1972 CanLII 140 (SCC).

Baker v. Canada, [1999] 2 SCR 817, 174 DLR (4th) 193.

Chaoulli v. Quebec (Attorney General), 2005 SCC 35, [2005] 1 SCR 791.

Committee for Justice and Liberty et al. v. National Energy Board et al., [1978] 1 SCR 369, 1976 CanLII 2 (SCC).

Eldridge v. British Columbia (Attorney General), [1997] 3 SCR 624, 151 DLR (4th) 577.

Falkiner v. Ontario (Director of Income Maintenance, Ministry of Community & Social Services) (2002), 212 DLR (4th) 633, 59 OR (3d) 481 (ON CA)..

Federated Anti-Poverty Groups of BC v. Vancouver (City), 2002 BCSC 105, 40 Admin LR (3d) 159.

Finlay v. Canada (Minister of Finance), [1993] 1 SCR 1080, 101 DLR (4th) 567.

Gosselin v. Quebec (Procureur général), 2002 SCC 84, [2002] 4 SCR 429.

Harper v. Canada (Attorney General), 2004 SCC 33, [2004] 1 SCR 827.

Lovelace v. Ontario, 2000 SCC 37, [2000] 1 SCR 950.

MacDonald v. MacDonald, [1976] 2 SCR 259, 1975 CanLII 28 (SCC).

New Brunswick (Minister of Health and Community Services) v. G.(J.), [1999] 3 SCR 46, 177 DLR (4th) 124.

Quebec (Attorney General) v. A., 2013 SCC 5, [2013] 1 SCR 61.

Quebec (Attorney General) v. Canada, 2011 SCC 11, [2011] 1 SCR 368.
R. v. Banks (2007), 275 DLR (4th) 640, 84 OR (3d) 1 (ON CA).
R. v. Bryan, 2007 SCC 12, [2007] 1 SCR 527.
R. v. Butler, [1992] 1 SCR 452, 89 DLR (4th) 449.
R. v. D.D., 2000 SCC 43, [2000] 2 SCR 275.
R. v. Hamilton (2003), 8 CR (6th) 215, 172 CCC (3d) 114 (ON Sup Ct J).
R. v. Khela, 2009 SCC 4, [2009] 1 SCR 104.
R. v. Lifchus, [1997] 3 SCR 320, 150 DLR (4th) 733.
R. v. Marquard, [1993] 4 SCR 223, 108 DLR (4th) 47.
R. v. Mohan, [1994] 2 SCR 9, 114 DLR (4th) 419.
R. v. Parks (1993), 24 CR (4th) 81, 65 OAC 122 (ON CA)
R. v. Parks, [1994] 1 SCR x.
R. v. S.(R.D.), [1997] 3 SCR 484, 151 DLR (4th) 193.
R. v. Walle, 2012 SCC 41, [2012] 2 SCR 438.
RJR-MacDonald Inc. v. Canada (Attorney General), [1995] 3 SCR 199, 127 DLR (4th) 1.
Sauvé v. Canada (Chief Electoral Officer), 2002 SCC 68, [2002] 3 SCR 519.
Snell v. Farrell, [1990] 2 SCR 311, 72 DLR (4th) 289.
Tranchemontagne v. Ontario (Director, Disability Support Program), 2006 SCC 14, [2006] 1 SCR 513.
Vetrovec v. The Queen, [1982] 1 SCR 811, 136 DLR (3d) 89.

SECONDARY SOURCES

Allen, Ronald A. "Common Sense, Rationality, and the Legal Process." *Cardozo Law Review* 22, nos 5–6 (2000): 1417–31.
Allen, Walter E. "Henry Fielding." In *Encyclopaedia Britannica*. https://www.britannica.com/biography/Henry-Fielding.
Arbour, Louise. "'Freedom from Want': From Charity to Entitlement." LaFontaine-Baldwin Lecture, 2005. https://www.icc-icc.ca/site/site/uploads/2016/11/LaFontaineBaldwinLecture2005_LouiseArbour.pdf.
Arendt, Hannah. "The Crisis in Culture." In *Judgment, Imagination and Politics: Themes from Kant and Arendt*, ed. Jennifer Nedelsky and Ronald Beiner, 3–25. Lanham, MD: Rowan and Littlefield, 2001.

– *Eichmann in Jerusalem: A Report on the Banality of Evil*. London: Penguin, 2006.
– *The Human Condition*. Chicago: University of Chicago Press, 1958.
– *Lectures on Kant's Political Philosophy*. Ed. Ronald Beiner. Chicago: University of Chicago Press, 1982.
– "Reflections on Little Rock." In *Responsibility and Judgment*, ed. Jerome Kohn, 193–213. New York: Schocken Books, 2003.
Aune, James Arnt. "Review of *Saving Persuasion: A Defense of Rhetoric and Judgment*, by Bryan Garsten." *Philosophy and Rhetoric* 41, no. 1 (2008): 94–9.
Austin, J.L. *How to Do Things with Words*. Oxford: Clarendon, 1962.
Bakan, Joel. *Just Words: Constitutional Rights and Social Wrongs*. Toronto: University of Toronto Press, 1997.
Baker, Gordon P. "Philosophical Investigations S. 122: Neglected Aspects." In *Wittgenstein's Method: Neglected Aspects*, ed. Gordon P. Baker and Katherine J. Morris, 22–51. Malden, MA: Blackwell, 2004.
Bala, Nicholas. "Double Victims: Child Sexual Abuse and the Canadian Criminal Justice System." *Queen's Law Journal* 15, nos 1–2 (1990): 3–32.
Beiner, Ronald. "Hannah Arendt on Judging." In Hannah Arendt, *Lectures on Kant's Political Philosophy*, ed. Ronald Beiner, 89–156. Chicago: University of Chicago Press, 1982.
– "Rereading Hannah Arendt's Kant Lectures." In *Judgment, Imagination and Politics: Themes from Kant and Arendt*, ed. Jennifer Nedelsky and Ronald Beiner, 91–101. Lanham, MD: Rowan and Littlefield, 2001.
Beiner, Ronald, and Jennifer Nedelsky. "Introduction." In *Judgment, Imagination and Politics: Themes from Kant and Arendt*, ed. Jennifer Nedelsky and Ronald Beiner, vii–xxvi. Lanham, MD: Rowan and Littlefield, 2001.
Benhabib, Seyla. "Judgment and the Moral Foundations of Politics in Hannah Arendt's Thought." In *Judgment, Imagination and Politics: Themes from Kant and Arendt*, ed. Jennifer Nedelsky and Ronald Beiner, 183–204. Lanham, MD: Rowan and Littlefield, 2001.

Berger, Benjamin L. "Trial by Metaphor: Rhetoric, Innovation, and the Juridical Text." *Court Review: The Journal of the American Judges Association* 39, no. 3 (2002): 30–8.

Bilsky, Leora Y. "When Actor and Spectator Meet in the Courtroom: Reflections on Hannah Arendt's Concept of Judgment." In *Judgment, Imagination and Politics: Themes from Kant and Arendt*, ed. Jennifer Nedelsky and Ronald Beiner, 257–85. Lanham, MD: Rowan and Littlefield, 2001.

Bohman, James. "The Moral Costs of Political Pluralism: The Dilemmas of Difference and Equality in Arendt's 'Reflections on Little Rock.'" In *Hannah Arendt: Twenty Years Later*, ed. Larry May and Jerome Kohn, 53–80. Cambridge, MA: MIT Press, 1997.

Boulter, Stephen. *The Rediscovery of Common Sense Philosophy*. London: Palgrave Macmillan, 2007.

Boyd, Susan B. "Some Postmodernist Challenges to Feminist Analyses of Law, Family and State: Ideology and Discourse in Child Cutody Law." *Canadian Journal of Family Law* 10 (1991): 79–113.

Boyle, Christine, Brenna Bhandar, Constance Backhouse, Marilyn MacCrimmon, and Audrey Kobayashi. "*R. v. R.D.S.*: An Editor's Forum." *Canadian Journal of Women and the Law* 10, no. 1 (1998): 159–63.

Boyle, Christine, and Marilyn MacCrimmon. "To Serve the Cause of Justice: Disciplining Fact Determination." *Windsor Yearbook of Access to Justice* 20 (2001): 55–85.

Brems, Eva. *Diversity and European Human Rights: Rewriting Judgments of the ECHR*. Cambridge, UK: Cambridge University Press, 2012.

Broadie, Alexander. *The Scottish Enlightenment: An Anthology*. Edinburgh: Canongate Classics, 1997.

Brodsky, Gwen. "*Gosselin v. Quebec*: Autonomy with a Vengeance." *Canadian Journal of Women and the Law* 15, no. 1 (2003): 194–214.

Brodsky, Gwen, Melissa Buckley, Shelagh Day, and Margot Young. "Human Rights Denied: Single Mothers on Social Assistance in British Columbia." 2006. http://www.westcoastleaf.org/wp-content/

uploads/2014/10/2006-REPORT-Human-Rights-Denied-Single-Mothers-on-Social-Assistance-in-British-Columbia.pdf.

Brodsky, Gwen, Rachel Cox, Shelagh Day, and Kate Stephenson. "*Gosselin v. Québec (Attorney General)*." *Canadian Journal of Women and the Law* 18, no. 1 (2006): 193–249.

Canada Without Poverty. http://www.cwp-csp.ca.

Canadian Centre for Policy Alternatives. "Fact Sheets on Women's Poverty." http://www.policyalternatives.ca/publications/commentary/fact-sheets-womens-poverty-recession.

Canadian Council on Social Development. "Economic Security Fact Sheet #2: Poverty." http://www.ccsd.ca/factsheets/economic_security/poverty/index.htm.

Canadian Judicial Council. *Commentaries on Judicial Conduct*. Cowansville, QC: Yvon Blais, 1991.

– *Ethical Principles for Judges*. Ottawa: Canadian Judicial Council, 2011. http://www.cjc-ccm.gc.ca/cmslib/general/news_pub_judicialconduct_Principles_en.pdf.

Cannon, Martin J., and Lina Sunseri, eds. *Racism, Colonialism, and Indigeneity in Canada: A Reader*. Don Mills, ON: Oxford University Press, 2011.

Carter, Peter. "Do Courts Decide According to the Evidence?" *University of British Columbia Law Review* 22 (1988): 351–67.

Chakrabarty, Dipesh. *Provincializing Europe: Postcolonial Thought and Historical Difference*. Princeton, NJ: Princeton University Press, 2000.

Choudhry, Sujit. "So What Is the Real Legacy of Oakes? Two Decades of Proportionality Analysis under the Canadian Charter's Section 1." *Supreme Court Law Review* 34 (2006): 501–35.

Coates, John. *The Claims of Common Sense: Moore, Wittgenstein, Keynes and the Social Sciences*. Cambridge, UK: Cambridge University Press, 1996.

Cochran, Patricia. "Notes on 'Judicial Edgework: Judgment Re-writing Projects from Around the World,' Roundtable Discussion at 'Law on the Edge,' Annual Meeting of the Canadian Law and Society Association and the Law and Society Association of Australia and New Zealand, University of British Columbia, 2 July 2013." Unpublished.

Collin, Chantal, and Hilary Jensen. "A Statistical Profile of Poverty In Canada." Library of Parliament, 2009. http://www.parl.gc.ca/content/lop/researchpublications/prb0917-e.htm.

Conservative Party of Ontario. "Common Sense Revolution." https://www.scribd.com/doc/57099326/Common-Sense-Revolution.

Cooper, Davina. *Challenging Diversity: Rethinking Equality and the Value of Difference*. Cambridge, UK: Cambridge University Press, 2004.

Cossman, Brenda, and David Schneiderman. "Beyond Intersecting Rights: The Constitutional Judge as Complex Self." *University of Toronto Law Journal* 57, no. 2 (2007): 431–48.

Crenshaw, Kimberle. "Mapping the Margins: Intersectionality, Identity Politics, and Violence against Women of Color." *Stanford Law Review* 43, no. 6 (1991): 1241–99.

Cunliffe, Emma. "Without Fear or Favour? Trends and Possibilities in the Canadian Approach to Expert Human Behaviour Evidence." *International Journal of Evidence and Proof* 10 (2006): 280–315.

Dauvergne, Mia. "Adult Correctional Statistics in Canada, 2010/2011." Statistics Canada, 2012. http://www.statcan.gc.ca/pub/85-002-x/2012001/article/11715-eng.htm#a7.

Degryse, Annelies. "Sensus communis as a Foundation for Men as Political Beings: Arendt's Reading of Kant's Critique of Judgment." *Philosophy and Social Criticism* 37, no. 3 (2011): 345–58.

D'Entreves, Maurizio Passerin. "Hannah Arendt." In *The Stanford Encyclopedia of Philosophy*, ed. Edward N. Zalta. Fall 2008. http://plato.stanford.edu/archives/fall2008/entries/arendt.

Devlin, Richard F., A. Wayne MacKay, and Natasha Kim. "Reducing the Democratic Deficit: Representation, Diversity and the Canadian Judiciary, or Towards a 'Triple P' Judiciary." *Alberta Law Review* 38, no. 3 (2000): 734–811.

Dua, Enakshi, and Angela Robertson, eds. *Scratching the Surface: Canadian Anti-racist Feminist Thought*. Toronto: Canadian Scholars' Press, 2000.

Edlin, Douglas E. "Kant and the Common Law: Intersubjectivity in Aesthetic and Legal Judgment." *Canadian Journal of Law and Jurisprudence* 23, no. 2 (2010): 429–60.

Faraday, Fay, Margaret Ann Denike, and M. Kate Stephenson, eds. *Making Equality Rights Real: Securing Substantive Equality under the Charter*. Toronto, ON: Irwin Law, 2006.

Falco, Maria J., ed. *Feminist Interpretations of Mary Wollstonecraft*. University Park: Pennsylvania State University Press, 1996.

Feldthusen, Bruce. "The Gender Wars: 'Where the Boys Are.'" *Canadian Journal of Women and the Law* 4, no. 1 (1990): 66–95.

Femia, Joseph V. *Gramsci's Political Thought: Hegemony, Consciousness, and the Revolutionary Process*. New York: Clarendon, 1981.

– "Hegemony and Consciousness in the Thought of Antonio Gramsci." *Political Studies* 23, no. 1 (1975): 29–48.

Ferguson, Kennan. *The Politics of Judgment Aesthetics, Identity, and Political Theory*. Lanham, MD: Lexington Books, 2007.

Fielding, Henry. *Pasquin: A Dramatick Satire on the Times: Being the Rehearsal of Two Plays, Viz. A Comdy Call'd The Election; And a Tragedy Call'd, The Life and Death of Common-Sense*. Cambridge, UK: Chadwick-Healey, 1997.

Finkel, Norman J. *Commonsense Justice: Jurors' Notions of the Law*. Cambridge, MA: Harvard University Press, 1995.

Flood, Colleen, and Sujith Xavier. "Health Care Rights in Canada: The Chaoulli Legacy." *International Journal of Law and Medicine* 27, no. 3 (2008): 617–44.

Forguson, Lynd. *Common Sense*. London: Routledge, 1989.

Foucault, Michel. *History of Sexuality*. 3 vols. Paris: Éditions Gallimard, 1976.

– *Power/Knowledge: Selected Interviews and Other Writings, 1972–1977*. Ed. Gordon Conlin. New York: Pantheon, 1980.

Fraser, Nancy. "Mapping the Feminist Imagination: From Redistribution to Recognition to Representation." *Constellations: An International Journal of Critical and Democratic Theory* 12, no. 3 (2005): 295–307.

– "Rethinking the Public Sphere: A Contribution to the Critique of Actually Existing Democracy." In *Habermas and the Public Sphere*, ed.

Craig Calhoun, 109–42. Cambridge, MA: MIT Press, 1992.
– *Scales of Justice: Reimagining Political Space in a Globalizing World.* New York: Columbia University Press, 2009.
– "What's Critical about Critical Theory? The Case of Habermas and Gender." In *Feminism as Critique: On the Politics of Gender*, ed. Seyla Benhabib and Drucilla Cornell, 31–56. Minneapolis: University of Minnesota Press, 1987.
Fraser, Nancy, and Axel Honneth. *Redistribution or Recognition? A Political-Philosophical Exchange*. London: Verso, 2003.
Fuller, Lon. "Positivism and Fidelity to Law: A Reply to Professor Hart." *Harvard Law Review* 71, no. 4 (1957): 630–72.
Garsten, Bryan. *Saving Persuasion: A Defense of Rhetoric and Judgment*. Cambridge, MA: Harvard University Press, 2006.
Gaudreault-DesBiens, Jean-François. "The Quebec Secession Reference and the Judicial Arbitration of Conflicting Narratives about Law, Democracy, and Identity." *Vermont Law Review* 23, no. 4 (1999–98): 793–843.
Gavigan, Shelley. "Poverty Law, Theory, and Practice: The Place of Gender and Class in Access to Justice." In *Locating Law: Race/Class/Gender Connections*, ed. Elizabeth Comack, 208–30. Halifax: Fernwood, 1999.
Geertz, Clifford. "Common Sense as a Cultural System." In *Local Knowledge: Further Essays in Interpretive Anthropology*, 73–93. New York: Basic Books, 1983.
Gibbon, Angus. "Social Rights, Money Matters and Institutional Capacity." *National Journal of Constitutional Law* 14 (2003): 353–401.
Gill, Krystle, and Alycia Shaw. "Representing Canada on the Bench: On Gender Balance, Equality and Judicial Appointments." *Empowering Women Law Journal*, 10 March 2013. https://empoweringwomenlawjournal.wordpress.com/2013/03/10/representing-canada-on-the-bench-on-gender-balance-equality-and-judicial-appointments.
Goldoni, Marco, and Christopher McCorkindale, eds. *Hannah Arendt and the Law*. Oxford: Hart, 2012.
Gotanda, Neil. "The 'Common Sense' of Race." *Southern California Law Review* 83, no. 3 (2010): 441–52.

Gramsci, Antonio. *Selections from the Prison Notebooks*. Trans. Quentin Hoare and Geoffrey Nowell Smith. New York: International Publishers, 1971.

Graycar, Regina. "The Gender of Judgments: Some Reflections on Bias." *University of British Columbia Law Review* 32, no. 1 (1998): 1–21.

Hall, Stuart, and Alan O'Shea. "Common-Sense Neoliberalism." In *After Neoliberalism? The Kilburn Manifesto*, ed. Stuart Hall, Doreen Massey, and Michael Rustin. London: Lawrence and Wishart, 2013. http://www.lwbooks.co.uk/journals/soundings/manifesto.html.

Hartsock, Nancy C.M. "The Feminist Standpoint: Developing the Ground for a Specifically Feminist Historical Materialism." In *Feminism and Methodology: Social Science Issues*, ed. Sandra Harding, 157–80. Bloomington: Indiana University Press, 1987.

Havercroft, Jonathan. "On Seeing Liberty As." In *The Grammar of Politics: Wittgenstein and Political Philosophy*, ed. Cressida Hayes, 149–64. Ithaca, NY: Cornell University Press, 2003.

Heyes, Cressida, ed. *The Grammar of Politics: Wittgenstein and Political Philosophy*. Ithaca, NY: Cornell University Press, 2003.

Honig, Bonnie, ed. *Feminist Interpretations of Hannah Arendt*. University Park: Pennsylvania State University Press, 1995.

Houston, J. *Thomas Reid: Context, Influence and Significance*. Edinburgh: Dunedin Academic, 2004.

Howard, Philip K. *The Death of Common Sense: How Law Is Suffocating America*. New York: Random House, 1994.

Hughes, Patricia. "A New Direction in Judicial Impartiality?" *National Journal of Constitutional Law* 9 (1998): 251–61.

Human Resources and Skills Development Canada. *Low Income in Canada: 2000–2006 – Using the Market Basket Measure*. Gatineau, QC: Human Resources and Skills Development Canada, 2008. http://www.cwp-csp.ca/resources/resources/low-income-canada-2000-2006-using-market-basket-measure.

Hunt, Alan. "The Ideology of Law: Advances and Problems in Recent Applications of the Concept of Ideology to the Analysis of Law." *Law and Society Review* 19, no. 1 (1985): 11–38.

Hunter, Rosemary C., Clare McGlynn, and Erika Rackley. *Feminist Judgments: From Theory to Practice*. Oxford: Hart, 2010.

Ives, Peter. *Language and Hegemony in Gramsci*. London: Pluto, 2004.

Jackman, Martha. "The Protection of Welfare Rights under the Charter." *Ottawa Law Review* 20 (1988): 257–338.

– "Reality Checks: Presuming Innocence and Proving Guilt in Charter Welfare Cases." In *Poverty: Rights, Social Citizenship and Legal Activism*, ed. Margot Young, Susan B. Boyd, Gwen Brodsky, and Shelagh Day, 23–39. Vancouver: UBC Press, 2007.

Jamieson, Amber, and Adam Gabbatt. "'You Don't Fit the Image': Hillary Clinton's Decades-Long Push against a Sexist Press." *Guardian* (London), 15 September 2016. https://www.theguardian.com/us-news/2016/sep/15/hillary-clinton-press-sexism-media-interviews.

Justice with Dignity. "Remember Kimberly Rogers." Report archived by the Canadian Association of Elizabeth Fry Societies. http://www.caefs.ca/wp-content/uploads/2013/04/rogers.pdf.

Kant, Immanuel. *Prolegomena to Any Future Metaphysics*. Indianapolis, IN: Bobbs-Merrill, 1950.

Kateb, George. "The Judgment of Arendt." In *Judgment, Imagination and Politics: Themes from Kant and Arendt*, ed. Ronald Beiner and Jennifer Nedelsky, 121–38. Lanham, MD: Rowan and Littlefield, 2001.

Kim, Natasha, and Tina Piper. "*Gosselin v. Quebec*: Back to the Poorhouse ..." *McGill Law Journal* 48 (2003): 749–81.

Kohn, Jerome. "Reflecting on Judgment: Common Sense and a Common World." In *Pragmatism, Critique, Judgment: Essays for Richard J. Bernstein*, ed. Richard J. Bernstein, Seyla Benhabib, and Nancy Fraser, 261–94. Cambridge, MA: MIT Press, 2004.

Law Reform Commission of Canada. *Report on Evidence*. Ottawa: Law Reform Commission of Canada, 1975.

Lazarus-Black, Mindie, and Susan F. Hirsch. *Contested States: Law, Hegemony, and Resistance*. New York: Routledge, 1994.

Lemos, Noah. *Common Sense: A Contemporary Defense*. Cambridge, UK: Cambridge University Press, 2004.

Litowitz, Douglas. "Gramsci, Hegemony, and the Law." *BYU Law Review* 2000, no. 2 (2000): 515–51.

MacCrimmon, Marilyn T. "Fact Determination: Common Sense Knowledge, Judicial Notice and Social Science." In *The Judicial Role in Criminal Proceedings*, ed. Sean Doran and John Jackson, 31–50. Oxford: Hart, 2000.

– "What Is 'Common' about Common Sense? Cautionary Tales for Travelers Crossing Interdisciplinary Boundaries." *Cardozo Law Review* 22, nos 5–6 (2001): 1433–60.

Macdonald, David, and Daniel Wilson. *Poverty or Prosperity: Indigenous Children in Canada*. Canadian Centre for Policy Alternatives, 19 June 2013. https://www.policyalternatives.ca/publications/reports/poverty-or-prosperity.

MacIvor, Heather. *Women and Politics in Canada*. Toronto: University of Toronto Press, 1996.

Maher, F.K.H. "Common Sense and Law." *Melbourne University Law Review* 8, no. 4 (1972): 587–624.

Majury, Diana. "Introducing the Women's Court of Canada." *Canadian Journal of Women and the Law* 18, no. 1 (2008): 1–12.

Makin, Kirk. "Of 100 New Federally Appointed Judges 98 Are White, Globe Finds." *Globe and Mail*, 17 April 2012.

Marcil-Lacoste, Louise. *Claude Buffier and Thomas Reid, Two Common Sense Philosophers*. Montreal and Kingston: McGill-Queen's University Press, 1982.

Maroney, Terry A. "Emotional Common Sense as Constitutional Law." *Vanderbilt Law Review* 62, no. 3 (2009): 851–917.

Marx, Karl. *Critique of Hegel's "Philosophy of Right."* Ed. Joseph O'Malley. Cambridge, UK: Cambridge University Press, 1982.

Marx, Karl, and Friedrich Engels. *The German Ideology*. New York: International Publishers, 1970.

Matsuda, Mari J. "Pragmatism Modified and the False Consciousness Problem." *Southern California Law Review* 63, no. 6 (1990): 1763–82.

– "When the First Quail Calls: Multiple Consciousness as Jurisprudential Method." *Women's Rights Law Reporter* 11, no. 1 (1989): 7–10.

Mayeda, Graham. "Between Principle and Pragmatism: The Decline of Principled Reasoning in the Jurisprudence of the McLachlin Court." *Supreme Court Law Review* 50 (2010): 41–88.

– "Uncommonly Common: The Nature of Common Law Judgment." *Canadian Journal of Law and Jurisprudence* 19, no. 1 (2006): 107–31.

McInturff, Kate. "Closing Canada's Gender Gap: Year 2240 Here We Come!" Canadian Centre for Policy Alternatives, 23 April 2013. http://www.policyalternatives.ca/publications/reports/closing-canadas-gender-gap.

McIntyre, Sheila. "Studied Ignorance and Privileged Innocence: Keeping Equity Academic." *Canadian Journal of Women and the Law* 12, no. 1 (2000): 147–96.

– "The Supreme Court and Section 15: A Thin and Impoverished Notion of Judicial Review." *Queen's Law Journal* 31, no. 2 (2006): 731–69.

Meyer, Linda Ross. "Between Reason and Power." *University of Cincinnati Law Review* 67, no. 3 (1999): 727–59.

Moore, G.E. "A Defense of Common Sense." In *Philosophical Papers*, 32–59. London: George Allen and Unwin, 1959.

Mootz, Francis J. "Vico and Imagination: An Ingenious Approach to Educating Lawyers with Semiotic Sensibility." *International Journal for the Semiotics of Law* 22, no. 1 (2009): 11–22.

Morgan, Brian G. "Proof of Facts in Charter Litigation." In *Charter Litigation*, ed. Robert J. Sharpe, 159–86. Toronto: Butterworths, 1987.

Morrison, Barry R., and Warren Comeau. "Judging Credibility of Witnesses." *Advocates' Quarterly* 25, no. 4 (2002): 411–40.

Mosher, Janet. "Managing the Disentitlement of Women: Glorified Markets, the Idealized Family, and the Undeserving Other." In *Restructuring Caring Labour: Discourse, State Practice, and Everyday Life*, ed. Sheila M. Neysmith, 30–51. Toronto: Oxford University Press, 2000.

– "The Shrinking of the Public and Private Spaces of the Poor." In *Disorderly People: Law and the Politics of Exclusion in Ontario*, ed. Joe Hermer and Janet Eaton Mosher, 41–53. Halifax: Fernwood, 2002.

Mossman, Mary Jane. "Choices and Commitments for Women: Challenging the Supreme Court of Canada in the Context of Social Assistance." *Osgoode Hall Law Journal* 42, no. 4 (2004): 615–24.

National Association of Women and the Law. *Factum of the Intervenor*. In *Gosselin v. Quebec (Procureur général)*, [2002] 4 SCR 429.
Nedelsky, Jennifer. "Communities of Judgment and Human Rights." *Theoretical Inquiries in Law* 1, no. 2 (2001): 245–82.
– "Embodied Diversity and Challenges to Law." *McGill Law Journal* 42 (1997): 91–118.
– "Judgment, Diversity, and Relational Autonomy." In *Judgment, Imagination and Politics: Themes from Kant and Arendt*, ed. Ronald Beiner and Jennifer Nedelsky, 103–20. Lanham, MD: Rowman and Littlefield, 2001.
– *Law's Relations: A Relational Theory of Self, Autonomy, and Law*. Oxford: Oxford University Press, 2012.
– "The Reciprocal Relation of Judgment and Autonomy." In *Being Relational: Reflections on Relational Theory and Health Law*, ed. Jocelyn Downie and Jennifer Llewellyn, 35–62. Vancouver: UBC Press, 2011.
Norris, Andrew. "Arendt, Kant, and the Politics of Common Sense." *Polity* 29, no. 2 (1996): 165–91.
Norris, John, and Marlys Edwardh. "Myths, Hidden Facts and Common Sense: Expert Opinion Evidence and the Assessment of Credibility." *Criminal Law Quarterly* 38, no. 1 (1996): 73–103.
Northern/Irish Feminist Judgments Project. http://www.feministjudging.ie.
Nun, José. "Elements for a Theory of Democracy: Gramsci and Common Sense." Trans. William Cartier. *Boundary* 2 14, no. 3 (1986): 197–229.
Omatsu, Maryka. "The Fiction of Judicial Impartiality." *Canadian Journal of Women and the Law* 9, no. 1 (1997): 1–16.
Owen, David. "Genealogy as Perspicuous Representation." In *The Grammar of Politics: Wittgenstein and Political Philosophy*, ed. Cressida Heyes, 82–96. Ithaca, NY: Cornell University Press, 2003.
Palmater, Pamela, "Stretched beyond Human Limits: Death by Poverty in First Nations." *Canadian Review of Social Policy*, nos 65–6 (2011): 112–27.
Parret, Herman. "Common Sense in Philosophy." In *Common Sense: The Foundations for Social Science*, ed. Frits van Holthoon and David R. Olson, 17–32. Lanham, MD: University Press of America, 1987.

Petter, Andrew. "Wealthcare: The Politics of the Charter Re-visited." In *Access to Care, Access to Justice: The Legal Debate over Private Health Insurance in Canada*, ed. Colleen Flood, Lorne Sossin, and Kent Roach, 116–38. Toronto: University of Toronto Press, 2005.

Pitkin, Hanna. *The Attack of the Blob: Hannah Arendt's Concept of the Social*. Chicago: University of Chicago Press, 1998.

– "Justice: On Relating Private and Public." *Political Theory* 9, no. 3 (1981): 327–52.

Purvis, Trevor, and Alan Hunt. "Discourse, Ideology, Discourse, Ideology, Discourse, Ideology ..." *British Journal of Sociology* 44, no. 3 (1993): 473–99.

Rasch, William. "Judgment: The Emergence of Legal Norms." *Cultural Critique* 57, no. 1 (2004): 93–103.

Razack, Sherene. "*R.D.S. v. Her Majesty the Queen*: A Case about Home." In *Scratching the Surface: Canadian Anti-racist Feminist Thought*, ed. Enakshi Dua and Angela Robertson, 281–94. Toronto: Canadian Scholars' Press, 2000.

Réaume, Denise G. "Dignity, Equality and Comparison." In *Philosophical Foundations of Discrimination Law*, ed. Deborah Hellman and Sophia Moreau, 7–27. Oxford: Oxford University Press, 2013.

– "Dignity, Equality and Second Generation Rights." In *Poverty: Rights, Social Citizenship and Legal Activism*, ed. Margot Young, Susan B. Boyd, Gwen Brodsky, and Shelagh Day, 281–96. Vancouver: UBC Press, 2007.

Reid, Thomas. *Essays on the Intellectual Powers of Man*. 1785. Reprint, Edinburgh: Edinburgh University Press, 2002.

– *An Inquiry into the Human Mind on the Principles of Common Sense*. 1764. Reprint, Edinburgh: Edinburgh University Press, 1997.

Riddell, William Renwick. "Common Law and Common Sense." *Yale Law Journal* 27, no. 8 (1918): 993–1007.

Roberts, Thomas. "Legal Positivism and Scottish Common Sense Philosophy." *Canadian Journal of Law and Jurisprudence* 18, no. 2 (2005): 277–305.

Robinson, Andrew. "Towards an Intellectual Reformation: The

Critique of Common Sense and the Forgotten Revolutionary Project of Gramscian Theory." *Critical Review of International Social and Political Philosophy* 8, no. 4 (2005): 469–81.

Rodgers, Sandra, and Sheila McIntyre, eds. *The Supreme Court of Canada and Social Justice: Commitment, Retrenchment or Retreat*. Markham, ON: Lexis Nexis, 2010.

Rosenfeld, Sophia A. *Common Sense: A Political History*. Cambridge, MA: Harvard University Press, 2011.

Roughan, Nicole. *Authorities: Conflicts, Cooperation, and Transnational Legal Theory.* Oxford: Oxford University Press, 2013.

Rundle, Kristen. *Forms Liberate: Reclaiming the Jurisprudence of Lon L. Fuller*. Oxford: Hart, 2012.

Rupert, Mark. "Globalising Common Sense: A Marxian-Gramscian (Re-)vision of the Politics of Governance/Resistance." *Review of International Studies* 29 (2003): 181–98.

Salter, Michael. "Common Sense and the Resistance to Legal Theory." *Ratio Juris* 5, no. 2 (1992): 212–29.

Santos, Boaventura de Sousa. *Toward a New Legal Common Sense: Law, Globalization and Emancipation*. 2nd ed. London: Butterworths, 2002.

Scheingold, Stuart. *The Politics of Rights: Lawyers, Public Policy and Political Change*. Vol. 2. Ann Arbor: University of Michigan Press, 2004.

Scheman, Naomi. "Forms of Life: Mapping the Rough Ground." In *The Cambridge Companion to Wittgenstein*, ed. Hans Sluga and David G. Stern, 383–410. Cambridge, UK: Cambridge University Press, 1996.

– "Introduction." In *Feminist Interpretations of Ludwig Wittgenstein*, ed. Naomi Scheman and Peg O'Connor, 1–21. University Park: Pennsylvania State University Press, 2002.

Schneiderman, David. "Common Sense and the Charter." *Supreme Court Law Review* 45 (2009): 3–25.

– "Social Rights and 'Common Sense': *Gosselin* through a Media Lens." In *Poverty: Rights, Social Citizenship and Legal Activism*, ed. Margot Young, Susan B. Boyd, Gwen Brodsky, and Shelagh Day, 57–73. Vancouver: UBC Press, 2007.

Smith, Lynn. "What Can Judges Know?" Lecture at the Faculty of Law, University of British Columbia, 2010. Unpublished.

Snir, Itay. "Bringing Plurality Together: Common Sense, Thinking and Philosophy in Arendt." *Southern Journal of Philosophy* 53, no. 3 (2015): 362–84.

– "Experts of Common Sense: Philosophers, Laypeople and Democratic Politics." *Humana.Mente Journal of Philosophical Studies* 28 (2015): 187–210.

– "'Not Just One Common Sense': Gramsci's Common Sense and Laclau and Mouffe's Radical Democratic Politics." *Constellations* 23, no. 2 (2016): 269–80.

Taylor, Charles. "Comparison, History, Truth." In *Philosophical Arguments*, 146–64. Cambridge, MA: Harvard University Press, 1997.

– "Overcoming Epistemology." In *Philosophical Arguments*, 1–19. Cambridge, MA: Harvard University Press, 1997.

Thiele, Leslie Paul. "Judging Hannah Arendt: A Reply to Zerilli." *Political Theory* 33, no. 5 (2005): 706–14.

Thompson, Richard H. "Common Sense and Fact-Finding: Cultural Reason in Judicial Decisions." *Legal Studies Forum* 19, no. 2 (1995): 119–37.

United Nations Economic and Social Council. "Substantive Issues Arising in the Implementation of the International Covenant on Economic, Social and Cultural Rights: Poverty and the International Covenant on Economic, Social and Cultural Rights." 10 May 2001. UN doc. E/C.12/2001/10. http://www2.ohchr.org/english/bodies/cescr/docs/statements/E.C.12.2001.10Poverty-2001.pdf.

University of Queensland. "Australian Feminist Judgments Project." http://www.law.uq.edu.au/australian-feminist-judgments-project.

Valverde, Mariana. *Law's Dream of a Common Knowledge*. Princeton, NJ: Princeton University Press, 2003.

van Holthoon, Frits. "Common Sense and Natural Law: From Thomas Aquinas to Thomas Reid." In *Common Sense: The Foundations for Social Science*, ed. Frits van Holthoon and David R. Olson, 99–114. Lanham, MD: University Press of America, 1987.

van Holthoon, Frits, and David R. Olson. "Common Sense: An Introduction." In *Common Sense: The Foundations for Social Science*, ed. Frits van Holthoon and David R. Olson, 1–16. Lanham, MD: University Press of America, 1987.

Victoria Anti-Poverty Coalition. "Gosselin Decision." Press release, 9 February 2001. http://www.povnet.org/node/1135.

Webber, Jeremy. "A Judicial Ethic for a Pluralistic Age." In *Multiculturalism and Law: A Critical Debate*, ed. Omid A. Payrow Shabani, 67–100. Cardiff, UK: University of Wales Press, 2007.

White, James Boyd. "Law as Rhetoric, Rhetoric as Law: The Arts of Cultural and Communal Life." *The University of Chicago Law Review* 52, no. 3 (1985): 684–702.

White, Lucie E. "Subordination, Rhetorical Survival Skills and Sunday Shoes: Notes on the Hearing of Mrs. G." *Buffalo Law Review* 38, no. 1 (1990): 1–58.

Williams, Patricia. *The Alchemy of Race and Rights*. Cambridge, MA: Harvard University Press, 1991.

Wilson, Bertha. "Will Women Judges Really Make a Difference?" *Osgoode Hall Law Journal* 28, no. 3 (1990): 507–22.

Wiseman, David. "The Charter and Poverty: Beyond Injusticiability." *University of Toronto Law Journal* 51, no. 4 (2001): 425–58.

– "Competence Concerns in Charter Adjudication: Countering the Anti-poverty Incompetence Argument." *McGill Law Journal* 51 (2006): 503–46.

Wittgenstein, Ludwig. *On Certainty*. Malden, MA: Blackwell, 1975.

– *Philosophical Investigations*. Malden, MA: Blackwell, 1953.

Wollstonecraft, Mary. *A Vindication of the Rights of Woman: With Strictures on Political and Moral Subjects*. London: Unwin, 1891.

Wolterstorff, Nicholas. "Reid on Common Sense." In *The Cambridge Companion to Reid*, ed. Terence Cuneo, 77–100. Cambridge, UK: Cambridge University Press, 2004.

– *Thomas Reid and the Story of Epistemology*. Cambridge, UK: Cambridge University Press, 2001.

Women's Court of Canada. "Women's Court of Canada: Future Directions." https://www.law.utoronto.ca/documents/conferences/rewritingequality08_future.pdf.

Yaffe, Gideon, and Ryan Nichols. "Thomas Reid." In *The Stanford Encyclopedia of Philosophy*, ed. Edward N. Zalta. Winter 2009. http://plato.stanford.edu/archives/win2009/entries/reid.

Young, Iris Marion. "Asymmetrical Reciprocity: On Moral Respect, Wonder, and Enlarged Thought." In *Judgment, Imagination and Politics: Themes from Kant and Arendt*, ed. Ronald Beiner and Jennifer Nedelsky, 205–28. Lanham, MD: Rowan and Littlefield, 2001.

Young, Margot. "Introduction." In *Poverty: Rights, Social Citizenship and Legal Activism*, ed. Margot Young, Susan B. Boyd, Gwen Brodsky, and Shelagh Day, 1–19. Vancouver: UBC Press, 2007.

– "Rights, the Homeless and Social Change: Reflection on *Victoria (City) v. Adams (BCSC)*." BC *Studies*, no. 164 (2009): 103–13.

– "Unequal to the Task: 'Kapp'ing the Substantive Potential of Section 15." *Supreme Court Law Review* 50 (2010): 183–220.

Young, Margot, Susan B. Boyd, Gwen Brodsky, and Shelagh Day, eds. *Poverty: Rights, Social Citizenship, and Legal Activism*. Vancouver: UBC Press, 2007.

Zerilli, Linda M.G. "Doing without Knowing: Feminism's Politics of the Ordinary." In *The Grammar of Politics: Wittgenstein and Political Philosophy*, ed. Cressida Heyes, 129–48. Ithaca, NY: Cornell University Press, 2003.

– "Response to Thiele." *Political Theory* 33, no. 5 (2005): 715–20.

– "Toward a Feminist Theory of Judgment." *Signs: Journal of Women in Culture and Society* 34, no. 2 (2009): 259–317.

– "'We Feel Our Freedom.'" *Political Theory* 33, no. 2 (2005): 158–88.

Zuckerman, Adrian A.S. "Law, Fact or Justice?" *Boston University Law Review* 66 (1986): 487–508.

Index